THE QUIET RULES

Stop Bank Freezes, Keep Full Control of Your Money, Never Miss a Deadline, and Use the Exact Forms & Scripts That Protect What You Earned

THE QUIET RULES

Stop Bank Freezes, Keep Full Control of Your Money, Never Miss a Deadline, and Use the Exact Forms & Scripts That Protect What You Earned

First Edition • Printed in the United States of America

Contents

INTRODUCTION

The Rules Nobody Explains

By the end of this introduction you will know what this book can and cannot do for you, which ten things to do first if you do nothing else, and the ten rules that run underneath every chapter.

A STORY **Carol, 68, Tampa, Florida**

In March, Carol added her son Michael to her checking account. It seemed like the sensible thing. He lived twenty minutes away, he was good with paperwork, and if anything happened to her he could pay the bills. The teller had her sign a new signature card. It took eleven minutes.

In April she sold the house she and her late husband had lived in for thirty-one years and bought a smaller one near her daughter. Three days before closing, she asked the bank to wire $184,000 to the title company. The wire did not go. A polite voice at a call center said the transaction was "under review." Nobody could say why, or for how long. The closing was Friday.

A new name on an account, followed within weeks by a large wire to a payee the bank had never seen, is exactly the pattern the bank's software is built to catch. Nobody was accusing her of anything. Nobody was permitted to tell her much at all. And because she had never named a trusted contact, the bank had no one to call to confirm that this was Carol's money doing what Carol wanted.

Carol is a composite, not a real person. So is Walter, below.

> A STORY **Walter, 66, Erie, Pennsylvania**
>
> Walter retired at 66 from a plant where he had carried good health insurance for twenty-nine years. Human resources handed him a COBRA packet and told him he could keep the same plan for eighteen months. He liked the plan. He kept it.
>
> He signed up for Medicare Part B when the COBRA ran out. That was when the letter came. His eight-month window to enroll without penalty had opened the month after he left work, not the month his COBRA ended, because COBRA does not count as coverage from current employment. The window had closed months earlier. He would wait for the General Enrollment Period, January 1 through March 31, and he would pay a surcharge on his Part B premium, 10% for every full twelve months he could have had Part B and did not, for the rest of his life.
>
> Walter had asked. He asked the office that handled his insurance, and he got an answer that was true about COBRA and silent about Medicare. Nobody in that building was responsible for explaining the rule.

Why the Rules Are Quiet

Neither Carol nor Walter did anything foolish. They asked the person in front of them and took the answer they were given. The rules that caught them were not hidden; they were published in regulations and handbooks anyone could read. They were quiet for a different reason.

The rules that govern your money are written for institutions, not for customers. The regulation behind Carol's paused wire is addressed to her bank; it tells the bank what to watch for and what to file, and it says nothing to Carol. The Medicare rule that caught Walter lives in a government publication, and it is nobody's job at a plant in Erie to hand it to a retiring machinist. The bank's first duty runs to its regulator. The plan's duty runs to the plan. Your account agreement is the only document in the whole arrangement addressed to you, and it is forty pages long.

So the customer learns the rule at the moment of failure. That is what we mean by a quiet rule: a rule you only hear about when it has already cost you something.

Quiet rules share three habits. First, they run on clocks you did not know had started: business days, not calendar days; 60 days from the date a statement was sent, not the day you noticed; a 2026 Medicare surcharge based on your 2024 tax return. Second, they are enforced by software and by silence. When a bank files a suspicious-activity report, federal law forbids it from telling you so; the person on the phone who "can't say why" is often not allowed to. Third, the price is frequently permanent. Walter's Part B penalty is for life. A Roth conversion cannot be undone. A retirement check made payable to a non-spouse heir, instead of moved custodian to custodian, is taxable in full, and nobody, including the IRS, can fix it.

This is not mostly a book about crime, though crime appears where it belongs. In 2025 the FBI's Internet Crime Complaint Center logged 201,266 complaints from Americans age 60 and older, with reported losses of $7.7 billion. That is serious money, and the software built to catch it is the software that paused Carol's wire. But most of the money lost to quiet rules is not stolen. It is forfeited. The IRS estimated that $1.2 billion in refunds for tax year 2022 was still unclaimed as the April 15, 2026 deadline approached, a median of $686 per person. After that date it belonged to the Treasury. Nobody took it. It expired.

What This Book Is, and What It Isn't

This is a protection guide with tools. Each of the eight chapters covers one place where retirement money gets frozen, lost, or taxed by default. Each names its quiet rules in a box near the top, explains them with the actual 2026 numbers, and then hands you the exact thing to say on the phone, the exact letter to send, and the exact worksheet to fill in. Every chapter ends with a page called Your Next Steps: six to ten actions, each with the form number or phone number in the line.

It is not a lawyer, an accountant, or a financial planner. Nothing here is legal, tax, or investment advice for your situation. Where a rule varies by state, and many do, we say so and tell you which office or which question will get you your own answer. Where a decision is large and irreversible, we say that a fee-only planner, a CPA, or an elder-law attorney should confirm it, and we mean it.

It is not a market book. You will find nothing here about what to buy or when to sell. The calendar, not the market, decides most of the avoidable tax you will pay, and the calendar is knowable.

And it is not alarmist. If you arrived here after a video about "bank freezes," you should know that no federal law lets a bank freeze a senior's account for fourteen business days, whatever the video said. A brokerage can pause a suspicious withdrawal for up to 15 business days under a national rule, extendable in stages. Whether your bank can do the same depends on your state, and about half the states have such laws. The details are in Chapter 1, along with the free form that keeps most of these pauses short.

How to Use This Book

The eight chapters follow the shape of a retirement: the everyday account, the death of a spouse, the government programs, the legal documents, the annual calendar, the transition out of work, the handoff to heirs, and the fine print underneath all of it.

The eight rooms of this book

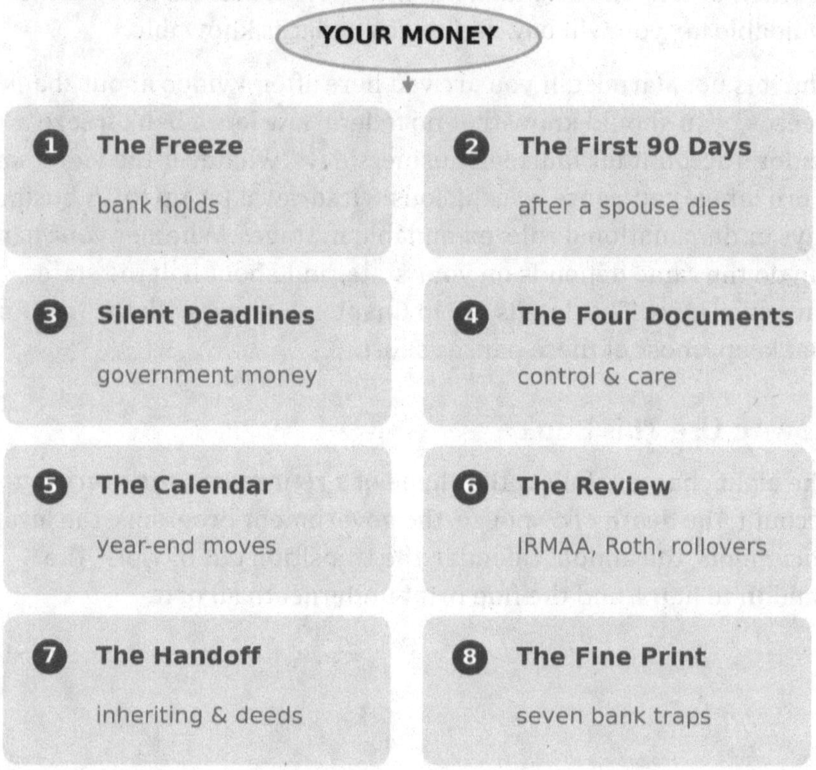

The eight places where retirement money gets frozen, lost, or taxed, and the chapter that covers each

Chapter	The quiet failure it prevents
1. The Freeze	A hold you did not expect, at the worst possible time
2. The First 90 Days	Irreversible mistakes made fast after a spouse dies
3. The Silent Deadlines	Government money that expires while you wait
4. The Four Documents	A power of attorney the bank will not accept
5. The Calendar	Tax you pay because a date passed
6. The Review	Permanent tax decisions made by default around retirement
7. The Handoff	Inheritances shrunk by a form filled out wrong
8. The Fine Print	Seven traps in the account agreement you did not read

You do not have to read in order. If your account is frozen this minute, go to Chapter 1 and find the checklist called If Your Account Is Frozen Right Now. If your spouse died this week, go to Chapter 2 and find First 72 Hours. Everyone else can read front to back or start with the two-hour plan below.

The three kinds of tools

Every chapter carries three kinds of tools, built to be used, not admired.

Scripts are word-for-word phone conversations: the opening line, the exact question, what to ask for in writing, the reference numbers to request before you hang up, and a polite line for escalating. The person answering has a script too; yours is designed to meet it.

Letters are complete templates with bracketed fields: date, address block, subject line, a request with a deadline, and the sentence "please respond in writing." Send them by a method that gives you a record.

Worksheets and checklists are meant to be photocopied. One action per line, verb first, with the form or phone number in the line. Some readers will tape them inside a cabinet door. That is a fine use of a book.

The appendices

Appendix A is the Master Calendar: every recurring deadline in the book, month by month, and every clock that starts when something happens to you. Appendix B is the Directory of phone numbers, forms, and agencies. Appendix C is the Glossary, and Appendix D is the Tool Library, an index of every script, letter, worksheet, and checklist by chapter.

The two-hour first pass

If you do nothing else, do these ten things. Most take fifteen minutes. None costs money.

> CHECKLIST **If You Do Only Ten Things**

- ☐ Name a trusted contact at every bank, credit union, and brokerage where you hold money; it is free, it gives the institution someone to call instead of freezing, and it grants that person no power over your account (Chapter 1).
- ☐ Open a my Social Security account and name up to three people, in order, as advance designees for representative payee; Social Security does not accept a power of attorney (Chapter 3).
- ☐ Pull the current beneficiary designation for every IRA, 401(k), life insurance policy, and POD or TOD account; check that each names a living primary and a contingent (Chapters 4 and 7).
- ☐ Locate your durable power of attorney; if your bank has never seen it, deliver a copy now, while you are healthy, and ask for written acceptance (Chapter 4).
- ☐ Fill in the My Deadline Sheet: the year you turn 73 or 75, the date you reach 70½, your Medicare enrollment window, your full retirement age (Chapters 3 and 5).
- ☐ Put four dates on next year's calendar in ink: December 31, April 1, April 15, and October 15 through December 7 (Chapter 5).
- ☐ Find the maturity date and grace period of every CD you own and calendar them; an unattended CD rolls into the same term at that day's rate (Chapter 8).
- ☐ Check that no bank holds more than $250,000 of your money in one ownership category, using the FDIC's EDIE calculator listed in Appendix B (Chapter 8).
- ☐ Open a modest second checking account at a different institution, so a hold or closure at one bank never leaves you unable to pay the electric bill (Chapter 8).
- ☐ Tell one person you trust where this book, your Four Documents Inventory, and your original documents are kept (Chapter 4).

The Ten Master Quiet Rules

Each chapter has its own rules, and you will meet them in their own boxes. Ten run underneath all eight chapters.

THE QUIET RULES The Ten Master Quiet Rules

1. *The bank's clock runs on business days, not calendar days.* Two business days is not two days. Fifteen business days is three weeks.
2. *When the bank cannot tell you why, it may be forbidden to.* Ask instead for the release date, in writing.
3. *Slow is safe.* In the ninety days after a death, nearly every irreversible mistake is one made quickly.
4. *Government money never comes looking for you.* Refunds, benefits, enrollment windows, and unclaimed property all expire quietly. You have to apply, on time.
5. *A power of attorney ends at death, a will begins at death, and Social Security accepts neither.* Each agency has its own form.
6. *The calendar, not the market, decides most of the tax you can avoid.* December 31 has no extension.
7. *The five years around retirement are when permanent tax decisions get made by default.* Make them on purpose instead.
8. *Assets move by title, designation, and form, never by wish.* The beneficiary form overrides the will, and a check made payable to you is the most expensive piece of paper in this book.
9. *Never add a helper as a joint owner.* A power of attorney, a payable-on-death designation, and a trusted contact do everything joint ownership does, without the exposure.
10. *Every statement is a deadline.* The windows to fix errors close at 30 days, 60 days, and one year, counted from the statement, not from when you noticed.

A Note on Numbers

Every figure in this book is a 2026 figure unless we say otherwise: the $275 and $6,725 thresholds for deposit holds, the $202.90 standard Part B premium, the $19,000 gift exclusion, the $7,500 IRA limit, the 2.8% cost-of-living adjustment. We took each from the agency that publishes it. Where we could not confirm a number from a primary source, we left it out or told you plainly that it varies.

Many of these numbers change every year, usually in the fall, when Social Security, Medicare, and the IRS announce the next year's figures. A few never change: the $255 lump-sum death payment, and the income thresholds that decide how much of your Social Security is taxed ($25,000 for a single filer, $32,000 for a couple), are not indexed at all. A few change on a longer cycle; the deposit-hold thresholds adjust every five years, next on July 1, 2030.

Appendix B tells you which agency owns each number, so that next year you can check it in five minutes. Where a rule changed recently, we say so and give the date, because the person helping you may be working from the old version. Where a rule differs between a bank and a brokerage, or between federal law and your state, we keep them apart, because the difference is usually the whole point. And when you see "days," check whether they are business days or calendar days; we say which every time.

Using This Book for a Parent

Many readers are the adult children in these stories, and this book was written with you at the table too. A few suggestions.

Start with Chapter 4, The Four Documents, and fill in the Four Documents Inventory with your parent, not for them. Knowing where the durable power of attorney is, when it was signed, and whether the bank has already accepted it will save you more grief than anything else in this book. Then read Chapter 1 and ask your parent to name you, or someone, as trusted contact at each institution. The bank may call you to confirm your parent's whereabouts or wellbeing, but a trusted contact cannot move money or make decisions. That limit is the point; it is why a bank will accept the designation without a lawyer.

Read Chapter 3 for the agencies that will not honor a power of attorney at all: Social Security (representative payee, Form SSA-11, and advance designation of up to three people), the IRS (Form 2848), Medicare (Form CMS-10106), and the VA (Forms 21-22a and 21-0845). Each is easier to set up before it is needed.

Do not add yourself to your parent's account as a joint owner, however convenient it seems. Chapter 8 explains why: your creditors, your divorce, an unintended inheritance, and the fact that adult children are the perpetrators in roughly 40% of the elder-theft reports financial institutions file. You are not that person. The bank's software does not know that.

If you are already acting under a power of attorney, the Consumer Financial Protection Bureau's plain-language guides, Managing Someone Else's Money, describe your duties in a few pages each; Appendix B lists them. The short version: keep the money separate, keep records, spend it only for your parent, and never pay yourself without written authority.

Helping is not controlling. The people in these stories are capable adults who ran into rules nobody explained. Your parent is too. Hand them the book, sit down with the worksheets, and let the scripts do the talking.

Now to the rules.

CHAPTER ONE

The Freeze — Stop Bank Holds Before They Start

By the end of this chapter you will know which of three very different things your bank means by "hold," how many business days each can last, and the one free form that keeps a hold from turning into a standoff.

A STORY **Marjorie, 69, Sarasota, Florida**

Marjorie had a roof problem and a plan. The plan was to wire the roofer's deposit, $9,500, on a Tuesday morning so the crew could start before the next storm. She had the invoice, the routing number, and thirty-one years at the same bank.

The week before, her old phone had given up, and she had stopped by the branch to update her number. Then she added the roofer as a new payee in online banking. The wire went "pending." Wednesday it was still pending. Thursday, a courteous voice from a "review team" said the transaction was being held "for her protection" and that they could not say more.

Her daughter Anne, in Columbus, Ohio, offered to call. The bank would not speak to Anne. She was not on the account, and Marjorie had never named her as anything. The roofer moved on to the next house.

Marjorie did not lose a dollar. She lost eight days, a roofing crew, and a fair amount of sleep, and nobody would answer the one question she kept asking: How long can they do this?

(Marjorie is a fictional composite. The rules that follow are not.)

The answer to Marjorie's question depends on which of three different things the bank is doing, because each has its own clock. Most of the fear around "bank freezes" comes from mixing the three together. Once you can tell them apart, what's left is a set of deadlines you can hold the bank to.

THE QUIET RULES The Quiet Rules in This Chapter

- *A "freeze" is one of three different things, and each one has its own clock.*
- *The bank's clock runs on business days, not calendar days.*
- *Your brokerage can pause a withdrawal for 15 business days. Whether your bank can depends on your state.*
- *A trusted contact is the free form that shortens every hold.*
- *Software flags patterns, not people. You can step around the patterns.*
- *Never split a cash withdrawal. Announce it instead.*
- *When the bank goes quiet, ask in writing and escalate on a schedule.*

Three Things People Call a Freeze

1. **A deposit hold.** You put a check in, and the bank makes you wait to spend it. A federal rule, Regulation CC, sets fixed dollar amounts and deadlines. Routine, legal, predictable.
2. **An exploitation or fraud hold.** You try to take money *out*, and the bank pauses it because something looks like a scam. At brokerages this runs under a national rule, FINRA Rule 2165. At banks and credit unions it runs under state law, and only about half the states have one.
3. **A compliance restriction.** The bank limits or closes your account after an internal review: an identity refresh you didn't answer, a suspicious-activity report it is forbidden to mention, or a decision to end the relationship. This one has the fewest deadlines.

The Deposit Hold: Regulation CC by the Numbers

Regulation CC is the federal rule that says how quickly a bank must let you use money you deposit. Its dollar figures were last adjusted on July 1, 2025, and by law they are re-checked for inflation every five years. **The next adjustment is scheduled for July 1, 2030.**

The standard schedule

What you deposit	Available no later than
Cash, deposited in person	Next business day
Wire or direct deposit (ACH)	Next business day
Treasury, government, cashier's, or certified check, handed to an employee	Next business day
A check drawn on the same bank ("on-us")	Next business day
The first $275 of any other checks deposited that day	Next business day
Everything else (ordinary checks)	Second business day

The next-day treatment for government and cashier's checks applies when you hand the check to a person; put it in an ATM or a mobile app and the bank may take until the second business day. The bank may also require a special deposit slip for those checks, so ask.

The **$275** is the "minimum amount" rule: whatever you deposit, the first $275 of a day's ordinary checks must be spendable the next business day. Enough for groceries and a prescription while the rest clears.

Business days, not calendar days

The bank's clock runs on business days, not calendar days. Saturdays, Sundays, and federal holidays do not count. A check deposited the Friday before a Monday holiday, with a second-business-day hold, becomes available on Wednesday. Five calendar days, every one of them legal.

When a teller says "two days," ask "two business days?" and count them on a calendar. That habit clears up most of the confusion people report about holds.

The "case-by-case" hold

Many banks release check funds faster than the law requires. When one decides to use its full legal time on a particular check, it calls that a **case-by-case hold**. It means your money lands on the second business day instead of sooner, and the bank must tell you so.

Exception holds: the seven-business-day hold

The bank may hold a deposit longer than the standard schedule only for one of six reasons:

- **New account:** less than 30 calendar days old.
- **Large deposit:** the portion of one day's check deposits over **$6,725**.
- **Redeposited check:** a check that already bounced once.
- **Repeated overdrafts:** negative on 6 or more days in the last 6 months, or negative by $6,725 or more on 2 or more days.
- **Reasonable cause:** a specific reason to doubt the check will be paid.
- **Emergency conditions:** power failures, disasters, and the like.

When one applies, the bank gets a "reasonable period" beyond the normal two business days, defined as **5 more business days**, which puts your money in your hands on the **seventh business day**. A bank may hold longer only if it can prove the extra time was reasonable.

The notice requirement is your friend. The bank must give **written notice** of an exception hold at the time of deposit or by the next business day, stating **the amount held, the reason, and the date the funds will be available.** If you did not get that notice, ask for it. If the bank cannot produce it, the hold is on shaky ground.

The $6,725 threshold applies to the *excess*. Deposit a $10,000 ordinary check and the bank can hold only the $3,275 above the line for the extra days.

New accounts: 30 days and the ninth business day

For the first 30 calendar days after you open an account, the bank has more room. Cash, wires, and the first $6,725 of government and cashier's checks still go next-day. The portion of those special checks above $6,725 must be available by the **ninth business day**. Ordinary checks in a brand-new account have no federal schedule at all during those 30 days. If you are moving a large sum into a new bank, send it by wire, or wait a month before depositing big checks.

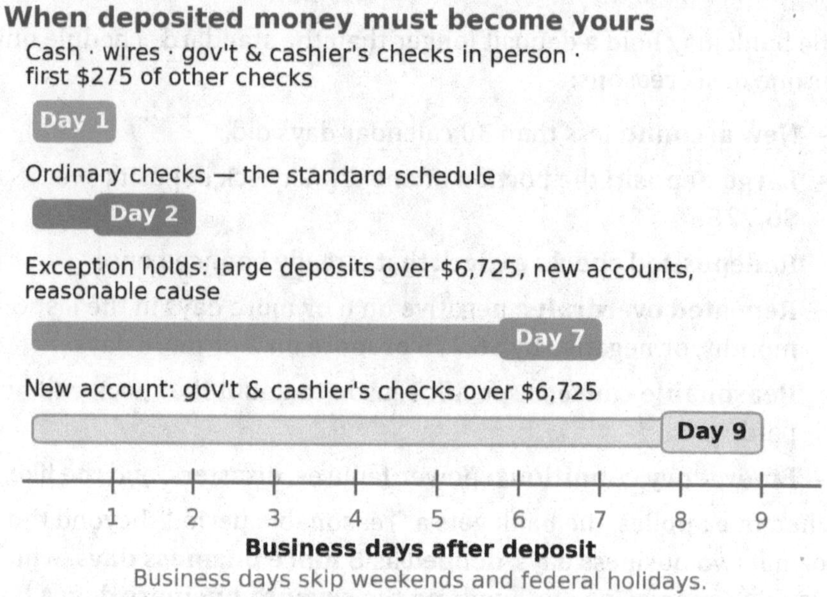

Figure 1.1. *Regulation CC availability timeline showing next-day, second, seventh, and ninth business-day landmarks*

KEY NUMBERS 2026 Numbers to Know

- **$275** — the first slice of a day's ordinary check deposits that must be available the next business day
- **$6,725** — the large-deposit and new-account threshold; only the amount *above* this can be held longer
- **2 business days** — standard availability for ordinary checks
- **7 business days** — the outer limit for most exception holds
- **9 business days** — large government and cashier's checks in a new account (first 30 calendar days)
- **15 business days** — a brokerage's initial exploitation hold under FINRA Rule 2165 (up to 55 with extensions); many state bank laws use 10 or 15
- **$10,000** — cash in one business day that triggers a routine Currency Transaction Report
- **60 days** — from the statement date to dispute an unauthorized electronic transaction under Regulation E (see Chapter 8, The Fine Print)
- **July 1, 2030** — next inflation adjustment to the Regulation CC figures

> QUIET TIP **The Fastest Money In Is Not a Check**
>
> Cash handed to a teller, a wire, and a direct deposit are all next-business-day money, with no exception hold for size. So are cashier's and government checks handed to an employee, up to $6,725. If someone owes you a large sum, ask for a wire or a cashier's check, and deposit that check with a person, not a machine.

Calling about a hold

The first phone call is where most people lose ground, because they ask "why is my money frozen" and get a script back. Ask narrower questions. The employee is allowed to tell you whether a hold is a Regulation CC hold and, if so, the release date.

> PHONE SCRIPT **Phone Script: Calling About a Hold**
>
> **You:** Good morning. My name is [YOUR NAME], and I'm calling about a hold on my account ending in [LAST FOUR DIGITS]. May I have your name and employee ID for my notes?
>
> **Them:** [Gives name and ID.]
>
> **You:** Thank you. Is this a Regulation CC deposit hold on a check I deposited, or a fraud or exploitation review on a withdrawal?
>
> **If they say deposit hold, you say:** Then under Regulation CC I should have a written notice with the amount, the reason, and the release date. What is the exact date the funds will be available, and which exception are you using: large deposit, new account, or reasonable cause?
>
> **If they say fraud or exploitation review, you say:** I understand you may not be able to tell me everything. What is the date the review must be completed, is there a case number, and will my trusted contact, [NAME], be called?
>
> **If they say "I don't have that information," you say:** Who does? Please transfer me, or give me the name and direct number of someone on the fraud team who can give me a release date.
>
> **You (closing):** Please note on the account that I requested the written hold notice, and mail or email it to me today. I have your name, [NAME], ID [NUMBER], and reference number [NUMBER]. If I don't receive the notice within two business days, I will follow up in writing and with the Consumer Financial Protection Bureau. Thank you.

The Fifteen-Business-Day Rule (and Who It Actually Applies To)

If you have seen a video about "banks legally freezing seniors' money for two weeks," this is the rule it was garbling.

At brokerages: FINRA Rule 2165

Every brokerage in the country operates under FINRA Rule 2165. It applies to a "specified adult": anyone **age 65 or older**, or any adult the firm reasonably believes has an impairment that keeps them from protecting their own interests.

If the firm reasonably believes financial exploitation has occurred, is occurring, or is about to be attempted, it *may* (not must) place a temporary hold on a **disbursement** of money or securities. Since **March 17, 2022**, it may also hold a **securities transaction**, such as a sudden order to sell everything and wire the proceeds.

The clock:

- **15 business days** for the initial hold.
- **10 more business days** if the firm's internal review still supports its belief (25 total).
- **30 more business days** if the firm has reported the matter to a state regulator, adult protective services, or a court (**55 business days** maximum without a court order).

The firm must notify everyone authorized on the account, and the trusted contact if you have named one, within **2 business days**. It cannot blanket-freeze the account; each disbursement is evaluated on its own. A firm that opens a hold is looking for someone who can confirm you are all right. If that person exists, the hold usually ends early.

In January 2026 FINRA proposed stretching the maximum to 145 business days and adding a short "speed bump" on suspicious disbursements for customers of any age. As of September 2026 that proposal awaited SEC approval and was not in effect.

At banks and credit unions: state law, or nothing

Here is the part the videos leave out. **No federal statute or regulation lets a bank or credit union hold a withdrawal for suspected exploitation.** Federal regulators, in a joint statement on December 4, 2024, *encouraged* banks to use holds "where legally appropriate." The authority itself comes only from state law.

As of the federal government's October 2024 count, 24 states had such a statute. Since then at least three have joined: Georgia, Maryland, and Oklahoma. California's bill failed in committee on February 2, 2026. We could find no bank hold statute in New York or Pennsylvania as of September 2026. The honest summary: **about half the states**.

Most of these laws cover customers age 65 or older, or any adult the state considers vulnerable; Oklahoma's starts at age 62. A sampling:

State	Initial bank hold	Extension
Florida	15 business days	Up to 30 more
Texas	10 business days	Up to 30 more, at an agency's request
Washington	5 business days (10 for securities)	Court order only
Georgia (since July 1, 2026)	15 business days	Up to 15 more
Oklahoma (from November 1, 2026)	10 business days	Extendable by investigation, agency, or court
Maryland (signed May 12, 2026)	Delay or denial permitted	Length and start date: confirm with your bank
Connecticut	7 business days	Up to 45 more
Delaware	10 business days	Up to 30 more
Mississippi	10 calendar days	Up to 10 more
Nebraska, South Carolina, Virginia	30 business days	None listed

Mississippi counts calendar days while nearly everyone else counts business days. Florida and Georgia require **written notice** to everyone on the account and to the trusted contact within **3**

business days. If you are in one of those states and got nothing in writing, say so.

Where to look up your own state

1. **Your state banking department** (sometimes the Department of Financial Institutions). Ask: "Does our state have a statute that lets banks place a temporary hold for suspected elder financial exploitation, and how many business days does it allow?"
2. **The Federal Trade Commission's state-by-state overview of financial-institution transaction holds**, a free document listing every state's law (the appendix directory says where to find it). It dates from October 2024, so use the newer information above for Georgia, Maryland, and Oklahoma.

No federal bank hold law, and one pending bill

You may read that Congress "passed a bank freeze law" in 2026. It did not. The House passed **H.R. 2478, the Financial Exploitation Prevention Act of 2025**, on June 25, 2026, by 414–2. It would let **mutual funds, ETFs, and transfer agents** delay a redemption for 15 business days, plus 10 more once exploitation is confirmed. It does not cover banks or credit unions, and as of this writing it was waiting in the Senate, where a nearly identical bill died in 2023.

> WATCH OUT **Watch Out: The "14 Business Days" Myth**
>
> A wave of articles in January 2026 claimed banks are "now legally allowed" to hold a senior's transfer for 14 business days. No such rule exists. The closest real rule is FINRA Rule 2165's 15 business days, and that applies to brokerages. If a bank employee quotes "14 days," ask which statute they are relying on and request the citation in writing. If they cannot name one, the hold is running on the bank's own policy, and your best tools are the account agreement and a polite written request for a release date.

The account agreement is the other clock

Even in a state with no hold statute, your bank can delay a transaction under its **account agreement**, which nearly always lets it take "reasonable time" to verify a transaction. What the state statutes add is a *time limit* and legal *immunity* for a bank acting in good faith. A bank without a statute has no fixed deadline, which is why the letter below asks for one.

The second figure shows the path a flagged transaction travels. Every box on it is a place where a named trusted contact and a written request shorten the trip.

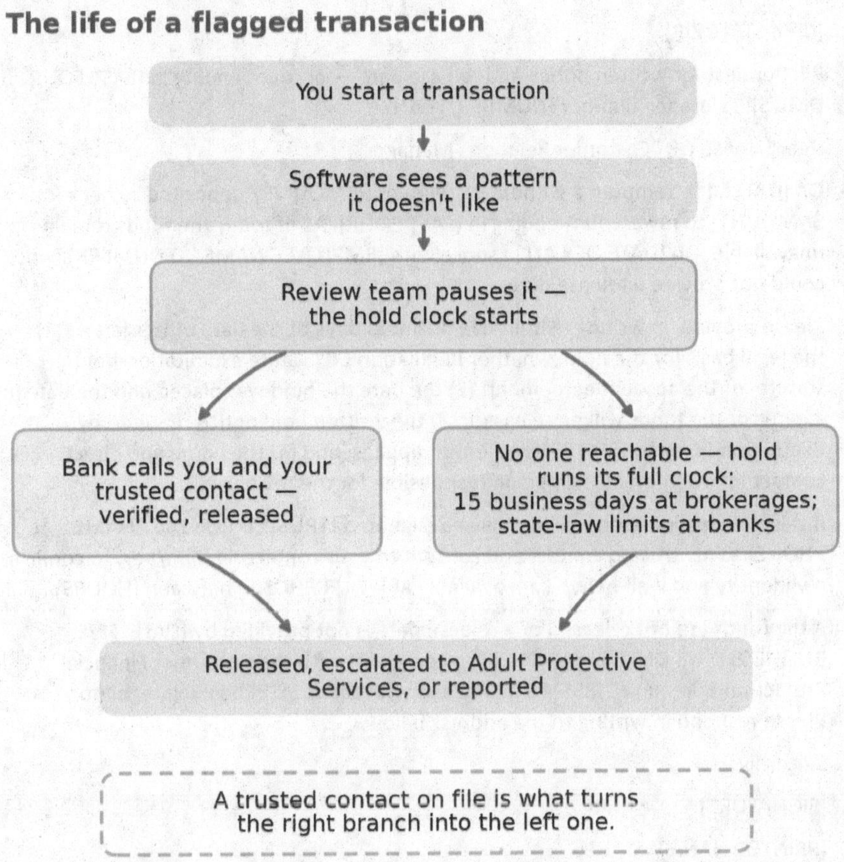

Figure 1.2. *What happens when a transaction is flagged, from trigger and review through hold, notice, the trusted-contact call, and release or escalation*

Putting it in writing

A phone call gets you a name and a date. A letter gets you a record. Send this one the day you learn of a hold with no release date, in a way you can prove: certified mail, the bank's secure message center, or hand delivery with a date-stamped copy.

LETTER TEMPLATE **Letter Template: Request for Written Explanation and Release Date of Hold**

[DATE]

[BANK OR BROKERAGE NAME]

Attn: Fraud Review / Customer Relations

[MAILING ADDRESS]

[CITY, STATE ZIP]

RE: Request for written notice and release date — account ending in [LAST FOUR DIGITS]; reference number [NUMBER, IF ANY]

Dear [NAME OR "Customer Relations Manager"]:

On [DATE], I [attempted a withdrawal/wire of $AMOUNT / deposited a check for $AMOUNT] to my account ending in [LAST FOUR]. As of today the funds remain unavailable. On [DATE OF CALL] I spoke with [EMPLOYEE NAME, ID NUMBER], who could not provide a release date.

Please provide, in writing, within **five business days** of the date of this letter: (1) the legal basis for the hold, whether Regulation CC, a state exploitation-hold statute, or the account agreement; (2) the date the hold was placed and the date it expires or the funds will be released; (3) the written hold notice required by Regulation CC or by [STATE] law, if either applies; and (4) the name and direct contact information of the person responsible for the review.

If this is an exploitation review, I have designated [TRUSTED CONTACT NAME, PHONE] as my trusted contact and consent to your contacting [him/her] to confirm my identity and well-being. I am available at [YOUR PHONE] between [HOURS].

If the funds are not released or a release date is not provided by [DATE, FIVE BUSINESS DAYS OUT], I intend to file a complaint with the Consumer Financial Protection Bureau at 1-855-411-2372 and with the [STATE] banking regulator. Please respond in writing to the address below.

Sincerely,

[SIGNATURE]

[PRINTED NAME]

[MAILING ADDRESS]

[PHONE]

Enclosures: copy of deposit receipt or wire request; copy of government-issued ID; copy of trusted contact designation (if on file)

The Free Form: Your Trusted Contact

Everything above moved faster when there was someone the institution could call. That is the entire point of the trusted contact designation, and it is free.

What it is

A **trusted contact person** is an adult you name on your account whom the institution may call if it suspects exploitation, cannot reach you, needs to confirm your health or whereabouts, or needs to find out who holds your power of attorney. It is a phone number on file, nothing more. At brokerages, **FINRA Rule 4512** requires the firm to make a reasonable effort to ask you for one when you open or update an account. You may decline, and the account opens anyway.

At banks and credit unions there is no federal requirement, but the designation is spreading. The December 2024 regulators' statement recommends it, and the Florida, Georgia, Maryland, and Oklahoma statutes all name the trusted contact as someone the bank should notify. Some banks call it an "emergency contact" or "designated contact." Ask by any of those names.

What a trusted contact can and cannot do

The institution may call them to...	They may NOT...
Address a possible exploitation concern	Withdraw, transfer, or spend anything
Confirm your current address and phone	See your balances as a matter of right
Confirm your health status	Make decisions about the account
Find your guardian, executor, trustee, or POA agent	Act as your power of attorney

A trusted contact is not an owner, not a signer, and not an agent. Naming one gives away nothing. It is the opposite of adding a child to your account as a joint owner, which gives away a great deal (see Chapter 4, The Four Documents).

Why it shortens every hold

A trusted contact is the free form that shortens every hold. A hold exists because a compliance officer cannot confirm you are acting freely. Without a trusted contact, the only person they can ask is you, and the whole worry is that you might be under someone's influence. With one, they have an independent voice who can say, "Yes, she's been talking about that roof for a month." Under Rule 2165 the firm must notify the trusted contact within 2 business days; in Florida and Georgia, within 3. That call is typically the moment the hold begins to end.

Who to pick, and how to set it up

Pick someone who is **not** on the account and not the person who helps you with day-to-day money; if a helper is the problem, a trusted contact who is also the helper defeats the purpose. Pick someone who answers the phone and lives at a stable address. They do not need to know your finances. They need to be able to say whether you are well.

1. Call or visit each bank, credit union, and brokerage and ask for the trusted contact form. Bring the contact's full name, phone, email, and address.
2. Ask whether the designation covers **all** your accounts there or only one; brokerages often apply it account by account.
3. Ask for **written confirmation** that it was recorded, and note the date on the worksheet.
4. Tell the person you named. A call from a bank about you is not a scam, and their job is to confirm you are well, not to discuss your accounts.
5. Review it once a year, alongside your beneficiary designations (Chapter 6, The Review).

WORKSHEET **Worksheet: Trusted Contact Designation & Institution Log**

Fill this out once, keep a copy with your important papers, and give a copy to the person you name. Update it whenever a phone number changes.

Part 1 — Your trusted contact

Your full name: ____________________

Trusted contact's full name: ____________________

Relationship to you: ____________________

Phone: ____________________ Second phone: ____________________

Email: ____________________

Mailing address: ____________________

Date you told them about this designation: ____________________

Backup contact (name and phone): ____________________

Part 2 — Institution log (one block per bank, credit union, or brokerage; copy this page for more)

Institution 1: ____________________ Account nickname: ____________________

[ ] Trusted contact form filed Date filed: __________ Written confirmation? [ ] Yes [ ] No

Institution's fraud/holds phone: ____________________

Institution 2: ____________________ Account nickname: ____________________

[ ] Trusted contact form filed Date filed: __________ Written confirmation? [ ] Yes [ ] No

Institution's fraud/holds phone: ____________________

Institution 3: ____________________ Account nickname: ____________________

[ ] Trusted contact form filed Date filed: __________ Written confirmation? [ ] Yes [ ] No

Institution's fraud/holds phone: ____________________

Part 3 — Annual review

Date of last review: __________ Next review date: __________

The Everyday Moves That Get Flagged

Banks do not have a person watching your account. They have software, and the software looks for a short list of patterns that show up again and again in exploitation cases. The list is public. In June 2022, the Financial Crimes Enforcement Network (FinCEN), the Treasury bureau that collects bank reports, issued an advisory spelling out the red flags it wants banks to watch for. The advisory does not tell banks to hold your cash; a withdrawal by itself triggers no federal hold. But it tells banks what to look at.

Software flags patterns, not people. The everyday moves that match the patterns:

- **Large cash withdrawals**, especially "frequent large withdrawals," which FinCEN names directly.
- **Daily-maximum ATM withdrawals**, several days running. This one is in the advisory word for word.
- **A sudden wire**, particularly to a person or country you have never sent money to before.
- **A new payee** added and paid within a day or two, as Marjorie did.
- **First-time gift-card purchases** in quantity, or a first visit to a cryptocurrency kiosk. The FBI counted $257.5 million in crypto-ATM losses by people age 60 and older in 2025.
- **Adding a name to an account**, then large outflows shortly after.
- **Changing your address or phone number, then withdrawing.** To the software this looks like a takeover: an impostor changes the contact details so you won't get the alert, then drains the account.
- **A dormant account that wakes up.** Years of silence, then movement, suggests someone new has found the account.
- **Checks to people the bank has never seen**, particularly in large round numbers.
- **A new caregiver or "friend"** at the branch with you or handling your paperwork.
- **Moving money right after a death.** Estate and joint accounts after a co-owner dies draw attention, and so, unhappily, do people who prey on the newly bereaved (see Chapter 2, The First 90 Days).

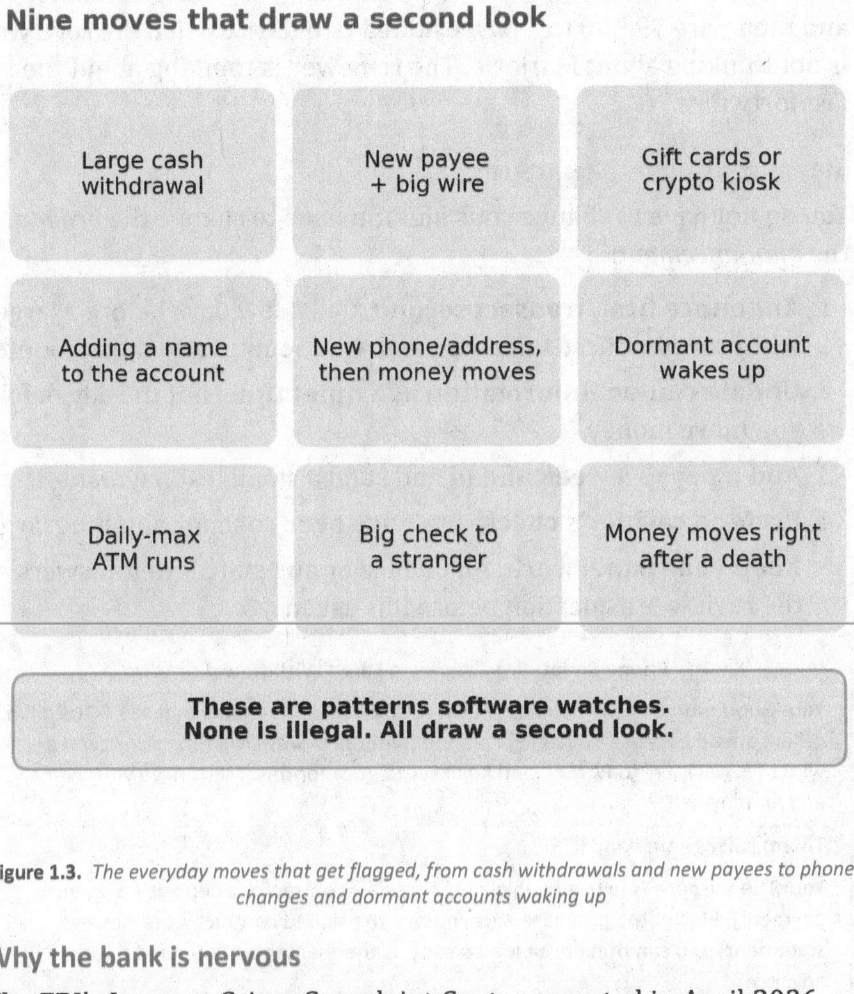

Figure 1.3. *The everyday moves that get flagged, from cash withdrawals and new payees to phone changes and dormant accounts waking up*

Why the bank is nervous

The FBI's Internet Crime Complaint Center reported in April 2026 that Americans age 60 and older lost **$7.7 billion** to internet-enabled fraud in 2025, across **201,266** complaints, roughly a 59% increase in losses over the year before. Separately, FinCEN found that financial institutions reported about **$27 billion** in suspicious activity linked to elder exploitation in the year ending June 2023. That is reported *suspicious activity*, including attempts and duplicates, not confirmed losses, but it shows the scale of what compliance teams see. In FinCEN's data, adult children were the perpetrators in about 40% of elder-theft reports.

So when a reviewer sees a 69-year-old change her phone number and then wire $9,500 to a payee added two days earlier, the reviewer is not thinking about Marjorie. The reviewer is thinking about the last forty files.

Stepping around the patterns

You do not have to change your life. You have to change the *order* and the *announcement*:

1. **Announce first, transact second.** Call a few days before a large withdrawal or first-time wire and ask them to note the account.
2. **Update contact information at a quiet time**, not the day before you move money.
3. **Add a payee a week ahead** and send a small test payment first.
4. **Prefer a cashier's check or a wire over cash** for anything large.
5. **Keep your paperwork.** An invoice or an estate letter answers the reviewer's question before it is asked.

PHONE SCRIPT **Phone Script: Pre-Clearing a Large Withdrawal or Wire**

You: Good morning. My name is [YOUR NAME], account ending in [LAST FOUR]. I'm calling ahead because on [DATE] I plan to [withdraw $AMOUNT in cash / send a wire of $AMOUNT to PAYEE], and I'd like it to go smoothly. May I have your name and employee ID?

Them: [Gives name and ID.]

You: The purpose is [a used-vehicle purchase / a contractor's deposit / a down payment]. I have [the purchase agreement / the signed contract / the closing statement] and can bring or upload a copy. Is there anything you need from me in advance?

If it is cash, you say: Does the branch need advance notice to have that much on hand, and how many days? I understand a cash transaction over $10,000 is reported routinely. I'm not asking to split it; I'd like to do it in one visit.

If it is a wire, you say: I'd like to add the payee today and send a small test wire first. What is the wire cutoff time, and will a wire of this size be reviewed before release?

If they say it might be held, you say: My trusted contact on file is [NAME], at [PHONE]; please call her if you need to confirm anything. What is the longest the review could take, in business days?

You (closing): Please note the account that I called today, and give me a reference number. Thank you, [NAME].

CHECKLIST **Checklist: Before Any Large Transaction**

- ☐ Call the bank 3–5 business days ahead using the pre-clearing script; get a reference number
- ☐ Gather the paperwork: invoice, contract, closing statement, or estate letter
- ☐ Confirm the trusted contact on file and tell them the transaction is coming
- ☐ Choose wire or cashier's check first; cash only if the other side cannot take anything else
- ☐ For a wire to a new payee, add the payee early and send a small test amount
- ☐ For cash over $10,000, ask how much notice the branch needs and plan one visit, not several
- ☐ Leave your address and phone unchanged in the week before, or explain the change to the bank
- ☐ Ask yourself the one question every reviewer asks: Did I decide to do this, or was I told to?

The Paperwork Behind the Counter: CTRs, SARs, and the $10,000 Line

Two federal reports shape what happens at the teller window with cash. Neither is aimed at you.

The Currency Transaction Report

When more than **$10,000 in cash** moves through a bank in one business day for one person, whether deposited, withdrawn, or exchanged, the bank must file a **Currency Transaction Report (CTR)** with FinCEN within 15 calendar days. Smaller cash transactions on the same day are added together. The teller records your ID. You are not notified, you cannot opt out, and a CTR on a legitimate withdrawal is no problem for you. A 2024 government audit found that of roughly 167 million CTRs filed over a decade, only about 5% were ever looked at.

CTRs cover **currency only**. Checks, cashier's checks, wires, and electronic transfers do not generate one.

Two bills in Congress would raise the threshold to $30,000; one cleared the House Financial Services Committee on January 22, 2026.

As of September 2026, **neither had passed, and $10,000 is still the line.**

Structuring: the one cash mistake that is a crime

Never split a cash withdrawal. Announce it instead. Breaking a cash transaction into pieces to stay under $10,000 is called **structuring**, and it is a federal crime even when the money is entirely yours and entirely legal. The penalty is a fine and up to 5 years in prison, rising to 10 years for a pattern involving more than $100,000 in a year. Banks must file a report when they suspect it, and their software is built to notice $9,500 on Monday and $9,500 on Tuesday.

> WATCH OUT **Watch Out: Never Split a Withdrawal to "Stay Under" $10,000**
>
> Well-meaning people do this constantly, sometimes on a teller's casual suggestion. Do not. Withdraw the full amount in one transaction, let the bank file its routine report, and keep the receipt. If anyone tells you to "keep each withdrawal under ten thousand so the bank doesn't ask questions," that instruction is itself proof you are being scammed. Hang up.

The Monetary Instrument Log

If you buy a cashier's check, money order, or traveler's checks **with cash** totaling **$3,000 to $10,000** in one day, the bank must *record* the purchase (your name, ID, and the serial numbers) in a log it keeps for five years. A record, not a report. Fund the cashier's check from your account instead of with cash, and the log does not apply.

Suspicious Activity Reports and "no tipping off"

A **Suspicious Activity Report (SAR)** is the bank's way of telling FinCEN that something looked wrong. Banks must file one for transactions of $5,000 or more with an identifiable suspect, $25,000 or more regardless of suspect, and $5,000 or more where structuring or money laundering is suspected, within 30 calendar days of detection.

Here is the part that makes people feel stonewalled: **federal law prohibits the bank from telling you that a SAR was filed** or what it says. This is "no tipping off." It is why the "review team" cannot say more, and why a bank that closes an account after a SAR will not explain itself. The silence is not personal. It is a legal requirement the employee would be breaking if they answered.

What you can do is ask the questions the law allows them to answer: is there a release date, a case number, is my trusted contact being called, and is my account being closed. The rest you may never learn, and it is better to know that up front than to spend a week demanding an answer that cannot legally be given.

The practical rules for cash

- **Announce large cash needs in advance.** Branches keep limited cash. A request for $15,000 may need a day or two of notice for purely logistical reasons; that is not a hold.
- **Prefer a cashier's check or wire.** They move next-business-day, avoid CTRs, and leave a paper trail that protects you.
- **Keep source-of-funds paperwork** for anything large. If a reviewer asks where the money came from, hand it over and the review ends.
- **Know your daily limits.** ATM cash limits are bank policy, not law; in 2026 they commonly run from a few hundred dollars to $1,000 or more per day, and most banks will raise them temporarily if you call. Hitting the limit day after day is one of the flags.

When the Bank Asks for Your ID Again

Long-time customers are sometimes startled when a letter arrives asking them to re-verify their identity, address, occupation, or source of funds. It feels like an accusation. It isn't.

The Customer Identification Program rule requires banks to verify who you are when you open an account. The Customer Due Diligence rule, in effect since 2018, requires them to understand the purpose of each customer relationship and to **keep that information current on a risk basis**. Old records or a routine sweep of accounts opened before the current rules can prompt a refresh.

Answer these requests **promptly**. An unanswered refresh is one of the quieter paths to a restricted or closed account, because the bank can no longer certify that it knows its customer. Bring what is requested, ask for confirmation that your file is complete, and keep a copy. If the letter seems suspicious, call the bank at the number on your statement, never the number in the letter.

When the Bank Closes the Door

Sometimes the restriction is not a hold at all. The bank ends the relationship.

The Consumer Financial Protection Bureau puts it plainly: a bank or credit union can close your account without your permission, for reasons including bounced checks, unpaid fees, dormancy, an unanswered identity request, or a compliance concern it will not name. **No federal law requires advance notice or a reason.** Some states may require notice, but none we could confirm. Federal regulators warned in 2024 against unfair "debanking" without process, but no rule yet makes notice mandatory.

What the bank must do is return your money, typically by check to the address on file. What you should do:

1. **Ask, in writing, for the balance by check** (or by wire to an account you already hold) and for a final statement. Confirm the mailing address on file first.
2. **Ask for the written reason.** You may not get one, especially if a SAR is involved. Ask anyway; the request goes in the file.
3. **Redirect your direct deposits the same day**: Social Security (1-800-772-1213), pensions, annuities. Then redirect automatic payments.
4. **File a complaint with the CFPB** at 1-855-411-2372 or through its online complaint form. The bank must respond in writing, which sometimes produces the explanation a phone call could not.
5. **Contact your state banking regulator**, particularly for a state-chartered bank or credit union.
6. **Keep a second account at a different institution.** Chapter 8, The Fine Print, calls this the lifeboat account. It turns a closure from a crisis into an inconvenience.

When the bank goes quiet, ask in writing and escalate on a schedule. A calm letter, a calendar reminder, and a complaint filed on the day you said you would file it get more done than any amount of frustration at the counter.

CHECKLIST **Checklist: If Your Account Is Frozen Right Now (The 72-Hour Plan)**

- ☐ Hour 1: Call the bank using the "Calling About a Hold" script; get the employee's name, ID, a reference number, and the answer to "Reg CC hold or fraud review?"
- ☐ Hour 1: Ask for the release date in business days and the written hold notice
- ☐ Hour 2: Call your trusted contact, tell them a call from the bank is legitimate, and ask them to answer it
- ☐ Day 1: If no trusted contact is on file, ask whether you can add one today by phone
- ☐ Day 1: Cover essentials from another account or card; do not open a new account at the same bank
- ☐ Day 2: Send the "Request for Written Explanation and Release Date" letter by certified mail or secure message
- ☐ Day 2: If you suspect someone is exploiting you or a parent, call Adult Protective Services; the Eldercare Locator at 1-800-677-1116 can connect you to your county office
- ☐ Day 3: If there is still no release date, file a complaint with the CFPB at 1-855-411-2372 and note the complaint number
- ☐ Day 3: Call your state banking department (or state securities regulator for a brokerage) and ask how long your state's hold law allows
- ☐ Every day: log each call, name, ID, and promise in one notebook

What Marjorie Did

Once Marjorie stopped asking "why" and started asking "which," the picture cleared. On her next call she asked whether the wire was under a Regulation CC hold or a fraud review. It was a review. She asked for the release date; under Florida law, the reviewer said, the bank could hold the disbursement up to 15 business days, but expected to finish sooner. She asked for a reference number, for the written notice Florida requires within 3 business days, and whether she could name her daughter Anne as a trusted contact. She could, by phone, that afternoon.

The bank called Anne the next morning. Anne confirmed the roof, the storm, and the fact that her mother had been grumbling about contractors for a month. The wire released that afternoon, and the bank's letter arrived two days later.

Marjorie found a second roofer. Before paying his deposit she called three days ahead, added him as a payee, sent a $50 test wire, and mentioned Anne's name. The full wire went through in under an hour. The worksheet now lives in the drawer with her passport, and Anne is on file at her brokerage and her credit union too.

Your Next Steps

CHECKLIST **Your Next Steps**

- ☐ Call each bank, credit union, and brokerage and ask for its trusted contact (or emergency contact) form; file one everywhere and log the date on the worksheet
- ☐ Tell the person you named and give them a copy of the worksheet
- ☐ Look up your state's bank hold rule by calling your state banking department or finding the FTC's state-by-state overview of transaction holds
- ☐ Read the "holds" and "reasonable time" sections of your deposit account agreement and note the wire cutoff time
- ☐ Write the Regulation CC numbers on an index card: $275 next day, 2 business days standard, 7 for exceptions, $6,725 threshold
- ☐ Open or confirm a lifeboat account at a different institution, with one small recurring transfer so it never goes dormant
- ☐ Gather source-of-funds paperwork for any large sum you expect to move this year
- ☐ Answer any pending identity-update request from your bank within a week, confirming it first by the number on your statement
- ☐ Copy the two scripts and the 72-hour checklist and keep them by the phone with the CFPB number, 1-855-411-2372
- ☐ Schedule an annual review of trusted contacts alongside your beneficiary designations (see Chapter 6, The Review)

CHAPTER TWO

The First 90 Days — When a Spouse Dies

By the end of this chapter you will know which calls to make in which order, which money to leave untouched, and which clocks started counting on the date printed on the death certificate.

A STORY **Marian, 68, Tucson, Arizona**

Dale died on a Tuesday in March, four days after a stroke. He was 74. They had been married 44 years, and for most of them he handled the accounts and she handled everything else. (This story is illustrative, not a real person.)

At the funeral home, the director asked for Dale's Social Security number. Marian gave it without thinking about why. On the drive home her son Kevin, who means well and talks fast, said they should move everything into her name that week, "before the bank freezes it."

In the second week of April, Dale's Social Security deposit landed in the joint checking account, same as always. A teller suggested Marian close the joint account and open a fresh one. A neighbor said to roll Dale's IRA into hers right away so it "wouldn't get stuck." The insurance agent left a voicemail. The mortgage company sent a letter.

Everyone had advice, and all of it was fast. Marian sat at the kitchen table with the checkbook, a legal pad, and a cup of coffee going cold, and wrote one question at the top of the page: *What has to happen this week, and what can wait?*

THE QUIET RULES The Quiet Rules in This Chapter

- *Slow is safe. The mistakes that cost the most in the first 90 days are the irreversible ones made fast.*
- *The last Social Security deposit is not yours to keep.*
- *Joint accounts pass by contract. Sole-name accounts wait for paper.*
- *A survivor does not have to choose one benefit forever. Survivors can switch.*
- *Losing a spouse is a "life-changing event" on a government form. File it before Medicare bills you as if nothing changed.*
- *An IRA rollover has no undo button.*
- *Tell one credit bureau, and all three lock the file.*

Slow Is Safe

There is no right way to feel in the weeks after your spouse dies, and nothing here asks you to feel any particular way. What this chapter asks is smaller: do a few things in a sensible order, and leave some things alone for a while.

Almost every costly mistake in the first 90 days is irreversible, and almost every one is made quickly, because someone with good intentions said "you should take care of that now." Rolling an IRA, closing an account, spending a deposit, selling a house, signing a disclaimer: each can be done in an afternoon and none can be undone.

The real deadlines are mostly measured in months: two years for the Social Security death payment, eight months for Medicare Part B, nine months for an estate tax return, sixty days for COBRA. The things that must happen in the first week are few. Think of the 90 days in five stretches, each with its own short list.

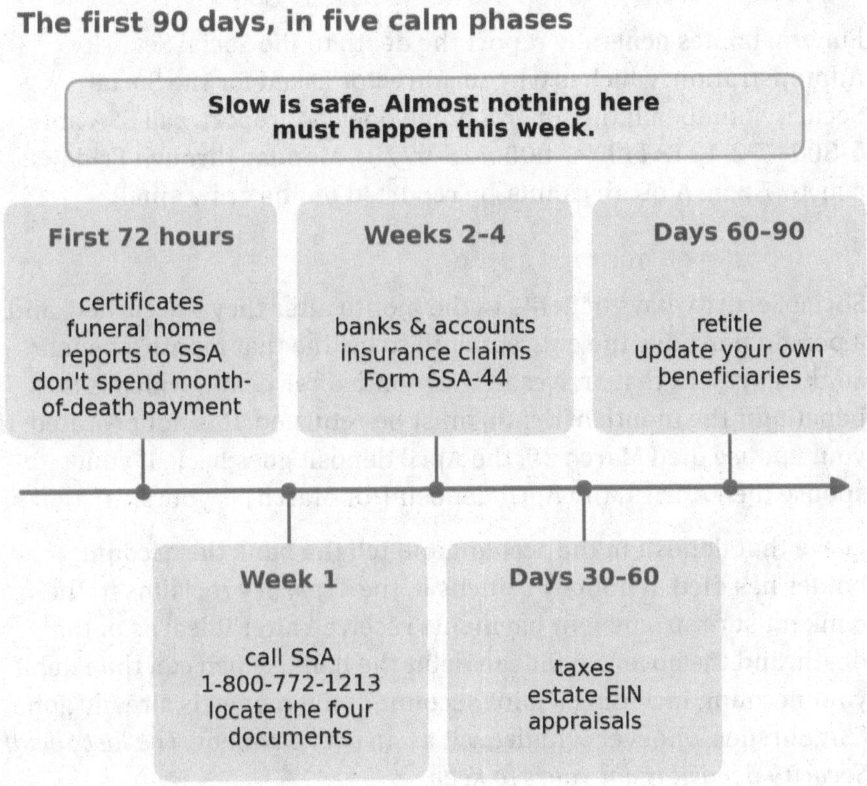

Figure 2.1. *The 90-day timeline after a spouse's death, from the first 72 hours through days 60–90*

The First 72 Hours

Death certificates

Order at least ten certified copies from the funeral home or county vital-records office. Most families use four to ten, and every bank, insurer, and agency wants its own. The first copy typically costs \$10–30 and additional copies \$5–15, so order them together. States have quirks: New York limits cause-of-death copies to immediate family, Texas issues short and long forms, and California distinguishes "authorized" copies (which banks want) from "informational" ones. Ask the funeral director which version your state's institutions accept.

Tell Social Security (the funeral home usually does)

Funeral homes generally report the death to the Social Security Administration, which is why the director asked for the Social Security number. If the funeral home does not report, call SSA at 1-800-772-1213 (TTY 1-800-325-0778), Monday through Friday, 8 a.m. to 7 p.m. A death cannot be reported online or by email.

The deposit you must not spend

Social Security pays benefits in the month after they are earned, and a person must live the entire month to be due that month's benefit. So the payment that arrives in the month after death, which is the benefit *for* the month of death, must be returned. It is not prorated. If your spouse died March 20, the April deposit goes back. If your spouse died April 1, the April deposit (for March) is yours.

Leave that deposit in the account and tell the bank the account holder has died. If nobody returns it, the Treasury reclaims it: the bank must return benefit payments received after it learns of the death, and the government can debit the bank, which can then debit your account, including a joint account. If the money is already gone, SSA pursues whoever withdrew it as an overpayment. *The last Social Security deposit is not yours to keep.*

Do not close the joint account

Kevin's advice was backwards. A joint account with right of survivorship already belongs to the survivor. Closing it means re-pointing every direct deposit and automatic payment, and it can interrupt the very deposits you are about to sort out. Keep it open and retitle it in weeks two through four.

Locate the four documents

Find the will or trust, the durable power of attorney, the health care directive, and the beneficiary designations (see Chapter 4, The Four Documents). The power of attorney is finished: a POA always ends at death. The will and the beneficiary forms are what matter now. You need not read them closely yet; you need to know where they are.

WATCH OUT **Watch Out: The Obituary Is a Shopping List**

Obituary-driven fraud starts within days: fake debt collectors, calls about a "lapsed" policy that needs a payment, funeral-home impersonators, burglars who read the service time, and identity thieves who open credit in the deceased's name ("ghosting").

- Leave the birth date, birthplace, mother's maiden name, and home address out of the obituary.
- Ask a neighbor to stay at the house during the service.
- Pay no one who calls about a debt. Debts are the estate's to sort out, in writing.
- Notify SSA, the IRS, and one credit bureau promptly so the file is flagged.
- Report attempts to the Federal Trade Commission; the appendix has the address.

CHECKLIST **Checklist: First 72 Hours**

- ☐ Order 10 or more certified death certificates from the funeral home or county vital-records office
- ☐ Give the funeral director your spouse's Social Security number so the death is reported to SSA
- ☐ Set aside, do not spend, the Social Security deposit for the month of death
- ☐ Keep every joint account open; close or empty nothing
- ☐ Locate the will or trust, POA, health care directive, and beneficiary forms
- ☐ Strip birth date, birthplace, maiden name, and address from the obituary
- ☐ Start the 90-Day Master Tracker (later in this chapter) for every call, name, and reference number

Week One: Social Security Survivor Benefits

Survivor benefits cannot be applied for online. Call 1-800-772-1213 or visit a local office. On that call you confirm the death has been reported, claim the $255 lump-sum death payment, and ask about survivor benefits.

The $255 lump-sum death payment

A one-time $255, payable first to a spouse living in the same household at the time of death. You must apply within 2 years. If you were already receiving spouse's benefits on your spouse's record, SSA says you need not file separately, but ask anyway.

Who qualifies, and how much

Your situation	Share of your spouse's benefit
At your full retirement age or later	100%
Age 60 up to full retirement age	71.5% to 99%, scaled by month
Age 50–59 and disabled	71.5%
Any age, caring for the deceased's child under 16	75%

You generally must have been married at least 9 months before the death (with exceptions, such as accidental death). A divorced spouse qualifies after a marriage of 10 years or more. Remarrying before age 60 (50 if disabled) bars the survivor benefit; remarrying at or after 60 does not.

You do not receive your own retirement benefit *plus* a survivor benefit; you receive the higher of the two, subject to your age. A survivor's full retirement age runs on a slightly different schedule from the retirement one, so ask the representative for your survivor FRA specifically.

The switch: a choice nobody else has

Since 2016, most people who file for any Social Security benefit are "deemed" to have filed for all of them at once. That rule does not apply to survivors. A widow or widower can take a reduced survivor benefit as early as 60, let their own retirement benefit grow until 70, then switch. Or take their own benefit first and switch to the survivor benefit at full retirement age.

A survivor does not have to choose one benefit forever. Survivors can switch. Before you file, ask SSA for the monthly amount of each benefit at each age, write them down, and pick the order that pays the most over time. A fee-only planner can run this in an hour; it is one of the few decisions here worth paying for.

Retroactive months

Past full retirement age, survivor benefits can be paid up to 6 months retroactively. Before FRA there is generally none, because back payments would deepen the reduction, with one exception: filing in the month immediately after the death allows one month back. Disabled widows and widowers may receive up to 12 months. So if you are past FRA, a few weeks of thought costs nothing; if you are under FRA and want that extra month, call within the month after the death.

> PHONE SCRIPT **Phone Script: Reporting a Death and Applying for Survivor Benefits**
>
> Call 1-800-772-1213 with your spouse's Social Security number, date of death, your own number, your marriage date, and a death certificate in front of you.
>
> **You:** Hello. My spouse, [FULL NAME], Social Security number [NUMBER], died on [DATE]. I want to confirm the death has been reported, apply for the lump-sum death payment, and ask about survivor benefits.
>
> **Them:** I can help with that. Can you verify your identity?
>
> **You:** Yes. [Answer their questions.] First, does your system show the death as reported? If not, I am reporting it now.
>
> **You:** Second, I am applying for the $255 lump-sum death payment. We lived in the same household. Please note today as my application date.
>
> **You:** Third, I need two figures: the survivor benefit I could receive now, and my own retirement benefit at full retirement age and at 70. I understand deemed filing does not apply to survivors and I can take one and switch later.
>
> **If they say:** You should file for everything today.
>
> **You say:** I would like the amounts in writing first. Please schedule an appointment for me to file, and note that I called within [one month / six months] of the death.
>
> **If they say:** The payment for the month of death was deposited.
>
> **You say:** I have set it aside. Will SSA reclaim it through the bank, or should I have the bank return it?
>
> **Close:** Please give me your name or employee ID, a confirmation number for this call, and the date and time of my appointment. Thank you.

Weeks Two Through Four: The Bank Accounts

Every account your spouse touched falls into a handful of categories, and each has its own rule. Sorting them first saves a dozen phone calls.

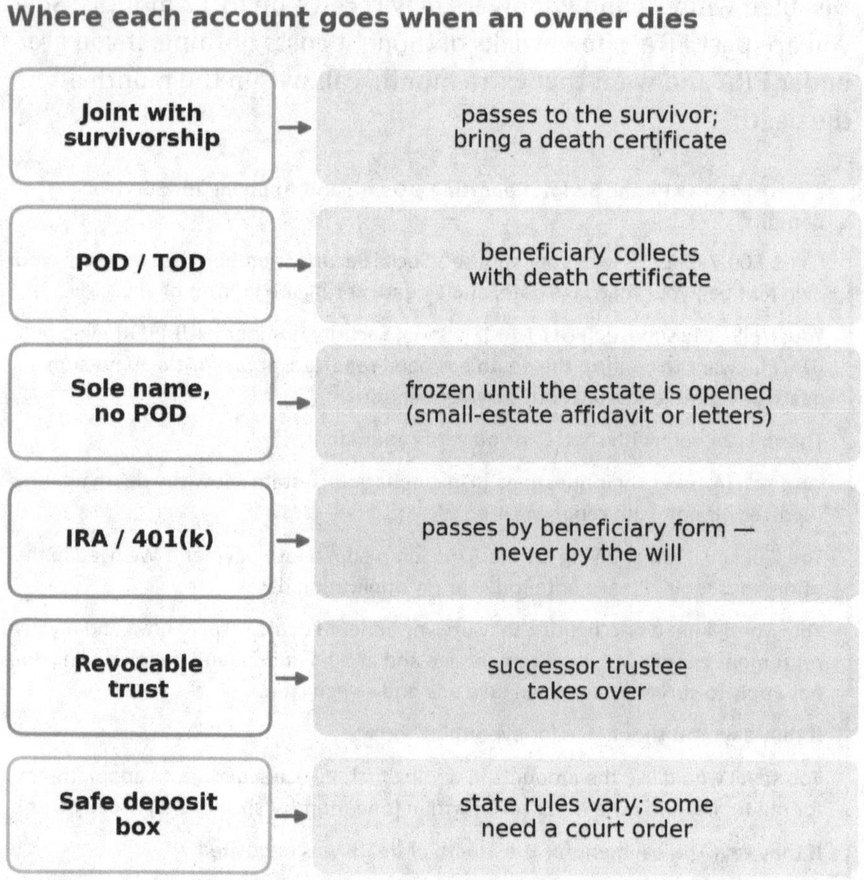

Figure 2.2. *What happens to each account type at death, from joint survivorship accounts to safe deposit boxes*

Joint with right of survivorship. The balance belongs to you by contract, outside probate. Banks generally do not freeze a survivorship account; you present a death certificate and the bank retitles it. Your spouse's half may still count for state inheritance tax and, in some states, be reachable by your spouse's creditors, but the money is yours to use.

Payable-on-death and transfer-on-death. If you were named as POD or TOD beneficiary, you collect by presenting a certified death certificate and your ID, typically within days. No probate, no letters.

Sole-name accounts. An account in your spouse's name alone, with no beneficiary, freezes when the bank learns of the death and stays frozen until a personal representative presents letters testamentary from the probate court or, for a small enough estate, a small-estate affidavit. One quiet exception: under the Uniform Commercial Code, a bank may keep paying checks your spouse wrote on or before the date of death for 10 days after that date, unless someone with an interest in the account orders it to stop. That is the window in which the last checks your spouse mailed will clear.

Joint accounts pass by contract. Sole-name accounts wait for paper.

State	Small-estate route	2026 limit
California	Personal-property affidavit	$208,850 (deaths on or after April 1, 2025)
Texas	Small-estate affidavit (no will; judge approves; 30-day wait)	$75,000, excluding homestead and exempt property
Florida	Summary administration	$75,000, excluding exempt property (or death over 2 years ago)
New York	Voluntary administration	$50,000 in personal property

Other states have their own figures. Ask the probate clerk at your county courthouse for the threshold and the form.

Convenience accounts. If your spouse added an adult child "to help with bills," the child is likely a signer, not an owner. A convenience account has no survivorship right; the money passes to the estate. But if the signature card says "joint with survivorship," courts often honor the card. Pull the card before assuming anything.

> QUIET TIP **Tip: Your Deposit Insurance Has a Six-Month Cushion**
>
> When a co-owner of a joint account dies, the FDIC keeps insuring the account as if that person were alive for 6 months. A $500,000 joint account does not become a $250,000-limit single account on the day of death. Use the six months to spread balances across ownership categories or institutions if you are over the limit (see Chapter 8, The Fine Print).

New Jersey and Pennsylvania: be precise

You may have read that "the bank must hold half the account" after a death. That is a **New Jersey** rule, and only New Jersey's. There, a tax lien attaches at death; a bank may release up to 50% of the date-of-death balance to the survivor or executor without a waiver but must hold the other 50% until a waiver arrives. For a surviving spouse (a "Class A" beneficiary), Form L-8 is a self-executing affidavit that releases the rest; Form L-9 covers real estate. Property held by spouses as tenants by the entirety needs no waiver.

Pennsylvania is different. Its banks must notify the Department of Revenue when a joint account owner dies, and transfers to a spouse are exempt at a 0% rate. No statute requires a Pennsylvania bank to freeze half, and the old REV-1543 notices that told survivors to pay a presumptive tax were suspended in April 2022. Some Pennsylvania banks may still hold funds as a matter of their own practice until an inheritance-tax return (REV-1500) is filed; if yours does, ask for the policy in writing and point out that spousal transfers are exempt. Pennsylvania's tax on non-spouse shares is delinquent 9 months after death, with a 5% discount if paid within 3 months.

The safe deposit box

Whether you can open the box depends on your state. About ten states, including New York, Georgia, Connecticut, and Nevada, require a court order first. Others, including California, Florida, Illinois, Minnesota, and Oregon, let a spouse or heir open it with a death certificate and ID, usually under bank supervision and often only to remove the will, burial instructions, and insurance policies. Virginia and Wisconsin permit a will search only. In Texas the executor may open the box with a copy of the will, but if the will is *in* the box, a court order is needed. If you co-rented the box, you may have access in your own right; ask the branch.

> PHONE SCRIPT **Phone Script: Calling the Bank About a Sole-Name Account**
>
> Call the number on the statement, or visit the branch with a death certificate.

You: Hello. My spouse, [FULL NAME], died on [DATE]. I am calling about account ending in [LAST FOUR DIGITS], which was in their name alone. What will the bank do with it, and what do you need from me?

Them: I'm sorry for your loss. We'll need a certified death certificate and we'll place the account in deceased status.

You: Three questions. First, is the account frozen now, and will you still pay checks my spouse wrote before the date of death during the 10-day window?

You: Second, what releases the funds: letters testamentary, or do you accept a small-estate affidavit for our state, and what is the limit?

You: Third, which automatic payments and direct deposits are on this account? Please list them so I can redirect them.

If they say: Your state requires us to hold half the balance.

You say: Please send me that policy in writing with the statute it relies on. [In New Jersey, ask for Form L-8. In Pennsylvania, note that spousal transfers are exempt.]

If they say: We need the original will.

You say: Please confirm in writing exactly which documents you require so I make one trip.

Close: Please give me your name, a reference number for this call, and the mailing address for the deceased-accounts department. I will follow up in writing.

LETTER TEMPLATE **Letter Template: Notification of Death to a Financial Institution**

[DATE]

[BANK OR BROKERAGE NAME]

Attn: Deceased Accounts / Estate Services

[STREET ADDRESS]

[CITY, STATE ZIP]

RE: Notification of death — [FULL NAME OF DECEASED], date of death [DATE]; account(s) ending in [LAST FOUR DIGITS]

Dear Estate Services:

I am writing to notify you that [FULL NAME OF DECEASED], an account holder at your institution, died on [DATE]. I am the surviving spouse [and joint owner / named beneficiary / executor named in the will].

Please place any accounts held solely in the deceased's name in deceased status and confirm in writing which documents you require to release or retitle each account. Please retitle joint accounts with right of survivorship into my name, and tell me how to claim any payable-on-death registration naming me.

> Please also send a list of automatic debits and direct deposits on each account, and confirm whether the Social Security payment received on [DATE] will be returned to the Treasury by the bank or must be returned by me.
>
> Please respond in writing within 10 business days to the address below, with a reference number for this matter.
>
> Sincerely,
>
> [YOUR NAME]
>
> [ADDRESS]
>
> [PHONE]
>
> Enclosures: certified death certificate; copy of my photo ID; [copy of the will / letters testamentary / small-estate affidavit, if applicable]

Health Coverage and the Widow's Penalty

If your health insurance came through your spouse's employer, or your Medicare premium is about to be set from a two-year-old joint return, the next four weeks matter.

Coverage decision	Window	What to file
Medicare Part B after losing a spouse's employer plan	8 months from when the job or coverage ended, whichever was first	Forms CMS-40B and CMS-L564
COBRA from the spouse's employer (20+ employees)	60 days to elect; up to 36 months of coverage	Plan's election form
ACA Marketplace	60 days after loss of coverage	Application, or 1-800-318-2596
Medigap (if new to Part B at 65 or older)	6 months from your Part B start; once only	Insurer's application
Lower your IRMAA surcharge	As soon as possible	Form SSA-44

Part B: eight months, and why COBRA does not stop the clock

If you were on your spouse's employer plan past 65 and have not enrolled in Part B, you have a Special Enrollment Period of 8 months beginning the month after the employment or the coverage ends, whichever is first. Use Form CMS-40B (Application for Enrollment in

Medicare Part B) and Form CMS-L564 (Request for Employment Information), which the employer completes.

COBRA does not count as employer coverage and does not extend the 8 months. Many widows take COBRA for the full 36 months, assume Medicare will be there when it ends, and then meet a Part B late-enrollment penalty of 10% of the standard premium for each full 12-month period they could have had Part B, for life. Elect COBRA if you need a bridge, but enroll in Part B inside the 8 months regardless. If you are under 65 and losing coverage, you have 60 days to elect COBRA and 60 days to enroll through the Marketplace. Free Medicare counseling is available from your State Health Insurance Assistance Program (SHIP) at 1-877-839-2675.

IRMAA: the same income, half the thresholds

Medicare's income-related surcharge (IRMAA) is set from your tax return of two years earlier. In 2026 the standard Part B premium is $202.90 a month, and the surcharge begins above $109,000 of modified adjusted gross income for a single filer, or $218,000 on a joint return. Cross the line by one dollar and the premium becomes $284.10, plus a $14.50 Part D surcharge, for the whole year.

Here is the trap. Two years from now, Medicare will look at a joint return from a year when you were married, but you will be filing single, and the single thresholds are exactly half the joint ones. Advisors call this the "widow's penalty": the same or lower income, taxed at single rates and measured against single IRMAA cliffs.

Death of a spouse is one of the eight "life-changing events" on Form SSA-44 (Medicare Income-Related Monthly Adjustment Amount – Life-Changing Event); the others are marriage, divorce or annulment, work stoppage, work reduction, loss of income-producing property, loss of pension income, and an employer settlement payment. File it with an estimate of your new income and evidence, by mail with copies, in person with originals, or by calling 1-800-772-1213 for an appointment. *Losing a spouse is a "life-changing event" on a government form. File it before Medicare bills you as if nothing changed.*

Pensions, Life Insurance, Employers, and the VA

Pensions. Federal law (ERISA) required your spouse's pension to be paid as a qualified joint-and-survivor annuity unless you signed a notarized waiver. Call the plan administrator with a death certificate and ask what survivor annuity you are due. If the Pension Benefit Guaranty Corporation took over the plan, report the death to PBGC at 1-800-400-7242 with a certified death certificate.

Life insurance. Claims typically pay in 14–60 days; policies less than 2 years old face a contestability review that takes longer. State laws require interest on late claims (Washington, for example, charges interest from the date of death on claims unpaid after 30 days, at the greater of the insurer's rate or 8%). If a policy may exist that you cannot find, the free NAIC Life Insurance Policy Locator asks participating insurers to search; allow 90 or more business days.

Employers. Ask your spouse's most recent employer about final pay and unused leave, group life insurance, the 401(k) or pension, COBRA paperwork, and any retiree health benefit that continues to a spouse.

Veterans. If your spouse served, ask the VA about survivor benefits, including the Survivors Pension for spouses with limited income and assets. Chapter 3, The Silent Deadlines, has the figures.

Retirement Accounts: Do Not Rush

The neighbor who told Marian to roll Dale's IRA into hers "right away" was repeating advice that is often right and occasionally very wrong, depending on the survivor's age and needs. *An IRA rollover has no undo button.* A surviving spouse has four options, and the first move is to understand them, not make one.

Option	Best for	The catch
Roll into your own IRA	Survivors over 59½, or older than the deceased	Irreversible; 10% penalty on withdrawals before 59½
Keep as an inherited (beneficiary) IRA	Survivors under 59½ who may need money	No 10% penalty at any age; RMDs wait until the deceased would have reached RMD age; can roll to your own IRA later

Option	Best for	The catch
Spousal election (since 2024)	Survivors who stay as beneficiary	Smaller RMDs from the Uniform Lifetime Table; ask the custodian
Disclaim all or part	Money that should go to children	Within 9 months; you cannot have touched it; irrevocable

The inherited-IRA route is the one most people do not know about. If you are 57 and widowed, rolling the money into your own IRA locks it behind the 10% early-withdrawal penalty until 59½. Leaving it as an inherited IRA lets you withdraw without penalty at any age, and you can still roll it into your own IRA two years later. Rolling over first and regretting it is irreversible.

Two dates apply whatever you choose. If your spouse was taking required minimum distributions and had not taken the full amount for the year of death, you as beneficiary must take the rest; under the 2024 final regulations the deadline is the later of your tax-filing deadline for that year (including extensions) or December 31 of the year following death, with an automatic penalty waiver if you meet it. Any RMD due must be taken before a rollover. And a disclaimer must be signed within 9 months of death.

> WATCH OUT **Watch Out: The Check Made Out to You**
>
> Never let a custodian mail you a check for your spouse's IRA or 401(k) payable to you personally. For a spouse that starts a 60-day clock and, from an employer plan, triggers 20% withholding. For any other beneficiary it is a fully taxable distribution the IRS cannot reverse. Ask for a trustee-to-trustee transfer, and say those words. Chapter 7, The Handoff, walks through the exact call.

Taxes in the First Year

The final joint return. You may file jointly for the year of death unless you remarry that year. Write "DECEASED," your spouse's name, and the date of death across the top. If you maintain a home for a dependent child, you may use Qualifying Surviving Spouse rates for the following 2 years.

Forms 1310 and 56. A surviving spouse filing a joint return does not need Form 1310 to claim a refund; it is required only when someone else claims the refund without court papers. Form 56 (Notice Concerning Fiduciary Relationship) tells the IRS who is acting for the estate.

The estate's own identity. If there is an estate to administer, get an estate Employer Identification Number with Form SS-4 (online, in minutes) and open an estate account. Do not pay estate bills from your personal account or deposit estate money into it.

Form 706 and portability. The federal estate tax return is due 9 months after death, with one 6-month extension on Form 4768 if requested before the deadline. Most estates owe nothing; the 2026 exemption is $15,000,000 per person. But filing a 706 anyway lets you claim your spouse's unused exemption ("portability"), which can matter if your estate grows or the law changes. If you miss the 9 months and the estate was not otherwise required to file, Rev. Proc. 2022-32 allows a portability-only 706 up to the fifth anniversary of death, with a required legend at the top. A CPA can tell you in one conversation whether it is worth filing.

Step-up in basis. Assets your spouse owned take a new cost basis equal to fair market value at death. Get a date-of-death appraisal for real estate and date-of-death brokerage statements now, while values are easy to document. In the nine community-property states (Arizona, California, Idaho, Louisiana, Nevada, New Mexico, Texas, Washington, and Wisconsin), both halves of community property step up, including yours. Elsewhere, only your spouse's half does. Retirement accounts and annuities never step up.

The house. If you sell within 2 years of your spouse's death and have not remarried, you may still exclude up to $500,000 of gain under Section 121, rather than the $250,000 single limit. Do not sell before you have the appraisal and understand the two-year window.

Credit, Identity, and the Paper Trail

Tell one credit bureau, and all three lock the file. Mail a certified death certificate with your spouse's name, Social Security number, date of birth, and date of death to any one of Equifax, Experian, or TransUnion; that bureau notifies the other two. TransUnion, for example, flags the file within 5 business days. SSA's death records reach the bureaus eventually, but a direct letter is faster and blocks new credit in your spouse's name.

> LETTER TEMPLATE **Letter Template: Credit Bureau Deceased Notification**
>
> [DATE]
>
> [CREDIT BUREAU NAME]
>
> [MAILING ADDRESS FROM THE APPENDIX]
>
> RE: Request to place a deceased indicator — [FULL NAME OF DECEASED], SSN [XXX-XX-XXXX], date of birth [DATE], date of death [DATE]
>
> Dear Consumer Relations:
>
> I am writing to notify you that [FULL NAME OF DECEASED] died on [DATE]. I am the surviving spouse [and executor of the estate].
>
> Please place a deceased indicator on the credit file so that no new credit is opened in this name, and notify the other two nationwide credit bureaus as your procedures provide.
>
> Please also send a copy of the deceased's current credit report to me at the address below so that I can identify open accounts and notify each creditor.
>
> Please confirm in writing, within 30 days, that the indicator has been placed and the other bureaus notified.
>
> Sincerely,
>
> [YOUR NAME]
>
> [ADDRESS]
>
> [PHONE]
>
> Enclosures: certified death certificate; copy of my photo ID; copy of my marriage certificate [or letters testamentary]

Credit cards. An authorized user on your spouse's card is not liable for the balance and should stop using the card. A joint cardholder remains liable. Check each card; the two look identical in your wallet.

Debts. Debts are the estate's to pay, from estate assets. You are not personally liable except as a co-signer, a joint account holder, a spouse in a community-property state, or where state law requires (some medical debt). Under federal rules a collector may contact a relative other than the representative only once, to learn who is handling the estate. A collector who calls repeatedly, or urges you to pay from your own pocket, is confused or a scammer. Send them to the executor, in writing.

The rest of the list. Notify the DMV to cancel the license and retitle any vehicle. Ask the post office to redirect mail if you are moving, and read every piece that arrives; statements you did not know about will show up. For online accounts, use the provider's own legacy tool first (Google's Inactive Account Manager, Apple's and Facebook's Legacy Contact); under the digital-assets law adopted in 49 states and D.C., that tool controls, then the will or trust.

CHECKLIST **Checklist: First 30 Days**

- ☐ Call SSA at 1-800-772-1213 to claim the $255 payment and get survivor and own-benefit figures at each age
- ☐ Ask the bank to return the month-of-death Social Security deposit and confirm in writing
- ☐ Deliver death certificates to each bank, brokerage, and insurer with the notification letter
- ☐ Retitle joint accounts; claim POD/TOD accounts; get letters or a small-estate affidavit for sole-name accounts
- ☐ Mail the deceased notification to one credit bureau and request the credit report
- ☐ File Forms CMS-40B and CMS-L564 for Part B if you were on your spouse's employer plan
- ☐ Elect COBRA or a Marketplace plan within 60 days if you are under 65 and losing coverage
- ☐ File Form SSA-44 to have your IRMAA recalculated for death of spouse
- ☐ Call the pension administrator or PBGC at 1-800-400-7242 about the survivor annuity
- ☐ Order date-of-death appraisals and brokerage statements for the step-up in basis

Days 30 Through 90: Rebuilding Your Own Plan

By the second month the urgent calls are done, and the work turns to your own affairs, which changed the day your spouse died even if the paperwork has not caught up.

Retitle and consolidate. Move remaining joint accounts and the house into your name (the deed goes to the county recorder).

Combine duplicate accounts where it makes sense. Add a trusted contact at each institution (Chapter 1, The Freeze).

Update your beneficiaries. Your own IRA, 401(k), life insurance, and POD/TOD forms almost certainly name your spouse. If you die with them unchanged, the money goes to a contingent beneficiary if you named one, and to your estate if you did not. Change every form, and name contingents.

Redo your four documents. Your will or trust, POA, and health care directive probably name your spouse as executor, agent, and proxy. Name new ones. An elder-law attorney or a fee-only planner can confirm the details for your state; this is the one place in the chapter where a professional hour is well spent.

Review the home. If there is a reverse mortgage in your spouse's name only, the servicer sends a "Due and Payable" letter within 30 days of learning of the death, and you should respond within 30 days. The estate has 6 months to sell, refinance, or pay, and HUD may approve two 90-day extensions. Heirs may keep the home by paying the lesser of the loan balance or 95% of appraised value. An Eligible Non-Borrowing Spouse may stay under a deferral as long as taxes, insurance, and upkeep continue; ask the servicer for that determination in writing.

Rebuild the budget. Two Social Security checks became one, a pension may have become a survivor annuity, and single-filer brackets and IRMAA thresholds are now yours. Write the new monthly income on one line, the fixed expenses beneath it, and see what is left. Chapter 6, The Review, covers the tax side, including the Roth conversion window that opens for many survivors.

CHECKLIST **Checklist: Days 30–90**

- ☐ Retitle the house and remaining joint accounts; record the new deed with the county recorder
- ☐ Change beneficiaries and add contingents on every one of your own accounts and policies
- ☐ Sign a new will or trust, durable POA, and health care directive naming new agents
- ☐ Name a trusted contact at each bank and brokerage
- ☐ Respond to any reverse-mortgage Due and Payable letter within 30 days; request the non-borrowing-spouse deferral in writing
- ☐ Decide on the IRA (own, inherited, or spousal election) after the year-of-death RMD is taken
- ☐ Ask a CPA whether to file Form 706 for portability before the 9-month deadline
- ☐ Draft the new single-income budget at the single tax and IRMAA thresholds

KEY NUMBERS **2026 Numbers to Know**

- **$255** — Social Security lump-sum death payment; apply within **2 years**
- **10 days** — after death, a bank may still pay checks your spouse wrote (UCC 4-405)
- **60 days** — to elect COBRA; to enroll in a Marketplace plan after losing coverage
- **8 months** — Medicare Part B Special Enrollment Period after employer coverage ends (COBRA does not count)
- **36 months** — maximum COBRA coverage for a surviving spouse
- **6 months** — FDIC grace after a co-owner's death; Medigap open enrollment; Form 706 extension; reverse-mortgage payoff period
- **9 months** — deadline for Form 706 and for a qualified disclaimer
- **$109,000 / $218,000** — 2026 IRMAA thresholds, single and joint; the widow's penalty lives in the gap
- **$202.90** — 2026 standard Part B premium; $284.10 in the first surcharge tier

CHECKLIST **Checklist: Do Not Rush**

- ☐ Do not roll your spouse's IRA into your own until you have compared the four options and taken any year-of-death RMD
- ☐ Do not sign a disclaimer without counsel; the 9-month clock is real and the decision is irrevocable
- ☐ Do not sell the home before the date-of-death appraisal and before you understand the 2-year $500,000 window
- ☐ Do not pay any creditor from personal funds; the estate pays its own debts
- ☐ Do not mix estate money with your own; get the EIN (Form SS-4) and an estate account first
- ☐ Do not skip the portability Form 706 without asking a CPA what it would preserve
- ☐ Do not close the joint checking account or "move everything now" to beat a freeze that survivorship accounts do not face

WORKSHEET **Worksheet: The 90-Day Master Tracker**

Photocopy one page per institution. Fill in the top block once, then log every call. Keep the certified death certificates in a folder with these sheets.

Date of death: ______________ Death certificates ordered: ______ Remaining: ______

Estate EIN (if any): ______________ Executor / personal representative: ______________

Institution: ____________________ Type: [ ] Bank [ ] Brokerage [ ] IRA/401(k) [ ] Insurer [ ] Pension [ ] Agency

Account nickname: ____________________ Last four digits: ______

How titled: [ ] Joint w/ survivorship [ ] POD/TOD to me [ ] Sole name [ ] Trust [ ] Convenience [ ] Unknown

Documents they require: ____

Date certificate delivered: __________ By: [ ] Mail [ ] In person [ ] Upload

Contact name: ____________________ Employee ID: __________ Phone/ext: ______________

Date of call: __________ Reference / case number: ____________________

What they said:

____

What they promised, and by when: ____________________________________

Follow-up date: __________ Done? [ ] Yes [ ] No

Deposits or auto-payments on this account to redirect:

____

Deadline tied to this institution (circle): $255 in 2 years / Part B 8 months / COBRA 60 days / 706 9 months / disclaimer 9 months / RMD by Dec. 31 next year / other:

____

Status: [ ] Notified [ ] Documents sent [ ] Retitled or paid [ ] Closed [ ] Waiting on:

____

A STORY **What Marian Did**

Marian did not move everything that week. She set the April deposit aside, kept the joint account open, and ordered twelve death certificates. When she called Social Security, she asked for three numbers: the survivor benefit now, her own benefit at full retirement age, and her own at 70. Her own at 70 turned out to be larger than Dale's, so she took the survivor benefit in April and wrote "switch to own benefit" on the calendar for her 70th birthday.

She left Dale's IRA where it was until his year-of-death RMD was taken, then rolled it into her own; at 68 the penalty question did not apply, and a fee-only planner confirmed it in one meeting. Because Arizona is a community-property state, the house and the brokerage account stepped up in full, and her CPA filed a portability return in month seven.

She mailed Form SSA-44 in May. Kevin, to his credit, stopped saying "now" and started saying "what's next on the pad?"

Your Next Steps

This checklist is for the reader whose spouse is alive and well. Everything Marian untangled in 90 days can be arranged in an afternoon, while both of you can still sign.

CHECKLIST **Your Next Steps**

- ☐ Confirm every joint bank account is titled "joint with right of survivorship" by asking the bank for the signature card
- ☐ Add POD or TOD beneficiaries, with contingents, to any account held in one name
- ☐ Print each of your Social Security benefit estimates from a my Social Security account and note the survivor amounts
- ☐ Locate every pension and confirm the joint-and-survivor annuity was never waived
- ☐ List all life insurance policies, insurers, and policy numbers on one page and tell your spouse where it is
- ☐ Record the cost basis of the house and each brokerage lot now so the step-up can be documented later
- ☐ Ask the bank what documents it will require at death and file the answer with your will
- ☐ Learn your state's safe deposit box rule and keep originals where a survivor can reach them without a court order
- ☐ Write 1-800-772-1213 (SSA), 1-800-400-7242 (PBGC), and 1-877-839-2675 (SHIP) inside the front cover of this book
- ☐ Copy the 90-Day Master Tracker and the First 72 Hours checklist and clip them to the folder with the will

CHAPTER THREE

The Silent Deadlines — Government Money That Expires

By the end of this chapter you will have a one-page sheet of your own government deadlines, and you will know which ones cost you money forever if you miss them by a day.

A STORY **Marlene, 64, Chattanooga, Tennessee**

Marlene claimed Social Security at 62, the year the printing plant cut her to three days a week. Two years later she was working spring and fall at a garden center, mostly because she liked the customers. The extra income was nice. She did not think much about it.

On a Saturday in late August she opened an envelope from the Social Security Administration. It said she had been overpaid $1,950 for the previous year because her earnings were higher than she had reported. If she did not respond, the agency would begin withholding from her monthly benefit. Her benefit is $1,640. She read the paragraph about "50 percent" three times.

The letter was dated July 29. It was now August 22. Underneath it sat a brochure about turning 65 and an unopened card from the county assessor.

Marlene did what most careful people do with a frightening government letter. She put it back in the envelope and set it on the counter where she would see it. This chapter is about why that is the one move that costs money, and what she did instead on Monday. (Marlene is illustrative, not a real person.)

THE QUIET RULES The Quiet Rules in This Chapter

- *Government money almost never comes looking for you. It expires quietly.*
- *A tax refund lives three years. After that, the Treasury keeps it.*
- *An overpayment notice is a clock, not a bill. The clock starts on the date printed at the top.*
- *Every Medicare window that closes leaves a penalty that never does.*
- *Waiting past 70 buys you nothing, and Social Security will only reach back six months.*
- *Nobody applies for you. The programs with the best terms have the fewest applicants.*
- *Money the state is holding for you is free to claim. Never pay a finder.*

Five Ways Government Money Disappears

Banks, as Chapter 1 showed, are noisy when they hold your money. Government money is the opposite. It sits, and then one day it is gone, and there was no phone call.

The silent deadlines fall into five bins, each with its own clock and its own fix.

1. **Refunds and credits with a statutory expiry.** A tax refund you never claimed. A Treasury check you never cashed.
2. **Benefits you must apply for.** Medicare Savings Programs, Extra Help, VA pension, property-tax exemptions. Eligibility does nothing on its own.
3. **Enrollment windows with permanent penalties.** Medicare Part B, Part D, and Medigap.
4. **Money that becomes an "overpayment" you must defend.** Social Security decides it paid you too much, and you have a short window to disagree.
5. **Unclaimed money.** Old accounts, policies, pensions, deposits. The state holds it indefinitely, but only if you ask.

At the end of the chapter you will put your own dates on a single sheet.

Bin One: Refunds That Expire

The three-year rule

Federal law gives you three years from a return's due date to claim a refund. After that, the money "becomes the property of the U.S. Treasury." No appeal, no hardship exception, no warning letter.

This catches retirees more than anyone, because the year you stop working is often the year you stop filing. Tax was withheld from a final paycheck or an IRA distribution, your income dropped, and a refund was waiting. You assumed there was nothing to file.

The 2022 deadline was April 15, 2026, and it has passed. The IRS estimated 1.3 million people left $1.2 billion behind for that year, with a median refund of $686. The dates still ahead:

- Tax year 2023 refunds expire **April 15, 2027**.
- Tax year 2024 refunds expire **April 15, 2028**.
- Tax year 2025 refunds expire April 15, 2029.

If you skipped a year, file the return. A late return showing a refund carries no penalty, although the refund can be applied to federal or state debts first.

The check you never cashed

A Treasury check, whether from the IRS, Social Security, or the VA, is payable for **12 months** from its issue date. After that the paper is void and the money returns to the agency. It is not lost; you ask the issuing agency to reissue it. For an IRS refund that means a refund trace on Form 3911 (Taxpayer Statement Regarding Refund). For Social Security, call 1-800-772-1213.

The 2026 tax figures retirees miss

The other way a refund goes unclaimed is quieter: you file, but the figures changed and you did not. For the 2026 return, due Thursday, April 15, 2027:

Item	Single	Married filing jointly
Standard deduction	$16,100	$32,200
Additional deduction, age 65 or older	$2,050	$1,650 per spouse

Item	Single	Married filing jointly
New senior deduction (tax years 2025–2028)	$6,000	$12,000 if both are 65 or older
Senior deduction starts shrinking above MAGI of	$75,000	$150,000
Social Security up to 50% taxable above "combined income" of	$25,000	$32,000
Social Security up to 85% taxable above	$34,000	$44,000

The **$6,000 senior deduction** is new under the 2025 tax law and runs only through 2028. You must be 65 by the last day of the tax year, married couples must file jointly, and it goes on Schedule 1-A. It sits on top of the regular 65-plus add-on whether or not you itemize, shrinks once modified adjusted gross income passes $75,000 (single) or $150,000 (joint), and is gone at roughly $175,000 and $250,000. It does not change how Social Security is taxed.

The **Social Security thresholds** have never been indexed. "Combined income" is adjusted gross income, plus tax-exempt interest, plus half your benefits. **Form 1040-SR** is the large-print return for people 65 and older, identical in substance to Form 1040.

Free help

- **AARP Foundation Tax-Aide**, 888-227-7669: the largest free program for older taxpayers, open roughly January through April, no membership needed in practice.
- **VITA and TCE**, 800-906-9887: VITA serves people earning $69,000 or less; TCE gives priority to taxpayers 60 and older and specializes in retirement questions.
- **IRS Free File** guided software was free for adjusted gross income of $89,000 or less this past season; the 2027 limit is announced each January.

Estimated taxes, and the retiree's shortcut

Once no employer withholds for you, the IRS expects you to pay as you go. For 2026 income the dates are April 15, June 15, and September 15, 2026, and January 15, 2027 (waived if you file and pay in full by February 1, 2027). The underpayment penalty is interest, running around 6–7% a year. You avoid it by paying in the smaller of 90% of this year's tax or 100% of last year's (110% if last year's AGI was over $150,000), or by owing under $1,000 at filing.

> QUIET TIP **Tip: Let Social Security and Your IRA Do the Withholding**
>
> Withheld tax counts as paid evenly through the year no matter when it came out, which estimated payments do not.
>
> - File **Form W-4V (Voluntary Withholding Request)** with Social Security to have 7%, 10%, 12%, or 22% withheld from your benefit.
> - Ask your IRA custodian to withhold from distributions, including a December required minimum distribution. Withholding in December counts as if paid in April.
>
> Many retirees can retire the four estimated-tax dates this way.

One more IRS tool: the **Identity Protection PIN**, a six-digit number that stops anyone else from filing in your name. Opt in through an IRS Online Account, or on Form 15227 if your AGI is under $84,000 (single) or $168,000 (joint). A new PIN arrives each January; the online tool is offline roughly mid-November to mid-January, so enroll in spring.

Every date in this section, and the Medicare dates ahead, repeats each year. The wheel below puts the whole year on one page.

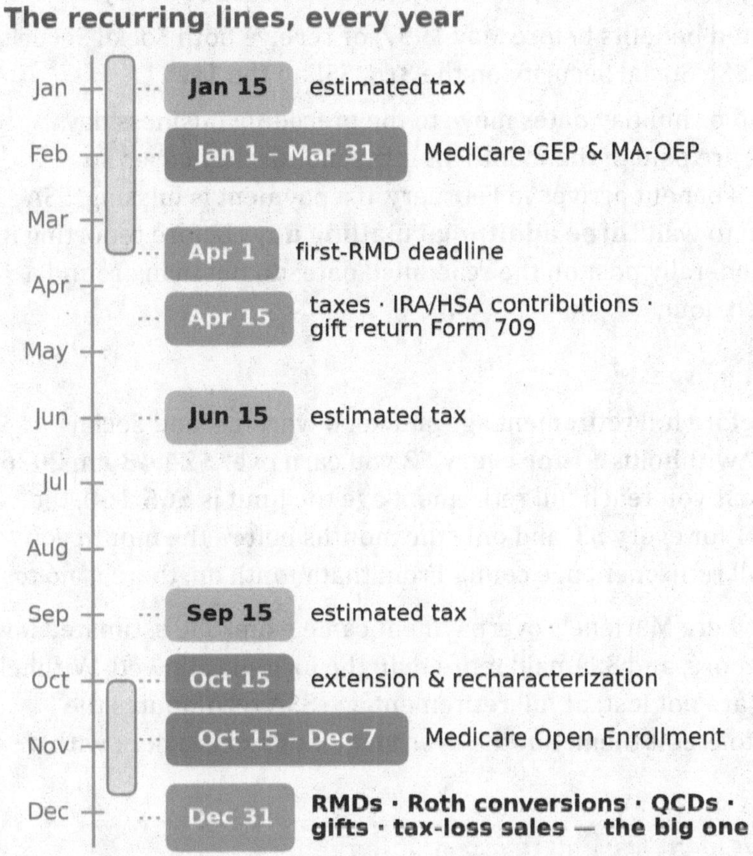

Figure 3.1. *The year at a glance: the government windows and due dates that come around every year, from the January enrollment periods to the January estimated-tax payment*

Social Security's Own Calendar

The 2026 figures

The 2026 cost-of-living adjustment is **2.8%**; the average retired worker saw about $56 more a month, for an average benefit of $2,071. The maximum at full retirement age is $4,152; for a worker who waited to 70, $5,181.

Payment dates depend on your birthday:

- Born the 1st through the 10th: the **second Wednesday**.
- Born the 11th through the 20th: the **third Wednesday**.

- Born the 21st through the 31st: the **fourth Wednesday**.
- Started benefits before May 1997, or receive both Social Security and SSI: Social Security on the **3rd**, SSI on the **1st**.

Weekend or holiday dates move to the preceding business day. Benefits are paid in the month after the month they cover, so January's benefit arrives in February. If a payment is missing, SSA asks you to wait **three additional mailing days** before reporting it. Banks generally post on the scheduled date; do not plan around a promised hour.

The earnings test

Claim before full retirement age and keep working, and Social Security withholds **$1 for every $2** you earn over **$24,480** in 2026. In the year you reach full retirement age the limit is **$65,160**, the rate is $1 for every $3, and only the months before the month you reach full retirement age count. From that month on, there is no test.

This is where Marlene's overpayment came from. She estimated low, earned more, and SSA paid more than the formula allowed. Withheld months are not lost; at full retirement age SSA recomputes the benefit to credit them. But the overpayment itself is a debt with a clock.

Full retirement age and the six-month rule

Birth year	Full retirement age
1943–1954	66
1955	66 and 2 months
1956	66 and 4 months
1957	66 and 6 months
1958	66 and 8 months
1959	66 and 10 months
1960 and later	67

Claiming at 62 cuts a worker's benefit 25% if full retirement age is 66 and 30% if it is 67. Delaying earns credits, and those credits stop at **70**.

Here is the silent deadline inside that sentence. Social Security pays retirement benefits retroactively for at most **six months** when you file after full retirement age, and never for a month before you reached it. There is no retroactivity at all for a reduced, pre-FRA benefit. A person who turns 70 in March and files the following January has lost four months of benefits, permanently, for no increase in the monthly amount. File no later than the month you turn 70.

The Overpayment Notice

What the notice means in 2026

Social Security overpays people for ordinary reasons: earnings reported late, a pension that started, a marriage, an agency error. When it notices, it sends a letter with an amount and a demand.

For notices sent on or after **April 25, 2025**, the default recovery for retirement, survivor, and disability benefits is **50% of your monthly check** until repaid. For SSI it remains 10%. If you no longer receive benefits, SSA can take your federal tax refund through the Treasury Offset Program or garnish wages.

Withholding begins if you have not filed an appeal or a waiver request within roughly 30 days of the notice — check the date on your notice, because SSA publications have described this window differently. Filing either one inside that window pauses collection until SSA decides.

Three forms and one phone call

An overpayment notice is a clock, not a bill. Three responses exist, and they do different jobs.

Form SSA-561 (Request for Reconsideration) says: *I was not overpaid, or the amount is wrong.* You have **60 days** from receiving the notice, and SSA presumes receipt 5 days after the printed date, so 65 days from the letter date. Miss it and the amount stands.

Form SSA-632-BK (Request for Waiver of Overpayment Recovery) says: *It was not my fault, and I cannot afford to repay.*

There is **no deadline**. File it online through my Social Security, by mail or fax to your local office, or in person.

Form SSA-634 (Request for Change in Overpayment Recovery Rate) says: *I owe it, but 50% will leave me unable to pay rent.* Longer repayment plans require the financial statement on the form.

And the phone call. Since November 22, 2024, SSA waives an overpayment of **$2,000 or less** on request, by phone, without a form, when there is no indication of fraud. The original amount governs; you cannot pay a $3,000 debt down to $2,000 to qualify. Marlene's $1,950 fits.

PHONE SCRIPT **Phone Script: Calling SSA About an Overpayment Notice**

Call 1-800-772-1213 (TTY 1-800-325-0778), Monday through Friday, 8 a.m. to 7 p.m., with the notice in front of you.

You: Good morning. I received an overpayment notice dated [DATE] for $[AMOUNT]. I want to confirm the notice date, understand the cause, and record my response today. May I have your name and employee ID?

Them: [Verifies your identity.]

You: Three questions. What months and what cause produced this overpayment? What is the last day I can file a reconsideration, and on what date will withholding start if I do nothing? And is the original amount $2,000 or less?

If the amount is $2,000 or less:

You: I am requesting an administrative waiver under your rules for overpayments of $2,000 or less. There is no fraud involved. Please record that request today and give me the confirmation number.

If the amount is over $2,000 and you believe it is wrong:

You: I disagree with the amount and will file Form SSA-561. Please note that I called on [TODAY'S DATE] and that collection should pause while it is pending.

If you agree but cannot afford 50%:

You: I am requesting a lower rate on Form SSA-634 and a waiver on Form SSA-632. Please note both requests today so collection pauses.

You: Please send written confirmation of what we discussed, and give me a reference number for this call.

If they say the request cannot be taken by phone:

You: I understand. Please schedule an appointment at my local office, and note that my request was made today so the deadline is protected.

Whatever form you send, add a short cover letter restating the notice date, the amount, what you are asking, and a request for a written reply. The letter template later in this chapter, written for Form SSA-44, works for SSA-561 with the subject line changed. Mail with tracking and keep copies.

Who Speaks for You at Social Security

Chapter 4 explains that Social Security does not accept a power of attorney. The agency has its own mechanism, the **representative payee**, and an advance version that is the closest thing to a free form this chapter offers.

Advance designation of representative payee lets any capable adult receiving Social Security, SSI, or Special Veterans Benefits name up to **three people**, in order, to manage benefits if the day comes when they cannot. Set it up through my Social Security, by calling 1-800-772-1213, or in person. Change it any time; SSA sends an annual notice listing your designees. Naming someone implies nothing about you today, and SSA still evaluates the person before appointing them. Without a designation, SSA picks.

Two housekeeping items, both new since 2025.

Identity proofing. The rule since April 28, 2025 is that stronger identity proofing applies only when you change **direct deposit** information. Do it online through my Social Security, by phone at 1-800-772-1213 using a one-time code you generate at ssa.gov/PIN, through your bank, or in person if nothing else works. Open the online account while you do not need it. People who still receive paper checks must visit an office before changing a mailing address.

Paper checks are ending. Federal benefits were required to go electronic as of September 30, 2025, and SSA says it will finish the transition during 2026. The choices are direct deposit or the **Direct Express** prepaid card (1-800-967-6857); Treasury waivers exist for people with mental-health barriers or no access to a bank. If a parent still gets a paper check, switch now.

Medicare: Windows That Close, Penalties That Don't

The 2026 prices

The standard Part B premium is **$202.90** a month with a **$283** annual deductible. The Part A hospital deductible is **$1,736** per benefit period. Part D out-of-pocket costs are capped at **$2,100** for the year (plan summaries put 2027 at $2,400; confirm with your plan). Insulin stays capped at $35 a month; adult vaccines are free.

The windows

- **Initial Enrollment Period: 7 months.** The three months before your 65th-birthday month, that month, and three after (born on the 1st, everything shifts a month earlier). Since 2023, signing up in the birthday month or later starts coverage the following month, so use the first three.
- **Special Enrollment Period: 8 months.** Still working at 65 with employer group coverage (yours or a spouse's)? You may delay Part B without penalty. The SEP runs 8 months from the month after employment or the coverage ends, whichever is first. **COBRA and retiree coverage do not count.** People take 18 months of COBRA, then enroll, and learn the window closed 10 months earlier.
- **General Enrollment Period: January 1–March 31.** The fallback if you missed both. Coverage begins the month after you enroll.
- **Open Enrollment: October 15–December 7.** Change Part D and Advantage plans, effective January 1.
- **Medicare Advantage Open Enrollment: January 1–March 31.** One change: switch Advantage plans, or drop Advantage for Original Medicare plus Part D.
- **Medigap open enrollment: 6 months**, starting the first month you are 65 or older and enrolled in Part B. Insurers must sell you any Medigap policy at the standard rate, no health questions. It happens once.

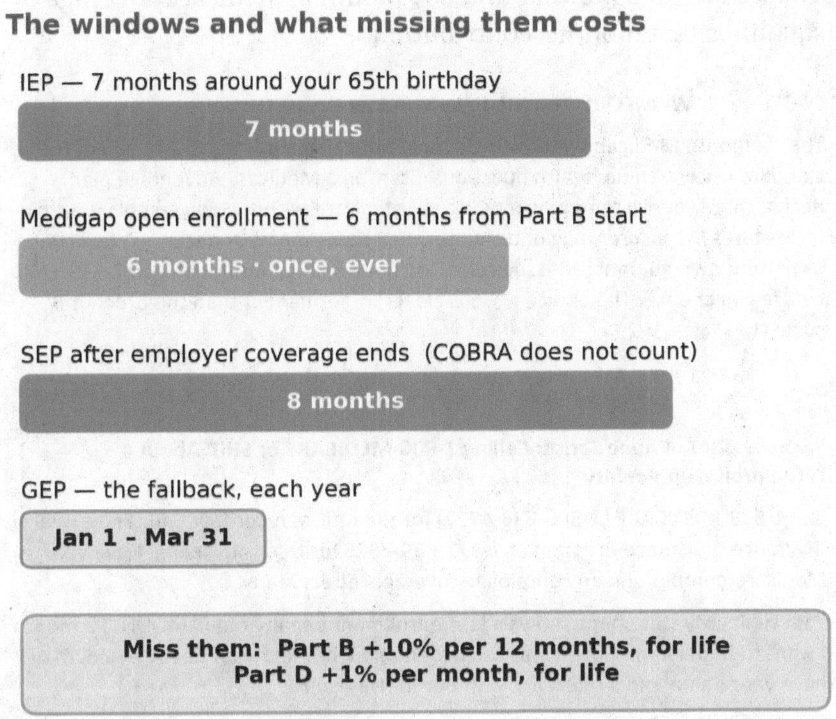

Figure 3.2. *Your Medicare windows: the seven-month initial period, the eight-month special period after employer coverage ends, the January–March general period, the once-only six-month Medigap window, and the lifetime penalties that follow a miss*

The penalties

Part B: 10% of the standard premium for every full 12-month period you could have had it and did not, for life. Two years late in 2026 adds $40.58 a month to $202.90, and the 10% rides along with every future increase.

Part D: 1% of the national base premium ($38.99 in 2026) for every full month without Part D or other creditable drug coverage after your IEP, rounded to the nearest 10 cents. Sixty-three consecutive uncovered days trigger it. Twenty-four months is about $9.40 a month, permanent, and recomputed each year against the new base ($41.33 for 2027).

HSA contributions: stop at least **6 months** before applying for Medicare or for Social Security after 65. Premium-free Part A is backdated up to 6 months, and any month of Medicare coverage disqualifies that month's contribution.

WATCH OUT **Watch Out: The Medigap Window Opens Once**

The six-month Medigap window is the only time an insurer must take you at the standard price with no health questions. Start on a Medicare Advantage plan, decide three years later you want Original Medicare with a Medigap policy, and in most states the insurer may underwrite you, charge more, or decline. A few states have their own guaranteed-issue rules; ask your SHIP counselor at 1-877-839-2675 before you choose. The choice at 65 is closer to permanent than the brochures suggest.

PHONE SCRIPT **Phone Script: Calling 1-800-MEDICARE or SHIP About a Late-Enrollment Penalty**

Call 1-800-MEDICARE (1-800-633-4227) for the official record, or your State Health Insurance Assistance Program at 1-877-839-2675 for free counseling. Have your Medicare number and any employer-coverage letters ready.

You: Hello. My statement shows a late-enrollment penalty of $[AMOUNT] a month. I want to understand how it was calculated and whether it can be reviewed. May I have your name and a reference number for this call?

You: Which months are counted as uncovered? What are the start and end dates of that period?

You: I had [employer group coverage / creditable drug coverage] through [EMPLOYER OR PLAN] until [DATE]. Was that counted? If not, what document do you need, and where do I send it?

If they say the coverage was not reported:

You: I will get a letter from [EMPLOYER] on letterhead confirming the dates and that the drug coverage was creditable. Please give me the address or fax number and the deadline for requesting a review.

If they say the penalty is correct:

You: Please send me the calculation in writing, with the months counted, and the address for the reconsideration process.

You: Last item: please confirm which enrollment period I am in right now and its last day.

If the answers are unclear:

You: Thank you. I am going to review this with my SHIP counselor and may call back. Please note on my record that I called today about the penalty calculation.

IRMAA: the surcharge that looks back two years

Higher-income enrollees pay an **Income-Related Monthly Adjustment Amount** on top of the standard premiums, and the quiet part is that 2026 premiums are set by your **2024** tax return. Retire in 2025, and Medicare still prices you as if you were working.

2024 MAGI, single	2024 MAGI, married filing jointly	Total Part B per month	Part D add-on
$109,000 or less	$218,000 or less	$202.90	$0
$109,000.01–$137,000	$218,000.01–$274,000	$284.10	$14.50
$137,000.01–$171,000	$274,000.01–$342,000	$405.80	$37.50
$171,000.01–$205,000	$342,000.01–$410,000	$527.50	$60.40
$205,000.01–under $500,000	$410,000.01–under $750,000	$649.20	$83.30
$500,000 and up	$750,000 and up	$689.90	$91.00

Each tier is a cliff. One dollar over $109,000 costs a single person $81.20 a month more for Part B all year, plus $14.50 on Part D; the Part B surcharges run from $81.20 to $487.00. A married person filing separately who lived with their spouse jumps from $0 straight to the $446.30 surcharge once MAGI passes $109,000. The Part D surcharge is deducted from your Social Security payment, not paid to the plan, and sits on top of the plan's own premium.

The eight events that let you ask for a redo

Form SSA-44 (Medicare Income-Related Monthly Adjustment Amount – Life-Changing Event) asks SSA to use a more recent year's income, including an estimate for the current year, after one of eight events:

1. Marriage
2. Divorce or annulment
3. Death of a spouse
4. Work stoppage (retirement)
5. Work reduction
6. Loss of income-producing property
7. Loss of pension income

8. Employer settlement payment

That is the whole list. A large capital gain, a Roth conversion, or a required minimum distribution is **not** a life-changing event, even though each can push you over a line (Chapter 6 covers the planning side). Retirement is on the list, and it is the one most people forget to claim.

File SSA-44 by mail with copies of your evidence, in person with originals, or by calling 1-800-772-1213 for an appointment. Send it with a cover letter.

LETTER TEMPLATE **Letter Template: IRMAA Life-Changing Event Cover Letter (Form SSA-44)**

[DATE]

Social Security Administration

[LOCAL OFFICE ADDRESS]

RE: Request for reduction of Medicare IRMAA based on a life-changing event

Name: [YOUR FULL NAME]

Social Security number: [XXX-XX-XXXX]

Medicare number: [YOUR MEDICARE NUMBER]

Dear Claims Representative:

I am enclosing Form SSA-44 requesting that my 2026 Medicare Part B and Part D income-related monthly adjustment amounts be determined using my [2025 / 2026] income rather than my 2024 tax return.

On [DATE OF EVENT], I experienced a life-changing event as defined on the form: [work stoppage / work reduction / death of spouse / other]. As a result, my modified adjusted gross income for [YEAR] is [$AMOUNT], compared with [$AMOUNT] in 2024. Documentation of the event and of my current income is enclosed.

I ask that you process this request, adjust my premiums beginning with [MONTH, YEAR], and refund any excess premiums already withheld from my Social Security benefit. Please respond in writing within 30 days with your determination or a list of any additional documents you require.

I can be reached at [PHONE NUMBER] between [HOURS].

Sincerely,

[SIGNATURE]

[PRINTED NAME]

[MAILING ADDRESS]

> Enclosures: Form SSA-44 (signed); copy of [retirement letter / final pay stub / death certificate]; copy of [2025 tax return or 2026 income estimate]; copy of the IRMAA notice dated [DATE]

Money You Must Ask For

The best terms in the federal benefit system belong to programs most eligible people never apply for. Eligibility is not enrollment.

Medicare Savings Programs

Three state-run programs pay Medicare premiums for people with modest income. The 2026 federal floors (monthly income, including the standard $20 disregard) are below; many states set higher limits or drop the asset test, so do not rule yourself out from this table alone.

Program	Monthly income, single / couple	Resources, single / couple	What it pays
QMB	$1,350 / $1,824	$9,950 / $14,910	Part A and B premiums, deductibles, coinsurance
SLMB	$1,616 / $2,184	$9,950 / $14,910	Part B premium ($202.90)
QI	$1,816 / $2,455	$9,950 / $14,910	Part B premium; annual funding, first come

Any of the three automatically qualifies you for Extra Help. Apply through your state Medicaid office; a SHIP counselor can hand you the form.

Extra Help with drug costs

Extra Help, the Part D Low-Income Subsidy, covers 2026 income up to **$23,940** a year ($32,460 for a couple) and resources up to **$18,090** ($36,100 for a couple, including a burial allowance). Since 2024 everyone who qualifies gets the full subsidy: no premium on benchmark plans, no deductible, copays no higher than $5.10 generic and $12.65 brand, and no late-enrollment penalty. Apply online, at 1-800-772-1213, or on Form SSA-1020.

Medicaid for a spouse in a nursing home

When one spouse needs long-term care, federal rules protect the other. For 2026 the community spouse may keep between **$32,532** and **$162,660** in countable assets (states pick a point in that range) plus a monthly income allowance of up to **$4,066.50**. The home is exempt up to **$752,000** of equity, or **$1,130,000** in states that chose the higher limit; a nationwide cap of $1,000,000 has been reported for January 1, 2028. The 60-month look-back on gifts runs on its own clock (Chapter 5). An elder-law attorney can confirm your state's figures before anyone moves money.

VA pension with Aid and Attendance

Wartime veterans and surviving spouses who need help with daily activities may qualify for a pension most families have never heard of. At rates effective December 1, 2025, the maximum annual pension with Aid and Attendance is **$29,093** for a veteran alone, **$34,488** with one dependent, and **$18,697** for a surviving spouse alone. The net-worth limit (assets plus annual income, excluding the home and one vehicle) is **$163,699** through November 30, 2026. An intent to file on VA Form 21-0966 generally holds your effective date while you gather paperwork; a Veterans Service Officer, whose help is free, can confirm.

The rest

- **Property-tax relief.** Most states offer senior homestead exemptions, credits, deferrals, or assessment freezes, and almost all require an application with a county deadline. Marlene's unopened assessor card was one of these. Ask the assessor: "What senior exemptions exist, and what is the deadline?"
- **LIHEAP and SNAP.** Heating and cooling help runs through your state or local agency, and many give priority to households with a member over 60. SNAP rules for households with a member 60 or older are typically more generous than people assume. Your Area Agency on Aging (Eldercare Locator, 1-800-677-1116) knows your state's rules.

Money That Is Already Yours

Where it hides

Every state runs an unclaimed-property program. When a bank account, utility deposit, brokerage account, or insurance payout sits with no owner contact for the state's **dormancy period**, 3 years in most states and 5 in a substantial minority, the holder must try to reach you and then turn the money over to the state treasurer, who holds it indefinitely. No deadline, no fee.

Two traps. A CD that renews automatically often does not count as owner activity, and interest posting never does; a 5-year CD you never touch can be reported as abandoned. And the bank's "inactive account" fee is separate from state dormancy. One owner-initiated contact a year keeps both at bay (Chapter 8 has more).

The free searches

- **MissingMoney.com**, the official multistate search. Search every state you have lived in, every name you have used, and your parents' names.
- **NAIC Life Insurance Policy Locator**, free for beneficiaries and people with legal authority over a deceased person's affairs. Insurers contact you only if they find a policy naming you. Allow 90 or more business days.
- **PBGC unclaimed pensions** (1-800-400-7242): benefits from terminated plans PBGC took over and its Missing Participants Program, searchable by last name and last four SSN digits.
- **Department of Labor Retirement Savings Lost and Found**, for private-sector pension and 401(k) plans you once belonged to. It requires an identity-verified Login.gov account, does not cover IRAs or government plans, and a hit only means you once participated.

> WATCH OUT **Watch Out: Never Pay a Finder**
>
> Letters arrive offering to "recover funds held in your name" for a percentage. Every search above is free, and states hold the money with no deadline. If a letter names an amount, that is your cue to search the state's site yourself. The only people who need a finder are people who have not been told the search is free. Now you have been.

What the Government Can and Cannot Take

Two protections, both narrower than the videos suggest.

Garnishment of federal benefits (31 CFR Part 212). When a bank receives a garnishment order it must, within 2 business days, look back **two months** for direct-deposited Social Security, SSI, VA, Railroad Retirement, or federal civil-service benefits. The protected amount is the lesser of the benefits deposited in that window or the balance on review day. The bank cannot freeze it, must let you use it, and may not charge a garnishment fee against it. The limits: orders from the United States (an IRS levy, say) and state child-support agencies are exceptions; benefits you moved to another account or received by paper check lose the automatic protection; and the rule says nothing about the bank's own setoff against your overdrafts and fees, on which courts are split. Keep benefits in the account where they land.

Treasury Offset Program. For delinquent federal non-tax debts, such as a defaulted federal student loan, the government may take the lesser of the debt, **15%** of your monthly Social Security benefit, or the amount by which the benefit exceeds **$750**. SSI is exempt. Written notice comes first. An IRS tax levy runs through a separate program at 15% with no $750 floor.

KEY NUMBERS **2026 Numbers to Know**

- **April 15, 2027:** last day to claim a 2023 tax refund (2024 refunds: April 15, 2028)
- **12 months:** life of an uncashed Treasury check before it must be reissued
- **2.8%:** 2026 Social Security COLA
- **$24,480 / $65,160:** earnings-test limits under FRA / in the FRA year
- **6 months:** maximum Social Security retroactivity, never before FRA; delayed credits stop at 70
- **50%:** default overpayment withholding for notices after April 25, 2025 (SSI 10%)
- **60 days + 5 mailing days:** deadline for Form SSA-561; no deadline for a waiver on SSA-632-BK
- **$2,000 or less:** overpayment waivable by phone
- **3:** people you may name in an advance designation of representative payee
- **$202.90 / $283 / $1,736 / $2,100:** Part B premium / Part B deductible / Part A deductible / Part D cap
- **$109,000 / $218,000:** 2024 income where IRMAA begins for 2026 (single / joint)
- **7 / 8 / 6 months:** Medicare initial window / special window after employer coverage / Medigap window
- **10% per 12 months; 1% per month:** Part B / Part D late penalties, for life
- **October 15–December 7; January 1–March 31:** Open Enrollment; General and Advantage enrollment
- **$23,940 / $32,460:** Extra Help income limits (single / couple)
- **3–5 years:** state dormancy period before an account goes to the state
- **15% / $750:** Treasury Offset cap and floor on Social Security

Your Deadline Sheet

Every date in this chapter is fixed either on the calendar or to your birthday, so you can compute all of them once. Fill this in, photocopy it, and tape a copy inside a kitchen cabinet.

WORKSHEET **Worksheet: My Deadline Sheet**

Fill in the dates that apply to you, using the FRA table and the Medicare windows in this chapter. Update each January.

Name: ____________________ Date of birth: ____________

Social Security

Full retirement age (from the table): _____ Month I reach it: ____________

Month I turn 70 (file no later than this month): ____________

My payment Wednesday: [ ] 2nd [ ] 3rd [ ] 4th [ ] The 3rd of the month

Direct deposit account (last 4 digits): _____ Bank: ____________

Advance designees (up to 3): 1. ____________ 2. ____________ 3. ____________

My Social Security account created: [ ] Yes [ ] No Date: ____________

Medicare

65th birthday month: ____________ IEP starts: ____________ IEP ends: ____________

Employer coverage ends (if working past 65): ____________ SEP ends (8 months later): ____________

HSA contributions must stop by (6 months before Medicare): ____________

Part B effective month: ____________ Medigap window ends (6 months later): ____________

Open Enrollment reminder set for October 15: [ ] Yes

Taxes

RMD year (age 73 if born 1951–1959; 75 if born 1960 or later; see Chapter 5): ____________

Estimated-tax dates I pay: [ ] April 15 [ ] June 15 [ ] September 15 [ ] January 15 [ ] None, I use Form W-4V withholding

Last tax year I filed: _____ Refund deadline for the first year I skipped: ____________

Identity Protection PIN enrolled: [ ] Yes [ ] No

Local

County senior property-tax exemption deadline: ____________ Applied: [ ] Yes [ ] No

State unclaimed-property search done (date): ____________

The Annual Sweep

Once the sheet exists, protecting it takes about two hours a year. January is the month: the General and Advantage enrollment periods are open, the new IRS PIN has arrived, tax documents are showing up, and the COLA has landed.

CHECKLIST **Checklist: Annual Government Money Sweep**

- ☐ Search MissingMoney.com for every name and state in your history, including a deceased spouse's
- ☐ Confirm your Social Security payment posted at the new COLA amount and direct deposit details are unchanged
- ☐ Compare your latest tax return MAGI against the IRMAA table; file Form SSA-44 if a life-changing event lowered your income
- ☐ Check whether any prior-year return went unfiled; file it before its April 15 three-year deadline
- ☐ Review Part D and Advantage plan changes during October 15–December 7
- ☐ Reapply for or confirm your county senior property-tax exemption by its deadline
- ☐ Recheck Medicare Savings Program and Extra Help limits against your income; apply if you are close
- ☐ Verify your advance designation of representative payee on SSA's annual notice
- ☐ Look for any uncashed government check; call the issuing agency if it is over 12 months old
- ☐ Confirm the trusted contact and beneficiary designations from Chapters 1 and 4 still name the right people

A STORY **Marlene, 64, Chattanooga, Tennessee**

On Monday morning, before her shift, Marlene called 1-800-772-1213 with the notice on the table. She asked the representative to confirm the notice date, July 29, and to explain the cause. It was the earnings test: she had told SSA in early 2025 to expect about $20,000 from the garden center, and she earned $27,300.

Then she used the sentence from the script. "The original amount is $1,950. I am requesting an administrative waiver under your rules for overpayments of $2,000 or less." The representative took the request, gave her a reference number and an employee ID, and said a written decision would follow. Marlene wrote all of it on the envelope.

That evening she filled in the Deadline Sheet. Her 65th birthday is in March 2027, so her Initial Enrollment Period runs December 2026 through June 2027, and her Medigap window opens the month Part B starts. She opened the assessor's card: a senior homestead credit, due in the spring. And she searched MissingMoney.com, where Tennessee was holding $140 from an apartment deposit she had forgotten in 2009.

Nothing dramatic happened. That was the point.

Your Next Steps

CHECKLIST **Your Next Steps**

- ☐ Create your my Social Security account and set up advance designation of up to three representative payees
- ☐ Fill in the Deadline Sheet above and photocopy it for the person who helps you
- ☐ Check whether you filed a 2023 return; if a refund is possible, file before April 15, 2027
- ☐ Search MissingMoney.com and, for a lost policy or pension, the NAIC locator and PBGC at 1-800-400-7242
- ☐ File Form W-4V with Social Security if you have been paying estimated taxes by hand
- ☐ Call SHIP at 1-877-839-2675 to confirm your enrollment window and Medigap deadline if you are within two years of 65 or working past it
- ☐ File Form SSA-44 if you retired, lost a pension, or lost a spouse and your 2026 premiums reflect 2024 income
- ☐ Respond to any overpayment notice by the date on the letter, by phone for $2,000 or less, or on Form SSA-561, SSA-632-BK, or SSA-634
- ☐ Call your county assessor for the senior property-tax exemption form and its deadline
- ☐ Switch any paper Social Security check to direct deposit or Direct Express at 1-800-967-6857 before the checks stop

CHAPTER FOUR

The Four Documents — Who Controls the Money and the Care

By the end of this chapter you will know which four documents decide who handles your money and your care, how to sign each one so a bank or a hospital honors it on the day it matters, and what to say when someone tells you no.

A STORY **Harold, 79, Toledo, Ohio**

Harold signed his power of attorney in 2015, the spring after his wife died. His lawyer drew it up, a notary stamped it, and Harold put it in the top desk drawer with the car title and the deed. His daughter Janet was the agent. "If anything happens," he told her, "it's in the drawer."

Something happened on a Tuesday in March 2026. A stroke, an ambulance, a hospital across town. By Friday Harold was stable but not himself, and Janet was at the counter of his bank with the document from the drawer and a list of bills due on the first.

The branch manager was kind and immovable. The power of attorney was eleven years old, she said. The bank preferred its own form. Could Harold come in and sign it? Janet explained that Harold could not currently sign his name. The manager said she would send the document to the legal department and someone would be in touch. She could not say when.

Back at the hospital, a nurse told Janet's sister over the phone that she could not discuss a patient with anyone who was not listed. Nobody was listed. Harold's file held one document, from 2015, and it covered his money, not his medical information. As far as the bank was concerned, it did not yet cover the money either.

An illustrative story; Harold and Janet are not real people.

THE QUIET RULES **The Quiet Rules in This Chapter**

- *A power of attorney ends at death; a will begins at death. No single document covers both sides of that line.*
- *The bank's clock on a notarized power of attorney runs in business days, and it starts the moment you hand the document over.*
- *A beneficiary form beats a will, every time, even when the will is newer.*
- *A trust controls only what has been retitled into it.*
- *Federal agencies do not honor your power of attorney. Each has its own form.*
- *Adding a name to an account is a gift, a risk, and almost always the wrong tool.*
- *File your documents while you are healthy. A document nobody has seen is a document that gets questioned.*

The Four Documents, and the Line Between Them

Most of what goes wrong in the months around an illness or a death goes wrong for one reason: the person holding the paperwork has the wrong paper for the moment. A daughter brings a will to the bank while her father is alive. A son brings a power of attorney the week after the funeral. Both are told, correctly, that the document "doesn't apply."

Here are the four documents and the moments each one covers.

Document	Controls	Works from	Stops at
Durable financial power of attorney	Bank and brokerage accounts, bills, taxes, property	Signing (or a trigger event)	Death
Health care proxy and living will, plus HIPAA release	Medical decisions; medical information	Incapacity (proxy); signing (HIPAA release)	Death
Will and/or revocable trust	Sole-name assets (will); assets titled to the trust	Death (will); signing (trust)	Final distribution
Beneficiary designations	IRAs, 401(k)s, life insurance, POD and TOD accounts	Death	When the custodian pays

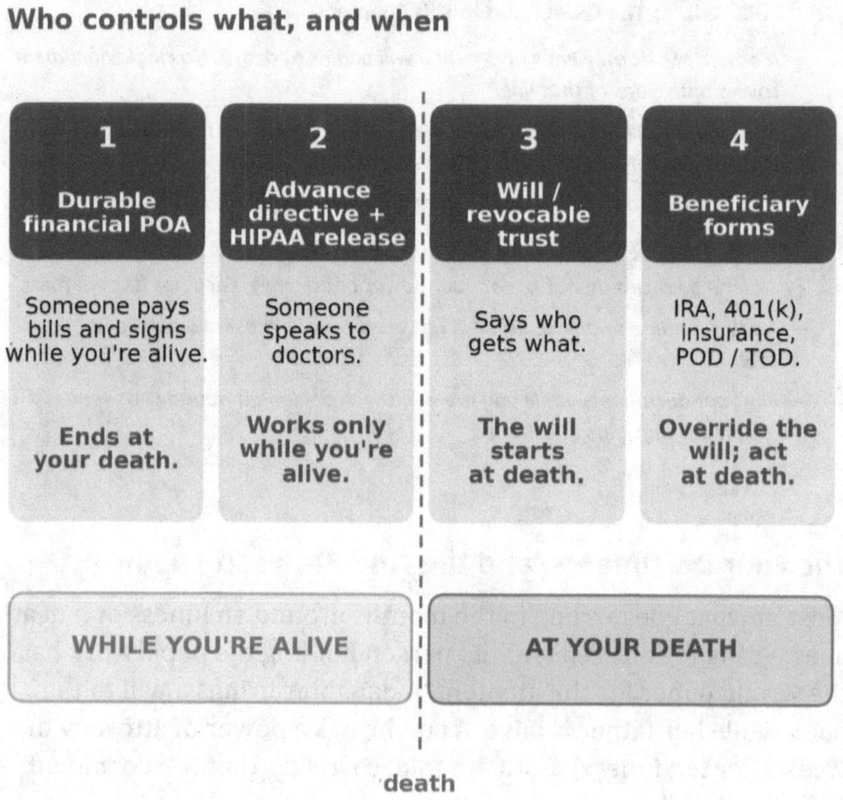

Figure 4.1. *The four documents, what each one controls, when it starts working, and when it stops*

The first Quiet Rule lives in that last column. *A power of attorney ends at death; a will begins at death.* The agent who writes a check the day after the funeral has no authority at all. The executor named in the will has none either until a court issues letters, which can take weeks (see Chapter 2, The First 90 Days). In that gap, the only things that move on their own are survivorship accounts, POD and TOD registrations, and beneficiary designations. That is why document four matters as much as the other three, and why people set up trusts.

Document One: The Durable Financial Power of Attorney

A financial power of attorney names an agent to act for you with money and property. "Durable" means it keeps working if you lose capacity, which is the entire point.

Durable, immediate, or springing

About 30 states plus the District of Columbia have adopted a version of the Uniform Power of Attorney Act, and under it a power of attorney is durable unless it says otherwise. States that have not adopted it, including California, Florida, New York, Illinois, and New Jersey, have their own statutes. California and Texas require durability language; without the word, the document dies at the moment you need it.

An immediate power of attorney works from the day you sign. A springing one waits for a trigger, usually a doctor's finding of incapacity. Springing sounds safer. In practice the agent must prove the trigger happened, with letters the bank's legal department gets to judge, and that is where weeks disappear. Florida bans springing powers of attorney signed on or after October 1, 2011; earlier Florida documents remain valid with a physician's affidavit.

The practical answer most people reach is an immediate, durable power of attorney given to someone they trust. If you do not trust the person enough to sign an immediate one, the problem is the person, not the document.

Why the bank says no

Banks reject powers of attorney for six reasons, and five have cures.

1. **The document is "stale."** No statute puts an expiration date on a power of attorney; banks apply their own age policies anyway. The cure is an agent's certification.
2. **It is not the bank's form.** In Uniform Act states, California, and Pennsylvania, this is not a lawful reason to refuse on its own.
3. **It lacks the "hot powers."** To change a beneficiary, make a gift, or add survivorship, the document must say so expressly.
4. **It is not durable.** A California or Texas document without the word ends at incapacity.

5. **It was never notarized.** The statutory acceptance deadlines apply only to acknowledged, meaning notarized, documents.
6. **The principal has died.** No cure. A power of attorney always ends at death, everywhere.

The cure: the agent's certification and the statutory clock

The agent's certification is a short sworn statement, on a form most statutes supply, in which the agent says under penalty of perjury that the principal is alive, that the power of attorney has not been revoked, and that the agent knows of nothing that would end it. It is the answer to "this is too old." It costs a notary fee and ten minutes.

The clock is the part nobody mentions at the counter. In Uniform Act states, a bank presented with a notarized power of attorney must, within seven business days, either accept it or ask for a certification, a translation, or an opinion of counsel. Once it receives what it asked for, it has five more business days to accept. It may not demand a different form for authority the document already grants. If it refuses anyway, a court can order acceptance and award the agent's attorney's fees.

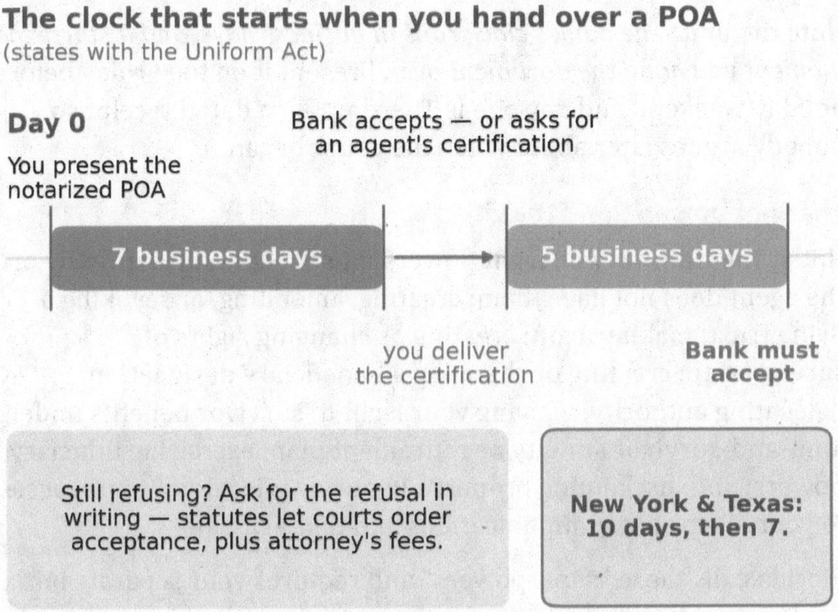

Figure 4.2. *What happens when you present a notarized power of attorney to a bank: seven business days to accept or ask for a certification, five more after it arrives, or ten plus seven in New York and Texas*

Several large states run their own versions.

Where	First deadline	After certification	If they still refuse
Uniform Act states (about 31 jurisdictions)	7 business days	5 business days	Court order plus attorney's fees
New York	10 business days, in writing with reasons	7 business days	Damages, including attorney's fees
Texas	10th business day	7 business days	Suit for wrongful refusal
Pennsylvania	7 business days	5 business days	Liability for financial harm; court order
California	No fixed day count; "not our form" is unreasonable per se for the statutory form	Agent's affidavit answers staleness	Mandatory attorney's fees

Note the unit. *The bank's clock runs in business days, and it starts the moment you hand the document over.* Present it on the Friday before a holiday weekend and day one is Tuesday. Get a dated receipt so nobody argues later about when the count began.

The "hot powers" and the gift cap

Under the Uniform Act, eight powers must be granted expressly or the agent does not have them: creating, amending, or revoking a living trust; making a gift; creating or changing rights of survivorship; creating or changing a beneficiary designation; delegating authority; waiving your right to survivor benefits under a joint-and-survivor annuity or retirement plan; exercising fiduciary powers; and disclaiming property. Pennsylvania adds a ninth: access to your electronic communications and digital assets.

Florida calls these "superpowers" and requires your separate initials or signature beside each. California's statutory form uses an initial-the-line layout, and a line you do not initial is a power you did not give. Read line by line. An agent who cannot change a beneficiary cannot fix a form that still names an ex-spouse, and an agent without digital-asset authority cannot get into the email account where the statements arrive.

Gifts have a default ceiling. Under the Uniform Act, unless the document says more, an agent may give no more than the federal annual gift-tax exclusion per recipient, $19,000 in 2026. New York's default is $5,000 per calendar year, up from $500 under the 2021 law. If you want your agent to pay a grandchild's tuition, the document must say so in dollars.

Signing it so it holds

Execution rules are state law, and they differ in ways that matter at the counter.

State	Witnesses	Notary	Extras
New York	2 (not the agent or a gift recipient; the notary may be one)	Required	Statutory short form; gifts go in "Modifications"

State	Witnesses	Notary	Extras
Florida	2 subscribing witnesses	Required	Superpowers need separate initials; no springing since October 1, 2011
California	2, or a notary instead	Either; notarize if real property is involved	Durability language required
Texas	None	Required	Durability language required
Pennsylvania	2 adults (not the agent; the notary may not double)	Required	Capital-letter notice on page one; agent acknowledgment before acting

Even where witnesses alone are legal, notarize. The acceptance clocks and court remedies attach only to a notarized document, and a power of attorney that will ever sign a deed must generally be recorded, which requires a notary. Use your state's statutory form where one exists; banks recognize it on sight.

CHECKLIST **Checklist: Document Execution (by State Formalities)**

- ☐ Confirm your state's rule: notary only (TX), notary or witnesses (CA), or notary plus 2 witnesses (NY, FL, PA)
- ☐ Use the statutory form if your state has one, with a "Modifications" section for gifts
- ☐ Include the word "durable" and language that the document survives incapacity
- ☐ Initial or sign beside every hot power you intend to grant, including digital assets
- ☐ State a dollar figure for gifts if you want more than the default ($19,000 Uniform Act; $5,000 New York)
- ☐ Name a successor agent
- ☐ Choose witnesses who are not the agent, not gift recipients, and, in Pennsylvania, not the notary
- ☐ Have the agent sign the acknowledgment (required in Pennsylvania; wise everywhere)
- ☐ Sign a separate health care proxy and HIPAA release; a financial power of attorney never covers medical matters

File it now, while you are healthy

Here is the move that would have saved Janet a week. Take the signed power of attorney to every bank and brokerage where you hold an account, while you are the one presenting it. Ask two questions: "Will you put this on file?" and "Do you have your own form you would like me to sign as well?" Sign the bank's form in addition to yours, never instead. A document that has sat in the bank's system for three years does not get called stale on the day the agent needs it.

> QUIET TIP **File It Once, Everywhere**
>
> List every institution: banks, credit unions, brokerages, the IRA custodian, the annuity company, the mortgage servicer. Deliver a copy of the power of attorney to each with the cover letter below, and log the date and the name of the person who took it. Ask whether they want the agent's certification now or at the time of use. Pair it with the trusted contact designation from Chapter 1, The Freeze, which gives the same institutions someone to call.

Agents have duties, and the best plain-English guide is free: the Consumer Financial Protection Bureau's "Managing Someone Else's Money: Help for Agents Under a Power of Attorney," in national and state editions. Its core fits on an index card: act only in the principal's interest, keep the principal's money separate from your own, keep records, and involve the principal in decisions as far as they are able.

> PHONE SCRIPT **In-Person Script: Presenting a Power of Attorney at the Bank**
>
> **You:** Good morning. I'm the agent under a durable power of attorney for [PRINCIPAL'S NAME], who has accounts here. I'd like to present the original and have it placed on the accounts. Here is the notarized document, my photo ID, and a signed agent's certification stating that the principal is alive and the document has not been revoked.
>
> **Them:** We'll need to send this to our legal department.
>
> **You:** I understand. Could you give me a dated receipt showing it was presented today, with your name and employee ID? Under [STATE] law, the bank has [7 / 10] business days from today to accept it or request a certification, and I've already provided one.
>
> **Them:** We usually require our own form.

You: I'm happy to complete your form as well, but the statute does not allow a refusal on that ground alone for authority this document already grants. Please treat today as the presentation date.

Them: This document is more than five years old.

You: There is no expiration date under the statute; the agent's certification is the legal answer to that concern. If the bank still declines, I'd like each reason in writing, with a reference number.

If they still refuse: "Please give me the name and direct number of the person in legal or compliance who reviews powers of attorney. I'll follow up in writing and, if needed, ask a court to order acceptance and award fees, as the statute provides."

LETTER TEMPLATE **Letter Template: Cover Letter Delivering a Power of Attorney to a Financial Institution**

[DATE]

[INSTITUTION NAME]

Attn: Legal / Power of Attorney Review

[STREET ADDRESS]

[CITY, STATE ZIP]

RE: Durable Power of Attorney of [PRINCIPAL'S FULL NAME], account(s) ending [XXXX]

Dear Sir or Madam:

I am the agent named in the enclosed durable power of attorney, signed by [PRINCIPAL'S NAME] on [DATE SIGNED] and acknowledged before a notary public in [STATE]. I am presenting it to be placed on file for the account(s) above.

Enclosed is my signed agent's certification stating that the principal is alive, that the power of attorney has not been revoked, and that I know of no event that would terminate it, along with a copy of my photo identification.

Under [STATE STATUTE, e.g., "the Uniform Power of Attorney Act as adopted in Ohio"], you must accept this document, or request a certification, translation, or opinion of counsel, within [7 / 10] business days of presentation, and must accept it within [5 / 7] business days after receiving any requested item. You may not require a different form for authority this document already grants.

Please confirm acceptance in writing by [DATE], or state in writing each reason for any refusal. Please respond in writing to the address below.

Sincerely,

[YOUR NAME], Agent for [PRINCIPAL'S NAME]

[YOUR ADDRESS] / [YOUR PHONE]

> Enclosures: (1) Durable Power of Attorney; (2) Agent's Certification; (3) Copy of agent's photo ID; (4) Copy of principal's photo ID

> WATCH OUT **Watch Out: A Power of Attorney Ends at Death**
>
> Every power of attorney, in every state, ends the moment the principal dies. An agent who moves money afterward, even to pay the funeral home, is acting without authority and may have to return it. On the day of death the agent's job becomes locating the will, securing the originals, and handing off to the executor or trustee. See Chapter 2 for what to do in that gap.

> **KEY NUMBERS 2026 Numbers to Know**
>
> - **7 + 5 business days:** the bank's clock to accept a notarized power of attorney in Uniform Act states and Pennsylvania
> - **10 + 7 business days:** the same clock in New York and Texas
> - **$19,000:** default annual gift per recipient an agent may make under the Uniform Act
> - **$5,000:** New York's default annual gift authority
> - **2 witnesses:** the nationwide norm for a will; required for a power of attorney in NY, FL, and PA
> - **3:** people you can name in advance as your Social Security representative payee
> - **46 states:** have a default-surrogate law (not MA, MN, MO, RI)
> - **49 states plus D.C.:** have the digital-assets access law; Louisiana has its own
> - **9–18 months:** a typical California formal probate; 6–18 months nationally

The Agencies That Will Not Take Your Power of Attorney

Here is the rule that surprises agents most. *Federal agencies do not honor your power of attorney. Each has its own form.* The Treasury Department does not recognize a power of attorney for federal payments, and the agencies that pay or insure retirees follow suit.

Agency	What it wants instead	How
Social Security	A representative payee appointed by SSA	Form SSA-11, generally in person; name up to 3 designees in advance; 1-800-772-1213

Agency	What it wants instead	How
IRS	Form 2848 (Power of Attorney and Declaration of Representative), signed by the representative too	Form 8821 for information only; Form 56 for a fiduciary
Medicare	Form CMS-10106 (1-800-MEDICARE Authorization to Disclose Personal Health Information), revised March 2026	Mail to 1-800-MEDICARE Written Authorization Dept., PO Box 1270, Lawrence, KS 66044, or file through a Medicare.gov account
VA	VA Form 21-22a (appoint a representative) or VA Form 21-0845 (authorize disclosure)	If a veteran is found incompetent, the VA appoints its own fiduciary

Social Security is the one to handle now. A capable adult receiving or applying for benefits can name up to three people, in order of preference, to serve as representative payee if the day comes: through a my Social Security account, by phone at 1-800-772-1213, or at a local office. You can change it any time, and SSA mails an annual notice listing your designees. Naming someone does not suggest you are incapable and does not appoint anyone automatically; SSA still evaluates the designee when a payee is needed. Without a designation, your agent files Form SSA-11 and waits, at the exact moment the mortgage is due. Chapter 3, The Silent Deadlines, covers the payee process.

For the IRS, a durable power of attorney is honored only if it meets the IRS's own regulatory requirements, and it cannot be recorded in the IRS's system unless a completed Form 2848 is attached. Sign the 2848 while you are healthy and keep it with the set. Medicare's authorization can last indefinitely or for a period you choose.

Document Two: The Health Care Documents

The proxy and the living will

A health care proxy (some states say medical power of attorney) names the person who decides when you cannot. A living will states your wishes about treatment. Most states combine them into one advance directive. A financial power of attorney never confers medical authority; California, for one, requires a separate instrument under a separate division of its code.

If you have no proxy, 46 states have a default-surrogate law that picks for you, usually in this order: spouse, adult children, parents, siblings, with some states adding a close friend. Massachusetts, Minnesota, Missouri, and Rhode Island have no such law; there, families rely on custom or go to court for guardianship. In every state, "adult children" as a group is a poor decision-maker when the children disagree. Name one.

The HIPAA release, and why it is a separate sheet

Janet's sister could not get a nurse to talk because of a gap that catches most families. A health care agent's authority typically begins only when the patient lacks capacity. Until a doctor makes that call, the agent is nobody, and the federal privacy rule (45 CFR 164.508) bars the hospital from discussing the patient with anyone not authorized in writing. Access to information is a different thing from authority to decide, and it needs its own document.

A stand-alone HIPAA authorization names the people who may receive your medical information now, while you can still decide for yourself. It takes one page. Sign it, list everyone you would want in the room, and give a copy to your primary doctor, your specialists, and the hospital where you would most likely be taken.

PHONE SCRIPT **Phone Script: Asking a Doctor's Office About the HIPAA Release**

You: Hello, this is [YOUR NAME], a patient of Dr. [NAME]; my date of birth is [DOB]. I'd like to make sure you have a HIPAA authorization on file naming [FAMILY MEMBER] so you can speak with them about my care. Can you check?

Them: I don't see one.

You: Do you have your own authorization form, or may I send a signed one? I'd like it to cover test results, appointments, and billing, and to stay in effect until I revoke it in writing.

Them: We'd prefer our form.

You: That's fine. Please mail or email it today. Once it's returned, could you confirm by phone that it's been scanned into my chart, with the date and the name of the person who entered it?

Them: Your family member can call and we'll talk to them.

You: I'd rather not rely on that. Please put the written authorization in the chart so any staff member can see it. Could you also tell me whether my health care proxy and living will are on file? If not, I'll bring copies to my next visit.

If they say it must be renewed yearly: "Please tell me the renewal date so I can calendar it."

Close: "Thank you. May I have your name and a direct extension in case there's a question when a family member calls?"

POLST, Five Wishes, and the papers people carry

For someone seriously ill, a POLST is different from an advance directive: it is a signed medical order, completed with a clinician, that tells emergency staff what to do. Every state and D.C. belongs to the National POLST Collaborative, but the form and its name vary: POLST in California, Florida, and Pennsylvania; MOLST in New York, Maryland, and Massachusetts; POST or MOST elsewhere; and some states have no mature program yet. Ask the treating physician.

Five Wishes is a plain-language advance directive valid in all 50 states and D.C. Four states may require extra steps (New Hampshire, Kansas, Ohio, Texas), and four require notarization (North Carolina, South Carolina, West Virginia, Missouri); elsewhere two witnesses suffice. Whatever form you use, under the Patient Self-Determination Act any hospital that takes Medicare or Medicaid must ask about your advance directive at admission, record whether one exists in a prominent part of your chart, and never condition care on having one.

> QUIET TIP **Carry Copies; Do Not Rely on a Registry**
>
> Some states run advance-directive registries, a few free and some for a small fee. Hospitals are not required to check them, and many do not. The document that gets honored is the one in the chart or in the bag. Keep a copy of the proxy and the HIPAA release with each named agent and your primary doctor, and a photo of each on the agent's phone.

Document Three: The Will, the Trust, or Both

What a will does not control

A will governs the assets in your sole name that have no beneficiary. That is a shorter list than most people think. Retirement accounts, life insurance, annuities, joint accounts with survivorship, POD and TOD registrations, and anything titled to a trust all pass outside the will, and the designation or the title controls even if the will says otherwise. Chapter 7, The Handoff, maps each asset to its path.

Probate: months and a fee schedule

Probate is the court process that proves the will and appoints the executor. Nationally, 6–18 months is a fair range; California's courts say formal probate "typically takes 9 to 18 months and can sometimes take even longer." During most of that time the sole-name accounts sit still.

Cost is state-specific. California sets it by statute, for the attorney and, separately, for the executor: 4% of the first $100,000, 3% of the next $100,000, 2% of the next $800,000, and 1% of the next $9 million. On a $600,000 gross estate, that is $15,000 for the attorney and another $15,000 if the executor takes the fee: $30,000 before court costs. Most other states use "reasonable" fees instead of a schedule.

Small estates skip most of this. California allows a personal-property affidavit up to $208,850 for deaths on or after April 1, 2025, and a simplified petition for a primary residence up to $750,000. Texas allows a small-estate affidavit up to $75,000, excluding the homestead, for people who died without a will, after a 30-day wait. Florida allows summary administration for estates of $75,000 or less, or when the death was more than 2 years ago. New York's voluntary administration covers personal property up to $50,000, with a $1 filing fee.

The trust, and the unfunded-trust mistake

A revocable living trust holds title to assets during your life, with you as trustee, and passes them at death without probate. It works only for what is titled to it. *A trust controls only what has been retitled into it.* The most common estate-planning failure is a beautifully drafted trust in a binder and a house, two bank accounts, and a brokerage account still in the owner's own name. The pour-over will catches those leftovers, but everything it catches goes through probate, which is what the trust was for.

Fund the trust the week you sign it: a new deed for the house, retitled bank and brokerage accounts, and the trust named as beneficiary where a form exists. Then notify your homeowner's insurer and lender of the new deed (Chapter 7 covers the due-on-sale protection).

One asset never gets retitled: the IRA or 401(k). Moving a retirement account into a trust is a taxable distribution of the whole thing. If you want the trust to receive it, name the trust as beneficiary, and only if it is drafted as a "see-through" trust. Under the SECURE Act, most non-spouse beneficiaries, including most trusts, must empty an inherited account within 10 years.

Signing a will that holds up

Two adult witnesses is the nationwide norm. Add a self-proving affidavit, a notarized statement by you and the witnesses, so the court can admit the will without finding witnesses years later; D.C. and Ohio do not allow it, and California, Illinois, Indiana, Maryland, and Nevada get the same result by having witnesses sign under penalty of perjury. Roughly half the states recognize a handwritten, unwitnessed holographic will; Florida, New York (except for military members), Ohio, and many others do not. Electronic wills are spreading, with more than a dozen states permitting some form, but a paper original with two witnesses remains the safe choice.

Where the originals live

Keep the original will, trust, and powers of attorney in a fireproof home safe, your attorney's vault, or the probate court's will-deposit service where one exists. Avoid a safe deposit box in a state where the box cannot be opened after death without a court order; New York, Georgia, Connecticut, and Nevada are among them. Add a one-page letter of instruction: where the accounts are, who the advisors are, where the passwords live.

Digital assets have their own law. The Revised Uniform Fiduciary Access to Digital Assets Act is in force in 49 states and D.C.; Louisiana has its own statute. Its priority order matters: the provider's own online tool comes first (Google's Inactive Account Manager, the legacy-contact settings at Apple and Facebook), then your will, trust, or power of attorney, then the terms of service. Set the legacy contacts. It takes ten minutes and outranks anything your lawyer writes.

Document Four: Beneficiary Designations

A beneficiary form beats a will, every time, even when the will is newer. The custodian of your IRA, the insurer, and the bank holding your POD account will pay the person on their form; the will is not their concern. That makes the beneficiary form the most powerful document in the set and the one reviewed least.

The errors repeat from family to family:

- **No beneficiary named.** The account falls to the estate and into probate.
- **The estate named on purpose.** Same result, on purpose.
- **An ex-spouse still named.** The form controls; a divorce decree and a new will do not change it at the custodian.
- **A minor named directly.** A custodian will not pay a child; a court appoints someone, at cost.

- **No contingent beneficiary.** If the primary dies first, you are back to "none named."
- **"Per stirpes" and "per capita" confused.** Per stirpes sends a deceased child's share down to that child's children; per capita splits it among survivors at the same level. Pick on purpose.

Employer plans add a rule. Federal law protects a spouse's survivor benefit in a pension or 401(k), and it cannot be waived without the spouse's written consent. Naming a child on a 401(k) form while married does not work unless the spouse signs. An IRA has no such rule, which is one reason the form matters more there.

Review every designation after each marriage, divorce, birth, death, and account transfer, and once a year regardless.

WORKSHEET **Worksheet: Beneficiary Audit Grid**

Instructions: List every account with a beneficiary form. Ask each custodian for written confirmation of the current primary and contingent beneficiaries (Chapter 7 has a letter for this). One block per account.

Account 1 (type, institution): ____________________

Primary beneficiary and share: ____________________

Contingent beneficiary and share: ____________________

Per stirpes or per capita: ____________________

Last confirmed in writing (date): ____________________

Account 2 (type, institution): ____________________

Primary beneficiary and share: ____________________

Contingent beneficiary and share: ____________________

Per stirpes or per capita: ____________________

Last confirmed in writing (date): ____________________

Account 3 (type, institution): ____________________

Primary beneficiary and share: ____________________

Contingent beneficiary and share: ____________________

Per stirpes or per capita: ____________________

Last confirmed in writing (date): ____________________

Red flags found: [ ] None named [ ] Estate named [ ] Ex-spouse [ ] Minor named [ ] No contingent [ ] Trust named without see-through review

Fixes to file, with deadline: ____________________

The Wrong Tool: "Add My Daughter to the Account"

When a parent starts needing help with the bills, the most common move in America is a trip to the branch to add the helper's name to the checking account. It feels like the small option. It is the large one.

There are two ways to add a name, and the signature card decides which one you got. A convenience account, which some states call an agency account, lets the second person sign checks and nothing more; the money stays yours, and at your death it goes to your estate. A joint account with right of survivorship makes the helper a co-owner today and the sole owner the day you die, regardless of what the will says. Florida, Illinois, New York, and Texas have statutes that distinguish the two, and many states follow the Uniform Probate Code's version. But if the card says "joint with survivorship," courts tend to honor the card.

The problems arrive from directions nobody was watching. A joint owner's creditors can reach the account. A joint owner's divorce can put it on the table. The other children discover at the funeral that the checking account went to one sibling by contract. And the bank's fraud software, as Chapter 1 explains, treats a newly added name followed by withdrawals as a red flag. Financial institutions told the Treasury's financial-crimes unit that adult children are the perpetrators in about 40% of elder-theft reports. Most helpers are honest; the account structure should not depend on it.

> WATCH OUT **Watch Out: "Adding a Name" Is a Gift and a Transfer of Control**
>
> Use the right tool for each job. To let someone pay your bills, give them a durable power of attorney and file it with the bank. To let someone receive the account at your death, add a POD beneficiary, which costs nothing, changes nothing while you live, and lets the beneficiary collect with a death certificate and ID. To give the bank someone to call, name a trusted contact. Three forms, no co-owner, no gift, no surprise. Chapter 8, The Fine Print, covers joint-account exposure in detail.

Where to Get Help

None of these documents requires a lawyer by law, and all of them benefit from one. If cost is the obstacle, start with the Eldercare Locator at 1-800-677-1116, which connects you to your local Area Agency on Aging; those agencies fund legal assistance for people 60 and older under the Older Americans Act, with no income test. Legal Services Corporation grantees, roughly 130 nonprofit programs with more than 800 offices, generally serve people with income at or below 125% of the federal poverty guidelines. Most state bars run lawyer referral services with low-fee first consultations, and the National Academy of Elder Law Attorneys keeps a directory that flags Certified Elder Law Attorneys. An elder-law attorney can confirm the execution rules for your state, which is the one thing this chapter cannot do for you.

Keeping the Set Alive

The four documents are a set of four dates that need to stay within reach of each other. The inventory below is the page to photocopy; keep one with the originals and give one to each agent.

WORKSHEET **Worksheet: Four Documents Inventory**

Instructions: One block per document. "Filed with" means every institution that has a copy on record. Update this page whenever a document is signed, revoked, or delivered somewhere new.

1. Durable financial power of attorney

Date signed / state: ____________________

Agent / successor agent: ____________________

Original kept at: ____________________

Copies held by: ____________________

Filed with (institution, date, employee): ____________________

Hot powers granted: [ ] Gifts [ ] Beneficiaries [ ] Survivorship [ ] Trusts [ ] Digital assets

Last reviewed: ____________________

1. Health care proxy and living will; HIPAA release

Date signed / agent / alternate: ____________________

HIPAA release names: ____________________

On file with (doctor, hospital, date): ____________________

POLST in place: [ ] Yes [ ] No [ ] Not needed

Last reviewed: ____________________

1. Will and/or revocable trust

Date signed: ____________________ Self-proving affidavit: [ ] Yes [ ] No

Executor / successor trustee: ____________________

Original kept at: ____________________

Assets not yet retitled to the trust: ____________________

Last reviewed: ____________________

1. Beneficiary designations and agency forms

Beneficiary Audit Grid completed (date): ____________________

SSA advance designation: [ ] Yes [ ] No IRS Form 2848 signed: [ ] Yes [ ] No

Medicare CMS-10106 filed: [ ] Yes [ ] No Legacy contacts set: [ ] Yes [ ] No

Letter of instruction location: ____________________

CHECKLIST **Checklist: Annual Review**

- ☐ Reread all four documents on the same date each year and note it on the inventory
- ☐ Confirm every named agent, executor, and trustee is still alive, willing, and reachable
- ☐ Confirm primary and contingent beneficiaries in writing with each custodian, using the Beneficiary Audit Grid
- ☐ Ask each bank and brokerage whether the power of attorney is still on file and whether it wants a fresh agent's certification
- ☐ Check that the HIPAA release is in the chart at every doctor's office added this year
- ☐ List any new account, deed, or vehicle not yet retitled to the trust or given a POD or TOD beneficiary
- ☐ Verify your SSA advance designation on the annual notice and update legacy contacts on email, phone, and social accounts

What Janet Did

Janet did not get a new power of attorney; Harold could not sign one. She got the old one accepted. Her father's lawyer pulled the Ohio statutory agent's certification form, and Janet signed it before a notary on Monday. On Tuesday she hand-delivered it with the original document, the cover letter from this chapter, and a request for a dated receipt. She named the seven-business-day rule out loud, politely, once. The bank's legal department called on Thursday to say the accounts were open to her.

At the hospital, a doctor's finding of incapacity brought Harold's health care proxy into effect, and it named Janet. She signed the hospital's authorization so her sister could get updates too. Then she went to the Social Security office with Form SSA-11 and became her father's representative payee, a process Harold could have shortened years earlier by naming her in advance.

Harold came home in May. Once he was able, he and Janet sat at the kitchen table and completed the Four Documents Inventory: a new HIPAA release, a POD beneficiary on the checking account, an IRS Form 2848, an advance designation with SSA. The document in the drawer had been good. It had been alone.

Your Next Steps

CHECKLIST Your Next Steps

- ☐ Locate the originals of your four documents and record the date signed and storage place on the Four Documents Inventory
- ☐ Confirm your power of attorney says "durable," is notarized, and grants the hot powers you intend; if not, sign a new one under your state's formalities
- ☐ Deliver a copy of the power of attorney to every bank and brokerage with the cover letter, and log the date and receiving employee
- ☐ Ask each institution for its own power of attorney form and sign it in addition to yours
- ☐ Sign a stand-alone HIPAA release and confirm by phone that your primary doctor and hospital have it in your chart
- ☐ Name up to 3 advance designees for a Social Security representative payee through my Social Security or at 1-800-772-1213
- ☐ Sign IRS Form 2848 and Medicare Form CMS-10106 and file them with the set
- ☐ Complete the Beneficiary Audit Grid and fix any account with no beneficiary, no contingent, an estate, an ex-spouse, or a minor named
- ☐ Add a POD beneficiary to any account where you were tempted to add a co-owner, and name a trusted contact at each institution
- ☐ Call the Eldercare Locator at 1-800-677-1116 if you need a low-cost attorney to review the set for your state

CHAPTER FIVE

The Calendar — Asset Moves Before the Line

By the end of this chapter you will know which money moves must be finished by December 31, April 1, April 15, and October 15 — and what each missed line costs in real dollars.

A STORY **Pauline, 73, Grand Rapids, Michigan**

Pauline retired from the school district library in 2019. She turned 73 in March 2026, and her traditional IRA showed $400,000 on last December's statement. She also has a small 403(b) she never got around to moving.

Her plans for the year were ordinary. Give $5,000 to her church, as she does every fall. Write four $2,000 checks to the grandchildren at Christmas. And her daughter had suggested over coffee that Pauline "put my name on the house so it's easier later."

Her neighbor Ed, who reads the financial pages, added one more: she didn't have to touch the IRA until April. "First year, you get until April 1. Take your time."

Pauline wrote it all on a legal pad. Church, grandchildren, house, April. Every item felt harmless, and she had a feeling that at least one of them wasn't. She was right. Three of her instincts were sound, one was expensive, and Ed's advice was true in a way that would have cost her about $1,000. This chapter is the legal pad, filled in properly. (Pauline is a composite; the numbers are 2026 numbers.)

THE QUIET RULES The Quiet Rules in This Chapter

- *The calendar, not the market, decides most of the avoidable tax you will pay.*
- *December 31 has no extension. April 15 does. Know which line you are standing on.*
- *April 1 is a permission slip, not a gift. Waiting stacks two RMDs into one tax year.*
- *Charity first, then the RMD. The first dollars out of an IRA are the RMD.*
- *$19,000 is a tax rule, not a Medicaid rule.*
- *A check is a gift when it is deposited, not when it is written.*
- *Never give away a loss, and never give away a house without a calculator.*

Why the Calendar Beats the Market

Most people believe their tax bill in retirement is set by how their investments do. It is mostly set by dates. The same $400,000 IRA, the same church gift, the same Christmas checks produce different tax bills depending on which side of a line they land on — and the lines do not announce themselves.

Some lines have a repair window; miss an IRA contribution deadline and there is a form for that. Some are hard; miss a required minimum distribution by December 31 and there is a penalty, a form, and a letter to the IRS asking forgiveness. This chapter sorts the year into four dates, then covers the three slower clocks running underneath: the gift lines, the Medicaid look-back, and the house.

KEY NUMBERS 2026 Numbers to Know

- **RMD age:** 73 if born 1951–1959; 75 if born 1960 or later
- **Missed-RMD penalty:** 25% of the shortfall; 10% if corrected in time (Form 5329)
- **QCD limit:** $111,000 per person; one-time $55,000 split-interest election; age 70½ on the date of the gift
- **Annual gift exclusion:** $19,000 per recipient ($38,000 for a couple gift-splitting on Form 709)
- **Lifetime estate and gift exemption:** $15,000,000 per person; $30,000,000 per couple with portability
- **Gift to a non-citizen spouse:** $194,000
- **529 superfunding:** $95,000 per beneficiary
- **IRA contribution for 2026:** $7,500 plus $1,100 catch-up at 50+, due April 15, 2027
- **HSA contribution for 2026:** $4,400 / $8,750, plus $1,000 at 55+, due April 15, 2027
- **Capital-loss deduction against ordinary income:** $3,000 per year
- **0% capital-gains bracket:** taxable income up to $49,450 single / $98,900 joint
- **Medicaid look-back:** 60 months

December 31: The Line With No Extension

Everything in this section is a calendar-year rule. The IRS does not care that your custodian's phones close early on New Year's Eve or that your accountant is in Cabo. If the money has not moved by midnight, the year is over.

Required minimum distributions

A required minimum distribution (RMD) is the least you must withdraw each year from a traditional IRA, SEP, SIMPLE, 401(k), 403(b), or similar pre-tax account once you reach the starting age: **age 73** if you were born 1951 through 1959, **age 75** if born 1960 or later. Roth IRAs have no lifetime RMDs, and since 2024 neither do Roth 401(k)s.

The math is one division problem. Take the balance on December 31 of the *previous* year and divide by the factor for the age you reach *this* year, from the IRS Uniform Lifetime Table (Publication 590-B, Appendix B, Table III).

Age this year	Table factor	RMD on $400,000
73	26.5	$15,094
75	24.6	$16,260
80	20.2	$19,802
85	16.0	$25,000
90	12.2	$32,787

So a 75-year-old whose IRA held $400,000 on December 31, 2025 must withdraw at least $400,000 ÷ 24.6 = **$16,260** during 2026. Notice what the table does as you age: the factor shrinks, so the required percentage grows — about 3.8% of the balance at 73, about 8.2% at 90. This is why a large IRA in your 80s can push you into brackets you left decades ago, and why Chapter 6 spends so much time on Roth conversions before RMDs start. (If your spouse is your sole beneficiary and more than 10 years younger, the Joint Life table applies and the RMD is smaller; your custodian will calculate it.)

Where the money can come from. With several traditional IRAs, calculate each RMD, then take the total from any one or more of them. 403(b)s aggregate the same way among themselves. 401(k)s do not: each plan's RMD must come from that plan. And you never cross types — a 403(b) RMD cannot come from an IRA. This is Pauline's 403(b) problem: its RMD must come out of the 403(b) itself.

The still-working exception. If you still work for the company sponsoring your 401(k) and own no more than 5% of it, that plan alone may let you delay RMDs until April 1 after the year you retire. It never applies to IRAs or former employers' plans.

WORKSHEET **Worksheet: RMD Calculator**

One line per pre-tax account. Use last year's December 31 balance and the factor for the age you reach this year. Your custodian will confirm the figure; do the math yourself anyway.

Tax year: ________ Age I reach this year: ______ Uniform Lifetime factor: ______

Account 1: ____________________ Custodian: ____________________ Type (IRA / 403(b) / 401(k)): ________

Balance on December 31 of last year: $__________ RMD (balance ÷ factor): $__________

Account 2: ____________________ Custodian: ____________________ Type (IRA / 403(b) / 401(k)): ________

Balance on December 31 of last year: $__________ RMD (balance ÷ factor): $__________

Account 3: ____________________ Custodian: ____________________ Type (IRA / 403(b) / 401(k)): ________

Balance on December 31 of last year: $__________ RMD (balance ÷ factor): $__________

Total IRA RMDs (may come from any IRA): $__________ Each 401(k) RMD (from that plan only): $__________

QCDs planned first: $__________ Remaining taxable RMD: $__________ Already withdrawn: $__________

[ ] First RMD year (April 1 of next year allowed — see the trap below)

[ ] Spouse is sole beneficiary and more than 10 years younger (Joint Life table)

Withholding elected: ______% Date completed: ________ Confirmation number: __________

What it costs when missed. The penalty is an excise tax of **25%** of the shortfall, reduced to **10%** if you withdraw it and file a return reflecting it within the correction window, which generally runs to the end of the second tax year after the miss. Report it on Form 5329 (Additional Taxes on Qualified Plans). If the miss was an honest error — a custodian mistake, an illness, a misread statement — ask for a full waiver: take the missed amount, file Form 5329, write "RC" and the waived amount on the dotted line next to line 54, and attach a short explanation. People who fix the shortfall promptly and explain plainly are often forgiven. People who wait are not.

Qualified charitable distributions

If you give to charity at all, the qualified charitable distribution (QCD) is the most under-used line on a retiree's calendar. A QCD is a transfer **directly from your IRA to a qualified public charity**. The money never counts as your income, so it doesn't raise the tax on your Social Security, doesn't push you toward a Medicare IRMAA threshold, and doesn't erode the $6,000 senior deduction. And it counts toward your RMD, dollar for dollar.

The 2026 limit is **$111,000 per person**. You must be **age 70½ on the date of the transfer** — not merely turning 70½ that year — which means QCDs can start two or three years before RMDs. The money must come from an IRA (traditional, inherited, or an inactive SEP or SIMPLE), not a 401(k); roll the 401(k) to an IRA first. Donor-advised funds and private foundations don't qualify. You may receive nothing in return, and you need the charity's written acknowledgment. Since 2023 there is also a one-time election to send up to **$55,000** of QCD money into a charitable gift annuity or charitable remainder trust that pays income back to you or your spouse; it counts within the $111,000 cap.

> QUIET TIP **Do the QCD First**
>
> The tax code has a first-dollars-out rule: the first money out of an IRA in a year is deemed to be your RMD. Take your full RMD in February as a taxable distribution and send a QCD in November, and the QCD still excludes that November money — but it cannot reach back and "cover" the RMD you already paid tax on. Order matters. Send the charity its money first, then take what is left. Pauline's $5,000 church gift, done as a QCD in October, leaves a taxable RMD of $15,094 − $5,000 = $10,094.

Two paperwork notes. Your custodian's Form 1099-R will show the full distribution as ordinary income; you report the gross on Form 1040 line 4a, the taxable amount (without the QCD) on line 4b, and write "QCD" next to 4b. Tell your preparer, because the 1099-R alone won't say it. And while custodians may mail the check to you, payable to the charity, many want the charity to cash it before year-end for it to count on this year's 1099-R. Do QCDs in October or November, and ask your custodian its cut-off date.

> PHONE SCRIPT **Phone Script: Setting Up a QCD and Confirming Your RMD**
>
> **You:** Hello. I'm calling about my traditional IRA, account ending in [LAST FOUR DIGITS]. I'd like to confirm my required minimum distribution for [YEAR] and set up a qualified charitable distribution. Could I get your name and an employee or extension number first?

Them: [Name and number.]

You: Thank you. What does your system show as my RMD this year, and what December 31 balance and factor did you use?

Them: [Amount.]

You: That matches my figure of [YOUR AMOUNT]. Now the QCD. I am over 70½. I'd like [DOLLAR AMOUNT] sent directly to [CHARITY NAME], tax ID [EIN], at [ADDRESS]. Please make the check payable to the charity, with no withholding, and code it as a qualified charitable distribution.

If they say the check must be mailed to you: **You:** That's fine as long as it's payable to the charity, not to me. What's the last date I can request it and still have it count for this tax year?

If they need a form: **You:** Please email it today and tell me where to return it. What's your processing time in business days once you receive it?

You: Last thing. Please send written confirmation of the RMD figure and the QCD once processed, and give me a reference number for this call.

If they cannot answer the RMD question: **You:** Could you transfer me to the retirement distributions team, or give me a direct number? I'd like this resolved before [DATE], which leaves time before year-end.

LETTER TEMPLATE **Letter Template: QCD Instruction to IRA Custodian**

[DATE]

[CUSTODIAN NAME]

Attn: Retirement Distributions

[STREET ADDRESS]

[CITY, STATE ZIP]

RE: Qualified Charitable Distribution from Traditional IRA, Account No. [ACCOUNT NUMBER], Owner [YOUR FULL NAME], SSN ending [LAST FOUR]

Dear Retirement Distributions Team:

Please process a qualified charitable distribution under Internal Revenue Code section 408(d)(8) from the account above. I was born [DATE OF BIRTH] and am over age 70½ as of this request.

Please issue a check for $[AMOUNT] payable to [CHARITY LEGAL NAME], EIN [EIN], and mail it directly to the charity at [CHARITY ADDRESS]. If your procedure requires mailing the check to me, it must still be payable only to the charity. Do not withhold any federal or state income tax.

> Please apply this distribution toward my [YEAR] required minimum distribution and report it on Form 1099-R in the usual manner. I intend the transfer to reach the charity no later than [DATE, e.g., November 20, 2026].
>
> Please confirm in writing, within 10 business days, the amount and the dates the check was issued and mailed. If any additional form or signature is required, contact me at [PHONE] or [EMAIL] immediately so we do not miss the year-end deadline.
>
> Sincerely,
>
> [SIGNATURE]
>
> [PRINTED NAME]
>
> [MAILING ADDRESS]
>
> Enclosures: copy of government photo ID; charity's address and EIN confirmation; your QCD request form (if applicable)

Roth conversions

A Roth conversion — moving pre-tax IRA money into a Roth IRA and paying the tax now — must be completed by **December 31** of the year you want it taxed. There is no "for last year" option, and since 2018 a conversion cannot be undone. Many custodians stop taking requests in mid-December, so treat December 15 as the real deadline. Chapter 6, The Review, covers when and how much. One calendar effect to keep in view: Medicare looks back two years, so a 2026 conversion sets your 2028 premiums, and the first IRMAA tier — above $109,000 single or $218,000 joint — is a cliff, not a ramp.

Harvesting losses — and harvesting gains

In a taxable brokerage account, realized losses offset realized gains without limit. If losses exceed gains, up to **$3,000** of the excess ($1,500 married filing separately) reduces ordinary income, and the rest carries forward — indefinitely, but not to your heirs. Unused carryforwards die with you, so use them.

The trap is the wash-sale rule: buy substantially identical shares within **30 calendar days before or after** the loss sale and the loss is disallowed. The window includes purchases in your IRA and by your spouse, and a loss triggered by an IRA repurchase is gone for good, not deferred. Trade date, not settlement date, governs the December 31 line.

The mirror image is worth more to many retirees. In 2026, long-term capital gains are taxed at **0%** as long as taxable income stays under **$49,450** (single) or **$98,900** (joint). In a low-income year — retired, not yet drawing Social Security, RMDs not started — you can sell appreciated shares, pay nothing, and buy them right back at a higher basis. There is no wash-sale rule on gains. But gain-harvesting still raises adjusted gross income, which is what the IRMAA thresholds and the senior-deduction phase-out watch, so do the math before December.

Annual gifts and the December wire

You can give up to **$19,000** to as many people as you like in 2026 without filing anything. A married couple can give $38,000 per recipient if both spouses consent to gift-splitting on Form 709 (United States Gift Tax Return) — and the form is required for the split even when neither spouse's share exceeds $19,000.

> WATCH OUT **Watch Out: The Check That Arrives in January**
>
> For gift-tax purposes a gift by check is generally complete when the recipient deposits it, not when you write it. In *Estate of Metzger*, checks written in one year and deposited in the next counted in the year of deposit. A $19,000 check written December 28 and deposited January 4 is a January gift — it uses next year's exclusion, and if you give that person another $19,000 next December, you have a Form 709 to file. The fix is easy: send December gifts by wire or electronic transfer in the first week of the month, or hand over checks at Thanksgiving and ask that they be deposited by mid-December. The recipient's bank may hold a large check for up to seven business days (Chapter 1), but "deposited" is the recipient's act, so a December 20 deposit counts even if the funds are held into January.

To give more than $19,000 to a grandchild's 529 plan, you can "superfund": contribute up to **$95,000** per beneficiary in one year ($190,000 for a couple) and elect on Form 709 to treat it as five years of annual gifts. If you die within the five years, the unused portions return to your estate. A 529 contribution is also a December 31 item for most states' income-tax deductions.

CHECKLIST **December Checklist**

- ☐ Confirm every RMD with each custodian and record it on the RMD Calculator worksheet
- ☐ Send QCDs by mid-November, payable directly to each charity, before taking any remaining RMD
- ☐ Take the remaining RMD from the IRAs and from each 401(k)/403(b) separately by December 31
- ☐ Submit any Roth conversion request by December 15 with zero withholding (Chapter 6)
- ☐ Harvest losses or 0% gains in the brokerage account; check the 30-day wash-sale window in every account, including IRAs
- ☐ Wire annual gifts in the first week of December; ask check recipients to deposit promptly
- ☐ Make 529 contributions by December 31 and note any Form 709 five-year election
- ☐ Set withholding on the December RMD if estimated payments are short

April 1: The Permission Slip

Here is the rule Ed half-remembered. For your **first** RMD year only, the IRS lets you delay that distribution until **April 1 of the following year** — your "required beginning date." Every later RMD is due December 31 of its own year, no exceptions.

The permission slip is real. The trap is the second year. If Pauline, who turned 73 in 2026, delays her 2026 RMD to April 1, 2027, she still owes her 2027 RMD by December 31, 2027. Two taxable distributions land on one return.

Put numbers on it. Pauline's IRA held $400,000 on December 31, 2025, so her 2026 RMD is $400,000 ÷ 26.5 = **$15,094**. Suppose she leaves it alone and the account grows to $410,000 by December 31, 2026. Her 2027 RMD, at age 74, is $410,000 ÷ 25.5 = **$16,078**. Take the first one in 2026 and she reports $15,094 in 2026 and $16,078 in 2027. Wait until April and she reports $0 in 2026 and **$31,172** in 2027.

Her other taxable income — pension plus the taxable part of her Social Security, after her standard deduction — is about $40,000, inside the single 12% bracket, which ends at $50,400 in 2026. She has $10,400 of 12% room each year. The table uses 2026 brackets for both years to keep the arithmetic honest.

	Take first RMD in 2026	Delay to April 1, 2027
2026 taxable RMD income	$15,094	$0
2027 taxable RMD income	$16,078	$31,172
Amount taxed at 22%	$10,372	$20,772
Federal tax on the RMDs	$4,778	$5,818

Delaying costs Pauline **$1,040** — the 12% room she left empty in 2026, taxed at 22% in 2027 instead. On a larger IRA the same stacking can cross the $75,000 line where the $6,000 senior deduction starts to phase out, push more Social Security into taxable territory, or clear the $109,000 IRMAA threshold that sets 2029 premiums. The permission slip almost never pays. The exception is a first RMD year in which your income is unusually high — a final paycheck, a severance, a property sale — and next year's will be markedly lower. Run both columns before deciding.

April 15, 2027: The Line With Paperwork

April 15 is a softer line, because it is mostly about filing, and filing can be extended. But three things attach to it that people confuse with December.

IRA and HSA contributions for 2026. You can contribute for 2026 until **April 15, 2027**, not including extensions. The IRA limit is **$7,500** plus a **$1,100** catch-up at 50 or older — $8,600 total — with no upper age limit as long as you or your spouse have earned income. The HSA limit is **$4,400** self-only or **$8,750** family, plus **$1,000** at 55 or older. Stop HSA contributions six months before enrolling in Medicare, because Part A enrollment after 65 is retroactive; Chapter 6 explains.

Form 709. You must file a gift-tax return for 2026 by April 15, 2027 if you gave any one person more than $19,000, elected gift-splitting, made a 529 five-year election, gave a "future interest" (most gifts into trusts), or gave a non-citizen spouse more than **$194,000**. Filing does not mean paying. No gift tax is owed until lifetime taxable gifts pass **$15,000,000**; the return exists to keep count. Extending your income-tax return on Form 4868, or filing Form 8892 alone, extends Form 709 to October 15.

Estimated taxes. RMDs, conversions, and harvested gains arrive without withholding unless you ask. The safe harbor for 2026 is to pay in, through withholding and estimates, the smaller of 90% of your 2026 tax or 100% of your 2025 tax (110% if 2025 adjusted gross income was over $150,000). Owe less than $1,000 at filing and there is no penalty. The last 2026 quarterly payment is due **January 15, 2027** (waived if you file and pay in full by February 1, 2027). The 2026 return is due April 15, 2027; the automatic extension on Form 4868 runs to October 15, 2027 — for filing, never for paying.

> QUIET TIP **Withholding on a December RMD Counts All Year**
>
> Estimated-tax penalties are figured quarter by quarter, so a large November conversion or gain can produce a penalty for April and June even though the income didn't exist yet. Withholding is different: tax withheld at any point in the year is treated as paid evenly across all four quarters. Many advisors therefore have clients skip estimates and withhold a large percentage from a December RMD instead. The IRA covers the tax, the penalty math comes out clean, and no quarterly checks are mailed. Ask your custodian for its withholding election form when you schedule the RMD.

October 15: The Last Repair Window

October 15 is the extended filing deadline, and also the deadline for two repairs most people don't know exist.

Recharacterizing a contribution. If you made a 2026 Roth IRA contribution and then discover your income was over the limit, or you contributed to a traditional IRA and would rather it had been a Roth, you can recharacterize the *contribution* — move it, with its earnings, to the other type — until **October 15, 2027**, if you filed on time or extended. Contributions only; conversions have been un-fixable since 2018.

Removing an excess contribution. An excess in an IRA is charged **6%** for every year it remains, measured on December 31. Withdraw the excess plus its earnings by October 15 of the following year and you avoid the first year's 6%. Miss that and the tax runs annually until it is removed, reported on Form 5329.

The full ladder, from hardest line to softest, looks like this.

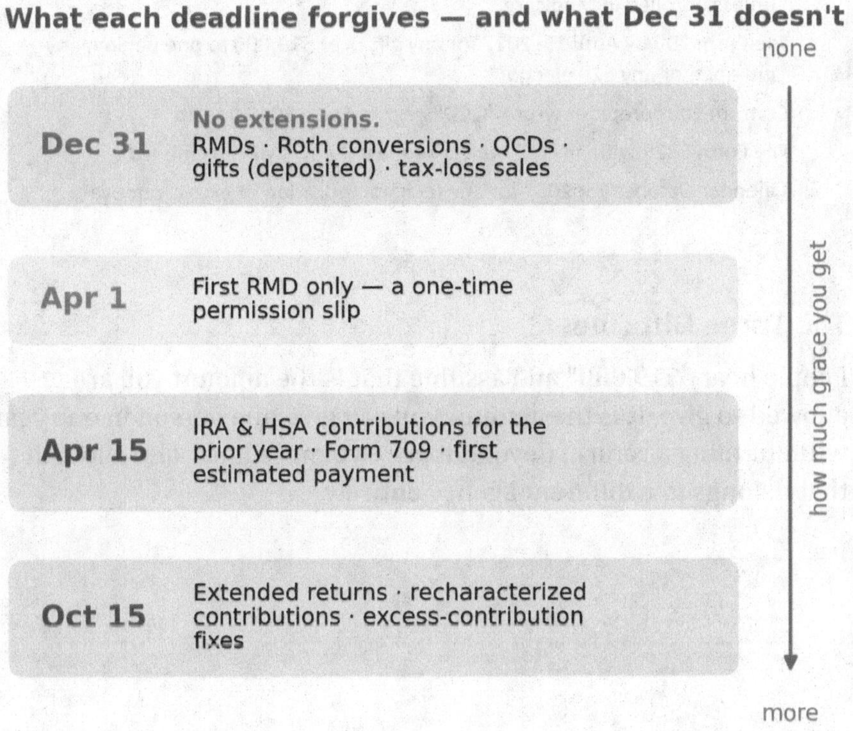

Figure 5.1. *The deadline ladder: what must be done by December 31, April 1, April 15, and October 15, and which lines can be extended*

CHECKLIST **April Checklist**

- ☐ Take the first RMD, if delayed, no later than April 1 — and schedule the second for December 31
- ☐ Make 2026 IRA contributions ($7,500 plus $1,100 catch-up) by April 15, 2027
- ☐ Make 2026 HSA contributions ($4,400 or $8,750, plus $1,000) by April 15, 2027, unless enrolled in Medicare
- ☐ File Form 709 by April 15, 2027 for any gift over $19,000 to one person, any gift-split, or any 529 election
- ☐ Confirm your preparer wrote "QCD" next to Form 1040 line 4b
- ☐ File Form 5329 with an "RC" waiver request if any RMD was missed
- ☐ Calendar October 15, 2027 for any recharacterization or excess removal

The Three Gift Lines

People hear "$19,000" and assume that is the amount you are allowed to give. It is the amount you can give one person in one year without filing a return. Beyond it are two more lines, and a fourth that belongs to a different agency entirely.

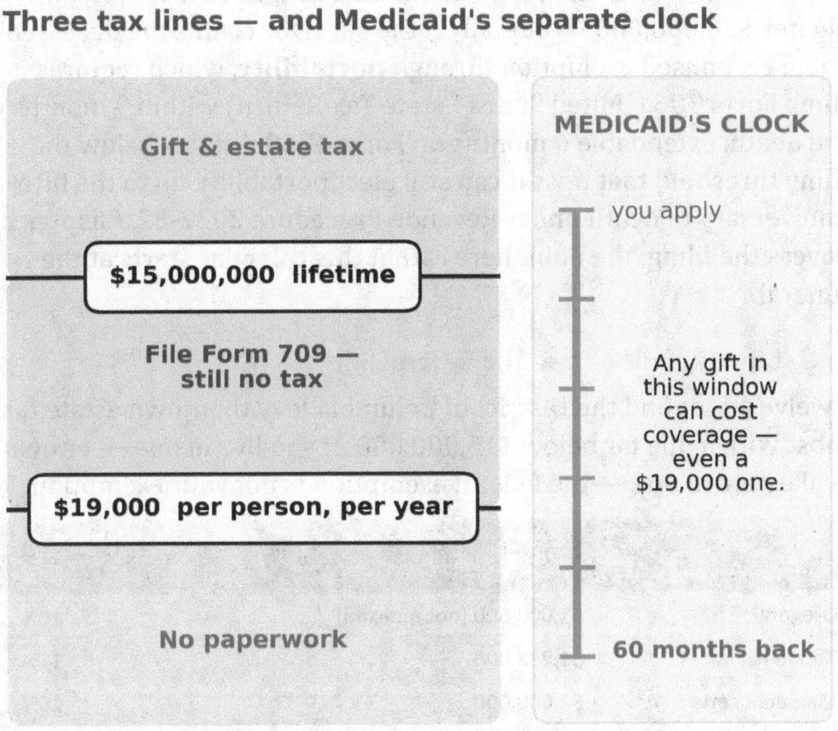

Figure 5.2. *The three gift lines — $19,000 annual exclusion, then Form 709, then the $15,000,000 lifetime exemption — with the Medicaid 60-month look-back running on its own clock beneath them*

Line one: $19,000 per person per year. No paperwork, no tax. Two exceptions make the line larger than it looks. **Tuition and medical bills paid directly to the school or provider** are unlimited and don't count against the $19,000 — but only tuition (not room, board, or books), and only if you pay the institution, not the student. Health-insurance premiums you pay for someone else qualify. Gifts to a citizen spouse are unlimited; gifts to a **non-citizen spouse** are capped at $194,000 a year before Form 709 is required.

Line two: Form 709. Cross $19,000 to one person and you file a return the following April. The excess is subtracted from your lifetime exemption. No check is written to the IRS.

Line three: $15,000,000. Under the 2025 tax law, the combined estate and lifetime-gift exemption is **$15,000,000 per person** for

2026, indexed after that, with no scheduled sunset. A couple can shelter $30,000,000 — but only if the survivor claims the deceased spouse's unused exemption through **portability**, which requires filing Form 706 (United States Estate Tax Return) within 9 months of the death, extendable 6 months on Form 4768. Estates below the filing threshold that miss it can still elect portability up to the fifth anniversary of death under Revenue Procedure 2022-32. Chapter 2 covers the filing; the point here is that this calendar starts at the funeral.

The states that don't use the federal line

Twelve states and the District of Columbia levy their own estate tax, most with a line far below $15,000,000. If you live in one — or own real estate in one — the federal exemption is not your exemption.

State	2026 exemption	Top rate
Oregon	$1,000,000 (not indexed)	16%
Rhode Island	$1,838,000	16%
Massachusetts	$2,000,000	16%
Minnesota	$3,000,000	16%
Washington	$3,000,000 (deaths on/after July 1, 2026)	20%
Illinois	$4,000,000 (cliff)	16%
District of Columbia	$4,988,400	16%

State	2026 exemption	Top rate
Maryland	$5,000,000 (also has inheritance tax)	16%
Vermont	$5,000,000	16%
Hawaii	$5,490,000	20%
Maine	$7,160,000	12%
New York	$7,350,000 (cliff)	16%
Connecticut	$15,000,000 (also has a gift tax)	12%

Three notes. A "cliff" state taxes the *whole* estate once you cross the line: in New York, an estate more than about 5% over the exemption loses it entirely. Washington's numbers changed on **July 1, 2026** — a flat $3,000,000 exemption replaced $3,076,000, and the top rate rolled back to 20% from the 35% that applied to deaths between July 1, 2025 and June 30, 2026. And most of these states do not let a surviving spouse inherit the other's unused exemption the way the federal rule does, which is why couples in Oregon or Massachusetts still hear about bypass trusts.

Five states charge an **inheritance tax** instead — a tax on the recipient, keyed to their relationship to you: **Kentucky, Maryland, Nebraska, New Jersey, and Pennsylvania** (Iowa repealed its tax for deaths on or after January 1, 2025). All five exempt a surviving spouse. Pennsylvania taxes transfers to children at **4.5%**, siblings at **12%**, and everyone else at **15%**. New Jersey exempts spouses, children, grandchildren, and parents; Nebraska exempts heirs under 22. Confirm current figures with the state revenue department or an estate attorney licensed there.

The Medicaid Clock

Underneath every gift line runs a clock that has nothing to do with the IRS. When someone applies for Medicaid to pay for nursing-home care (or, in most states, home-based long-term care), the state looks back **60 months** from the application for any transfer made for less than fair value. The gifts are added up and divided by the state's "penalty divisor" — roughly the average monthly cost of a private nursing-home bed there. The result is the number of months Medicaid refuses to pay.

> WATCH OUT **Watch Out: $19,000 Is a Tax Rule, Not a Medicaid Rule**
>
> The federal gift-tax exclusion means nothing to a Medicaid caseworker. A $19,000 birthday check, four $2,000 Christmas checks, a car signed over to a grandson, half a house deeded to a daughter — all are penalized transfers if they fall within 60 months of an application. Using rough 2026 divisors, $60,000 of gifts produces a penalty of about five and a half months in Florida (divisor near $10,645), about five months in Pennsylvania (near $11,500), and about seven and a half months in Texas (near $7,900). Those are months of nursing-home bills the family pays. Pauline's Christmas checks are fine as long as she is not applying for Medicaid before December 2031. If a nursing-home stay is a real possibility, every gift should go past an elder-law attorney first.

Some transfers are exempt: to a spouse; to a minor child or a blind or disabled child of any age; to a child who lived in the home and provided care for at least two years before the move to a facility; and to a sibling with an equity interest who lived in the home at least a year. States differ on the details, and this is one place where a consultation with an elder-law attorney licensed in your state earns its fee.

Other 2026 numbers on this clock: a spouse who stays home may keep between **$32,532** and **$162,660** of the couple's countable assets and up to **$4,066.50** a month of income. The home is exempt while a spouse lives in it, and otherwise up to a home-equity limit states set between **$752,000** and **$1,130,000**. The 2025 budget law has been reported to cap that limit at $1,000,000 nationwide from January 1, 2028, with exceptions for farms and homes occupied by a spouse or a minor or disabled child; confirm with your state Medicaid office before relying on it.

And after death there is **estate recovery**: states must seek repayment from the estates of recipients who were **55 or older** when they received long-term-care services, deferred while a surviving spouse, a child under 21, or a blind or disabled child is living. This is why "the house will go to the kids" is not a plan by itself, and why Chapter 7 exists.

The House: Moves That Look Free and Aren't

Pauline's daughter meant well. Adding a child's name to a deed feels like housekeeping. It is a transfer of property, and every clock in this chapter starts running on it at once.

It is a gift. Deeding half your house to a child is a completed gift of half its market value. Over $19,000, it requires Form 709 by the following April 15 — no tax until the $15,000,000 line, but the return is mandatory.

It surrenders half the step-up if the house is sold while you are alive. The child's half carries your original cost basis, so a lifetime sale means capital-gains tax on that half's appreciation, and the child cannot use your Section 121 exclusion unless the house is also the child's principal residence. At your death a non-spouse joint owner who contributed nothing generally does get a full step-up — but only after proving who paid for what. You have traded a clean rule for a paperwork burden. Chapter 7 covers step-up in detail.

It exposes the house to the child's life. The child's half is reachable by the child's creditors, a lawsuit, a bankruptcy trustee, or a divorcing spouse.

It is a Medicaid transfer. Half the house divided by the penalty divisor is a penalty period if you apply within 60 months.

It may trigger reassessment. In California, under Proposition 19, parent-child transfers on or after February 16, 2021 escape reassessment only for the family home the child makes a principal residence (claiming the homeowners' exemption within one year), and only up to the assessed value plus **$1,044,586** for transfers through February 15, 2027; rentals and second homes are fully reassessed, and Form BOE-19-P must be filed within three years. In Florida, a badly worded transfer can forfeit the homestead exemption and the 3% Save Our Homes cap. Call your county assessor before signing anything.

One fear you can set aside is the mortgage. The federal Garn-St Germain Act generally prevents a lender from calling a residential loan due when the home passes to a spouse or children, or into a revocable trust you continue to occupy. That protects you from the bank, and from nothing else on this list.

Section 121 on the calendar. When you sell, you can exclude **$250,000** of gain ($500,000 on a joint return) if you owned and used the home as your principal residence for 24 months of the five years before the sale. A surviving spouse keeps the full $500,000 if the sale closes **within two years** of the death and the survivor has not remarried. A sale that closes in month 25 gets $250,000. Chapter 2 puts it on the 90-day timeline; put it on yours.

Chapter 7, The Handoff, compares the deed options that pass a house without giving it away now — transfer-on-death deeds, life estates, trusts — and what each does to probate, Medicaid, and the step-up. Read it before the next conversation over coffee.

The Brokerage Account: Step-Up, Losses, and Charity

Three rules for taxable accounts, each turning on a date.

Appreciated assets held until death get a new basis. Stocks, funds, and real estate that pass through your estate take a basis equal to their value at death; the gain you never sold disappears. IRAs, annuities, and savings-bond interest do not get this treatment. So hold appreciated assets, and spend or give from cash and IRA money. Chapter 7 has the specifics.

Never gift a loss position. A gift carries your basis to the recipient, with a twist: if the shares are worth less than you paid, the recipient must use the lower market value to figure any loss. Your loss vanishes. Sell the shares yourself, harvest the loss, and gift the cash.

Give appreciated stock, not cash, to charity — from a taxable account. Donating long-term appreciated shares to a public charity avoids the capital-gains tax and, if you itemize, deducts full market value (subject to a 30%-of-AGI ceiling, versus 60% for cash). If you don't itemize — and most retirees with the 2026 standard deduction don't — the QCD is usually the better tool, because it removes income rather than adding a deduction you can't use. Many families do both.

Talking to Your CPA

Most of the mistakes in this chapter are made in April, when the year is closed. The most useful hour on this calendar is a year-end projection in October or November, while every line is still open. Bring both worksheets and ask five questions.

> PHONE SCRIPT **Phone Script: Asking Your CPA for a Year-End Projection**
>
> **You:** Hi, this is [NAME]. I'd like to schedule a year-end tax projection for [YEAR] — before December 1 if possible, so there's time to act. I'll send my year-to-date income, RMD figures, and brokerage gains and losses ahead of time. I have five questions.
>
> **You:** One. What will my taxable income be, which bracket does it land in, and how much room is left before the next one?

> **You:** Two. Where does my adjusted gross income sit relative to the IRMAA thresholds — $109,000 single or $218,000 joint — and the $75,000 or $150,000 line where the senior deduction phases out?
>
> **You:** Three. Given my charitable giving of [AMOUNT], should some or all of it be a qualified charitable distribution from my IRA instead of a check?
>
> **You:** Four. In my brokerage account, are there losses worth harvesting, or gains I could realize at the 0% rate?
>
> **You:** Five. Am I on track for the estimated-tax safe harbor, and if not, how much should I withhold from my December RMD to fix it?
>
> *If they say, "Let's handle it at tax time":* **You:** I understand it's the busy season, but every one of these is a December 31 decision — after that nothing can be changed. Could we do a 30-minute call or an emailed projection instead?
>
> *If they need more information:* **You:** Tell me exactly which documents you want and I'll send them this week. Could you confirm a date by which I'll have the projection back?
>
> **You:** Thank you. Please send a written summary afterward, so I have the numbers when I call my custodian.

A fee-only planner or enrolled agent can run the same projection; the questions don't change.

> WORKSHEET **Worksheet: Year-End Money Moves Planner**
>
> Complete in October. Update as each item is done. Keep with your tax records.
>
> Tax year: ______ Filing status: ____________ Projected taxable income: $____________
>
> Top of my bracket: $____________ Room remaining: $____________ IRMAA threshold to stay under: $____________
>
> RMDs — total due: $____________ Taken: $____________ Remaining and from which account: ____________________
>
> QCDs (age 70½ or older; up to $111,000)
>
> Charity: ____________________ Amount: $__________ Requested: ________ Confirmed: [ ]
>
> Charity: ____________________ Amount: $__________ Requested: ________ Confirmed: [ ]
>
> Roth conversion (by December 31; Chapter 6) — amount that fits my bracket: $____________ Withholding 0%: [ ] Tax paid from: ____________
>
> Gifts ($19,000 per person; all count toward the Medicaid look-back)

Recipient: ____________________ Amount: $__________ Wire / check / 529: ________ Sent: ________ Deposited: [ ]

Recipient: ____________________ Amount: $__________ Wire / check / 529: ________ Sent: ________ Deposited: [ ]

Recipient: ____________________ Amount: $__________ Wire / check / 529: ________ Sent: ________ Deposited: [ ]

Anyone over $19,000, any gift-split, any 529 five-year election → Form 709 due April 15: [ ]

Brokerage — realized gains: $__________ Realized losses: $__________

Losses to harvest: $__________ (no repurchase within 30 days in any account, including IRAs) [ ]

Gains to harvest at 0%: $__________ (taxable income under $49,450 / $98,900) [ ]

Contributions by April 15 — IRA: $__________ HSA: $__________ (stop six months before Medicare) [ ]

Safe-harbor amount needed: $__________ Paid in so far: $__________
Withholding to elect on December RMD: $__________ Confirmed: [ ]

A STORY **What Pauline Did**

Pauline took her legal pad to a CPA in October, with both worksheets filled in. Three of her four items survived.

The church gift became a $5,000 QCD, sent from the IRA payable to the church on October 22. She took the remaining $10,094 of her 2026 RMD on December 4 with 30% withheld, and took the small 403(b) RMD from the 403(b) itself, which the worksheet caught. She did not wait until April; the CPA showed her the same $1,040 arithmetic you saw above.

The grandchildren's $2,000 gifts went by bank transfer on December 3, with a note to the two who still use checkbooks that a check deposited in January is a January gift. She wrote "Medicaid clock — December 2031" in the margin and decided that was acceptable.

The house stayed in her name. She and her daughter read Chapter 7 together instead, and booked an elder-law attorney to talk about a deed that passes the house at death without giving it away now.

Ed got a copy of the RMD table. He was gracious about it.

Your Next Steps

CHECKLIST **Your Next Steps**

- ☐ Write your RMD starting age (73 or 75) and first RMD year on the RMD Calculator worksheet
- ☐ Pull last December 31 statements for every pre-tax account and calculate each RMD from the Uniform Lifetime Table in IRS Publication 590-B
- ☐ Call each IRA custodian to confirm the RMD figure, the QCD procedure, and the year-end cut-off, using the script in this chapter
- ☐ Decide which charitable gifts become QCDs and mail the QCD instruction letter by November 15
- ☐ Schedule a year-end projection with your CPA or enrolled agent before December 1 and ask the five questions
- ☐ Wire annual gifts in the first week of December and log each recipient on the Year-End Money Moves Planner
- ☐ Check whether you live in, or own property in, a state with its own estate or inheritance tax, and note its exemption next to your net worth
- ☐ Write down the date 60 months after your most recent gift as your Medicaid look-back date, and see an elder-law attorney before any gift if long-term care is on the horizon
- ☐ Calendar April 15, 2027 for 2026 IRA/HSA contributions and Form 709, and October 15, 2027 for any recharacterization or excess removal
- ☐ Hold off on adding anyone to a deed until you have read Chapter 7, The Handoff, and asked the county assessor about reassessment

CHAPTER SIX

The Review — Your Pre-Retirement Account Check

By the end of this chapter you will be able to run a one-page review of every retirement account you own, fill your tax bracket on purpose, move money between accounts without losing 20% of it, and stop Medicare from billing you for a year of income you no longer have.

A STORY **Diane, 64, Fort Collins, Colorado**

Diane had planned her last day at the water utility for years: Friday, December 18, 2026, cake in the break room. What she had not planned for was the packet from HR. It offered three boxes for her 401(k): leave it, roll it, or "distribute to participant." The last box came with a cheerful note that a check would be mailed within ten business days.

Her final year was a good one on paper: salary, a retention bonus, and a payout for 31 weeks of unused vacation. Her husband Ray, 66, was already drawing his pension. On a legal pad she figured their 2026 income would land near $232,000, the highest year of their marriage.

At a free steak-dinner seminar in October, a man with a nice watch told her to roll everything into an IRA he would manage and convert "a good chunk" to Roth before year-end. He did not ask about her 2026 income. He did not mention Medicare. He did say, twice, that he was "basically a fiduciary."

Diane did what she usually did with things that sounded too smooth. She put the packet in a folder, wrote REVIEW on the tab, and gave herself until Thanksgiving. (Diane is a composite; the numbers in this chapter are real.)

THE QUIET RULES The Quiet Rules in This Chapter

- *Medicare reads your tax return two years late.*
- *IRMAA is a cliff, not a slope: one dollar over costs you the whole tier.*
- *A Roth conversion cannot be undone, and its year ends on December 31.*
- *The rollover check is never payable to you.*
- *Once per 12 months means once, across every IRA you own.*
- *The plan protects you in ways an IRA may not. Ask before you roll.*
- *Nobody owes you the word "fiduciary" unless you ask for it in writing.*

Why the review happens now

The five years before retirement and the five years after are when most of your permanent tax decisions get made. Usually they get made by default: by an HR packet, by a custodian's standard withholding box, by a seminar, or by nobody at all.

Retirement income is different from a paycheck. You choose how much to take, from which account, and when. Those choices set your tax bracket, your Medicare premium, and, if you are married, the bill your surviving spouse will pay one day. This chapter is the review you do on purpose, once a year, so the defaults do not do it for you.

Medicare reads your tax return two years late

Medicare Part B has a standard premium: $202.90 a month in 2026. Above a certain income you pay more. The extra is the Income-Related Monthly Adjustment Amount, IRMAA, and it applies to Part D drug coverage too.

Here is the quiet part. Your 2026 premium is set by your **2024** tax return, the most recent one on file when Social Security ran the numbers. So the year you retire, with its last salary and vacation payout, keeps billing you two years after you stop working. And a Roth conversion you do in 2026 shows up in your 2028 premium.

The measure is modified adjusted gross income (MAGI): adjusted gross income plus tax-exempt interest. The full 2026 table, per person, per month:

Single MAGI (2024)	Joint MAGI (2024)	Part B total (surcharge)	Part D surcharge
$109,000 or less	$218,000 or less	$202.90 ($0)	$0
$109,000.01–$137,000	$218,000.01–$274,000	$284.10 ($81.20)	$14.50
$137,000.01–$171,000	$274,000.01–$342,000	$405.80 ($202.90)	$37.50
$171,000.01–$205,000	$342,000.01–$410,000	$527.50 ($324.60)	$60.40
$205,000.01–under $500,000	$410,000.01–under $750,000	$649.20 ($446.30)	$83.30
$500,000 and up	$750,000 and up	$689.90 ($487.00)	$91.00

The Part D surcharge is deducted from your Social Security check and goes to Medicare, on top of whatever your drug plan charges. Married people filing separately face a harsher two-line schedule; ask Social Security for it.

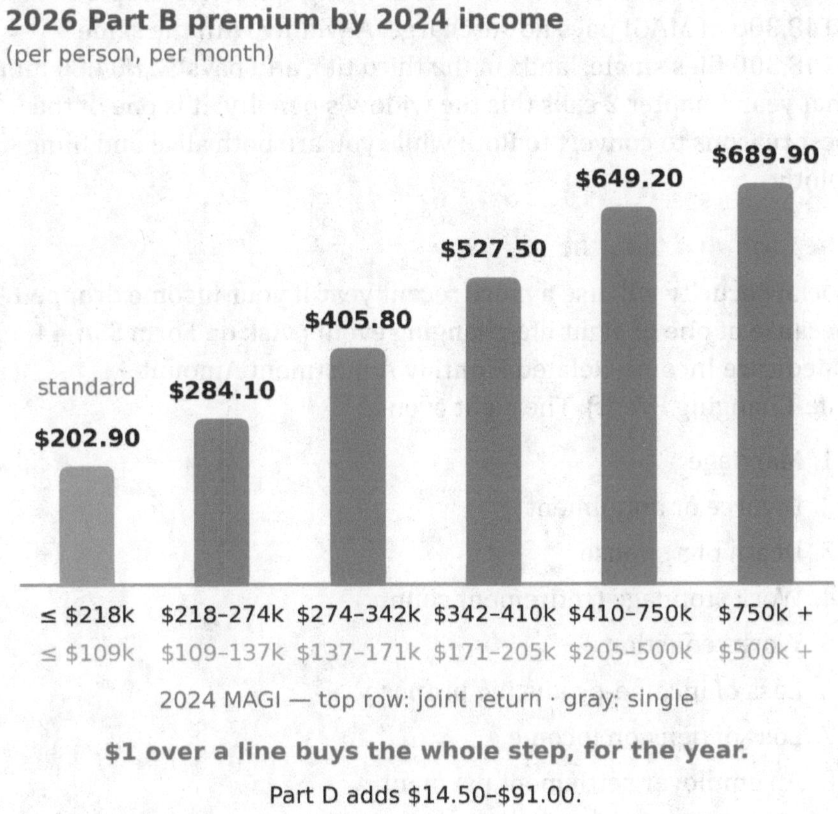

Figure 6.1. *The 2026 Part B premium cliff by income tier, single and joint filers*

It is a cliff, not a slope

Income tax brackets are gentle: only the dollars above the line get the higher rate. IRMAA is not. Cross a threshold by one dollar and you pay the full tier for the whole year.

- A single retiree with 2024 MAGI of $109,500 is $500 over the first line. That costs $81.20 (Part B) plus $14.50 (Part D) a month, or $1,148.40 for 2026.
- A couple both on Medicare with 2024 MAGI of $275,000 sit $1,000 into the third tier. Each pays $240.40 a month in surcharges, $5,769.60 for the year. At $274,000 they would have paid $2,296.80. The last $1,000 of income cost $3,472.80.

The cliff also runs in reverse for a surviving spouse. A couple with $148,300 of MAGI pays no surcharge. A widow with the same $148,300 files single, lands in the third tier, and pays $2,884.80 more that year. Chapter 2 calls this the widow's penalty; it is one of the best reasons to convert to Roth while you are both alive and filing jointly.

The form that fixes the lag: SSA-44

Social Security will use a more recent year if your income dropped because of one of eight life-changing events. Ask on Form SSA-44 (Medicare Income-Related Monthly Adjustment Amount – Life-Changing Event). The eight events:

1. Marriage
2. Divorce or annulment
3. Death of a spouse
4. Work stoppage (retirement counts)
5. Work reduction
6. Loss of income-producing property
7. Loss of pension income
8. An employer settlement payment

You give your estimate of the more recent year's MAGI with evidence (a retirement letter, a final pay stub), by mail with copies, in person with originals, or by calling 1-800-772-1213 for an appointment. Example: a single retiree earned $190,000 in 2024, retired in 2026, and expects $80,000 this year. Without the form she pays $587.90 a month counting the Part D surcharge; with it, $202.90 — a difference of $4,620 for the year.

What does not count: a one-time capital gain, a required distribution, or a Roth conversion. Those are your choices, and Medicare treats them as ordinary income. *Medicare reads your tax return two years late, and only a life event makes it read a newer one.*

A Roth conversion cannot be undone

A Roth conversion moves money from a traditional IRA or 401(k) to a Roth IRA. You pay ordinary income tax on the pre-tax amount in the year you convert. After that the money grows tax-free, there are no lifetime required distributions, and heirs inherit it tax-free (though they must empty it within ten years; see Chapter 7).

Four facts govern every conversion:

- **No income limit.** Anyone can convert any amount.
- **Taxed in the year of conversion.** No 10% early-withdrawal penalty at any age on the converted amount.
- **Irreversible.** Since 2018, conversions cannot be recharacterized. Contributions still can, until October 15.
- **December 31.** No extension, no "for last year." Custodians set internal cut-offs in mid-December; start in November.

The two five-year clocks

Each conversion starts its own five-year clock on January 1 of the conversion year. Withdraw converted money before five years and before age 59½, and you owe the 10% penalty on it. At 59½ this clock stops mattering.

The second clock covers earnings, which come out tax-free only when five years have passed since January 1 of the year of your first-ever Roth contribution or conversion, and you are 59½. This clock never restarts. A 65-year-old whose first Roth is a 2026 conversion has tax-free earnings from January 1, 2031. Open a small Roth early, even with $100, to start it.

The gap years

The best time to convert is when your income is lowest, and for many people that is a short, specific window: after the last paycheck, before Social Security, and before required minimum distributions begin at age 73 (born 1951–1959) or 75 (born 1960 or later). Every dollar converted in that window is a dollar that will not be forced out later, at a higher rate, on top of two Social Security checks.

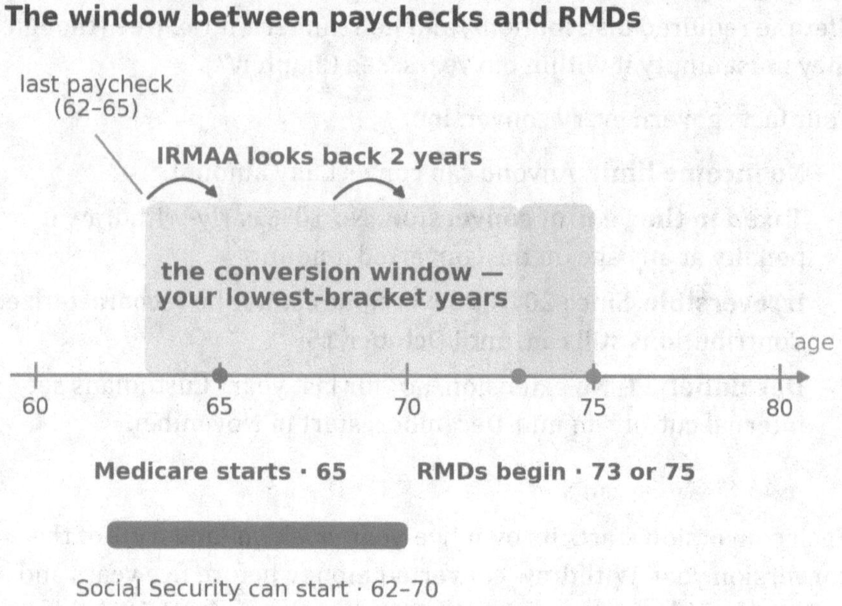

Figure 6.2. *From last paycheck to RMDs, the conversion window and the two-year IRMAA look-back*

Filling the bracket: the 2026 numbers

"Bracket filling" means converting exactly enough to reach the top of a bracket you are comfortable with, and no more. Here are the 2026 brackets on taxable income.

Rate	Single	Married filing jointly
10%	$0–$12,400	$0–$24,800
12%	$12,400–$50,400	$24,800–$100,800
22%	$50,400–$105,700	$100,800–$211,400
24%	$105,700–$201,775	$211,400–$403,550
32%	$201,775–$256,225	$403,550–$512,450

Taxable income is what is left after deductions. In 2026 a joint return gets a standard deduction of $32,200, plus $1,650 for each spouse 65 or older, plus the new $6,000 senior deduction per person 65 or older (2025 through 2028, claimed on Schedule 1-A). Single filers get

$16,100, plus $2,050 at 65, plus the $6,000. The senior deduction shrinks once MAGI passes $75,000 single or $150,000 joint, so a large conversion can eat part of it.

A worked example. Ann and Joe are 66 and 67, retired, and waiting until 70 to claim Social Security. In 2026 they have a $30,000 pension and $8,000 of interest and dividends: AGI $38,000. Their deductions are $32,200 + $3,300 + $12,000 = $47,500. Taxable income before any conversion is zero, and $9,500 of deductions would go to waste.

The top of the 12% bracket is $100,800 of taxable income. Their conversion room is $100,800 + $47,500 − $38,000 = **$110,300.** Convert that amount and AGI becomes $148,300, still under the $150,000 line where the senior deduction starts shrinking and well under the $218,000 IRMAA line. Taxable income is $148,300 − $47,500 = $100,800. Tax: 10% of $24,800 is $2,480; 12% of the next $76,000 is $9,120; total **$11,600**. They moved $110,300 into a Roth at an effective rate of about 10.5%. Left in the IRA, that money would come out later as required distributions, likely at 22% or more.

A single 66-year-old runs the same arithmetic with $24,150 of deductions: filling the 12% bracket means an AGI of $74,550, which keeps the full senior deduction and stays under the $109,000 IRMAA line.

WORKSHEET **Worksheet: Bracket-Filling Worksheet (2026)**

Fill this in each November using year-to-date figures and the 2026 brackets above. Bring it to your tax preparer before converting.

Filing status: [ ] Single [ ] Married filing jointly

Line 1. Income so far this year, before any conversion (wages, pension, interest, dividends, gains, taxable Social Security, RMDs): $____________________

Line 2. Standard deduction ($16,100 single / $32,200 joint): $____________________

Line 3. Age 65+ add-on ($2,050 single / $1,650 per spouse joint): $____________________

Line 4. Senior deduction ($6,000 per person 65+, if MAGI under $75,000 / $150,000): $____________________

Line 5. Total deductions (Lines 2 + 3 + 4): $____________________

Line 6. Top of the bracket I will fill ($50,400 / $100,800 for 12%; $105,700 / $211,400 for 22%): $____________

Line 7. Conversion room = Line 6 + Line 5 − Line 1: $____________

Line 8. IRMAA line ($109,000 single / $218,000 joint): $____________

Line 9. Income after conversion = Line 1 + Line 7 (keep under Line 8 unless I accept the surcharge in two years): $____________

Line 10. Amount I will convert: $____________

Line 11. Estimated federal tax on it: $____________ Paid from (not the IRA): ____________

Line 12. Basis on my last Form 8606, if any: $____________

Line 13. Custodian cut-off date: ____________ Instruction letter sent: ____________

What a conversion touches besides the bracket

A conversion raises your AGI, and several other rules key off AGI or MAGI:

- **Social Security taxation.** Conversion income counts toward "combined income" (AGI + tax-exempt interest + half your benefits). Over $25,000 single or $32,000 joint, up to 50% of benefits become taxable; over $34,000 or $44,000, up to 85%. If you already draw Social Security, every converted dollar can drag benefit dollars into taxable income with it.
- **IRMAA**, two years later.
- **The senior deduction**, above $75,000 / $150,000 MAGI.
- **Net investment income tax**, 3.8% on investment income once MAGI passes $200,000 single / $250,000 joint.
- **State income tax.** A conversion is taxed by the state you live in on the day you convert. Some states tax retirement income lightly or not at all; if a move is in your plans, the order of "move, then convert" can matter. Your state's department of revenue can tell you how it treats IRA income.

> WATCH OUT **Watch Out: Under 65 and on a Marketplace Plan? The Cliff Is Back**
>
> If you buy health insurance through the ACA marketplace before Medicare, be careful. The enhanced premium tax credits expired after 2025, and for 2026 the subsidy cliff at 400% of the federal poverty level has returned. A conversion that pushes household MAGI over that line can forfeit the entire year's premium credit, thousands of dollars for a couple in their early sixties. Run the numbers with your marketplace figure first, or wait until you are both on Medicare. Congress could change this; check before you act.

The pro-rata rule and Form 8606

If you ever made non-deductible contributions to a traditional IRA, you have "basis," money already taxed. You cannot convert only the basis. Every conversion is taxable in proportion to the after-tax share of **all** your traditional, SEP, and SIMPLE IRAs combined, measured at December 31 of the conversion year. Form 8606 (Nondeductible IRAs) tracks that basis. If you have never filed one, the IRS assumes your basis is zero, and you pay tax twice on the same dollars. Dig out old returns and file the missing 8606s before you convert.

Paying the tax the right way

> WATCH OUT **Watch Out: The Withholding Trap**
>
> Any tax withheld from a conversion is not converted. It leaves the IRA as a taxable distribution, and if you are under 59½, it is hit with the 10% penalty as well. Convert $100,000 with 20% withheld and only $80,000 reaches the Roth; the other $20,000 is gone, taxed, and possibly penalized. Elect zero withholding on the conversion and pay the tax from a checking or brokerage account.

The IRS still expects the money during the year. The safe harbor is to pay in, through withholding and estimated payments, the smaller of 90% of this year's tax or 100% of last year's tax (110% if last year's AGI was over $150,000). No penalty applies if you owe under $1,000 at filing. Estimated payments for 2026 are due April 15, June 15, September 15, 2026, and January 15, 2027. A December conversion with no payment until January can trigger a penalty for the earlier quarters unless you file Form 2210 with Schedule AI to show the income arrived late.

QUIET TIP **The December Withholding Trick**

Withholding is treated as paid evenly through the year, whenever it happens. If you must take a required distribution anyway, take it in December and have the custodian withhold enough from it to cover the tax on your conversion. That covers all four quarters, with no Form 2210. Voluntary withholding from Social Security (Form W-4V) works the same way.

Custodians have their own conversion forms; send this letter with the form so the zero-withholding election is on the record.

LETTER TEMPLATE **Letter Template: Instruction for a Partial Roth Conversion With Zero Withholding**

[DATE]

[CUSTODIAN NAME]

Attn: IRA Conversions Department

[STREET ADDRESS]

[CITY, STATE ZIP]

RE: Partial Roth conversion — Traditional IRA ending [LAST 4 DIGITS] to Roth IRA ending [LAST 4 DIGITS], owner [YOUR FULL NAME], SSN ending [LAST 4 DIGITS]

Dear Conversions Department:

Please convert [$AMOUNT] (or: [NUMBER] shares of [FUND NAME], in kind) from my Traditional IRA to my Roth IRA at your firm as a direct trustee-to-trustee conversion. Your conversion form is enclosed.

I elect **zero federal and zero state income tax withholding** on this conversion. I will pay the tax from funds outside the IRA. Please do not apply your default withholding rate.

Please complete this conversion by [DATE, at least two weeks before your cut-off] so it is reported for tax year 2026. If you cannot complete it by December 31, 2026, do not process it; call me first at [PHONE].

Please confirm in writing the date processed, the amount converted, and that no tax was withheld, and confirm that a Form 1099-R will be issued for 2026 and a Form 5498 for the Roth IRA. Please respond in writing within 10 business days.

Sincerely,

[SIGNATURE]

[PRINTED NAME]

[ADDRESS] | [PHONE] | [EMAIL]

Enclosures: Roth conversion form; copy of photo ID (if your firm requires it)

A Roth conversion cannot be undone, and its year ends on December 31. Convert the right amount, with the tax paid from outside money, and you have made one of the few retirement decisions that gets better with age.

The check is never payable to you

When you leave a job, FINRA requires brokers to weigh four options for your plan money: leave it in the plan, roll it to a new employer's plan, roll it to an IRA, or cash out. A seminar host who mentions only the IRA has skipped three.

If you do move money, there are two ways, and only one is safe.

A **direct rollover** (trustee-to-trustee transfer) sends the money from the plan straight to the new custodian. No withholding, no deadline, and it counts against no limit. If a paper check is involved, it is payable to the new custodian "FBO" (for the benefit of) you, for example "Fidelity Management Trust Co. FBO Diane Ortiz IRA." A check written that way is still a direct rollover even if it is mailed to your house for you to forward.

An **indirect rollover** pays the money to you. A plan must withhold 20% federal tax from any eligible rollover distribution paid to you, even if you say you will roll it over. You then have 60 days from the day you receive it to deposit the full amount, including the 20% you never saw, into the new account. Miss the deadline, or deposit only the 80% you got, and the difference is a taxable distribution (plus 10% penalty under 59½). The withheld 20% comes back on your tax return the following spring. On a $400,000 balance, that is $80,000 you must find from somewhere else for months.

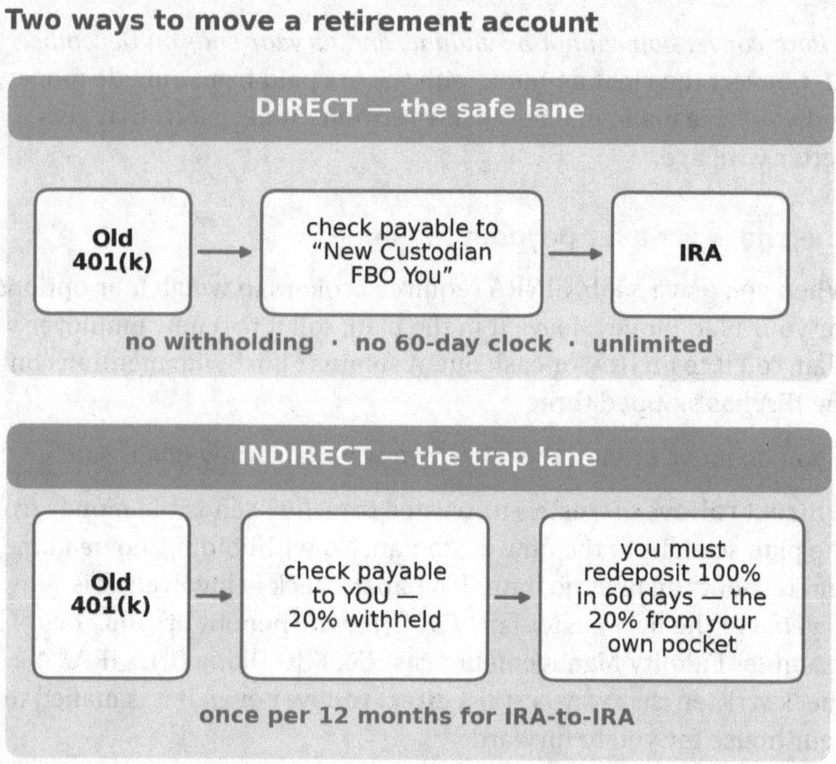

Figure 6.3. *Direct versus indirect rollover: who the check is payable to, withholding, the 60-day clock, and the once-per-12-months limit*

IRA-to-IRA distributions paid to you carry a default 10% withholding, which you can decline. They also carry a worse rule.

> WATCH OUT **Watch Out: The Once-Per-12-Months Rule**
>
> You may do only **one** indirect (60-day) IRA-to-IRA or Roth-to-Roth rollover in any 12-month period, counting every IRA you own together. This has been the rule since 2015, after a Tax Court case called *Bobrow*. A second 60-day rollover inside the window is a taxable distribution and an excess contribution, taxed 6% a year until removed. Direct transfers, plan-to-IRA rollovers, IRA-to-plan rollovers, and Roth conversions do not count. The fix is easy: never take the check. *Once per 12 months means once, across every IRA you own.*

Two more rules ride along:

- **The RMD comes out first.** In RMD years, the required amount cannot be rolled over. Take it, then move the rest.
- **Late rollovers can sometimes be rescued.** If you miss the 60 days for one of twelve listed reasons (the institution's error, a misplaced check, serious illness, a death in the family, a postal error, severe damage to your home, among others), you can self-certify to the receiving custodian under Revenue Procedure 2020-46 using the IRS model letter, if you complete the deposit within 30 days after the reason ends. It is not a waiver; the IRS can still disagree on audit.

PHONE SCRIPT **Phone Script: Requesting a Direct Rollover From a 401(k) Plan**

You: Hello, my name is [NAME], employee ID [NUMBER], date of birth [DATE]. I have separated from service and I am requesting a **direct rollover** of my [401(k) / 403(b)] balance to my IRA. I do not want any part of it paid to me.

Them: We can mail you a check.

You: That is fine if the check is payable to the custodian, not to me: "[CUSTODIAN NAME] FBO [YOUR NAME] IRA," with my IRA number [NUMBER] on the memo line. Please confirm you are coding this as a direct rollover with zero withholding.

Them: We'll need a letter of acceptance from the receiving firm.

You: I will get it. What fax number or upload address, and what exact wording do you need?

You: Before anything moves, please confirm in writing the balance of any [company stock / after-tax contributions] in the plan, and, if I am in RMD years, that this year's RMD will be paid to me first, not rolled.

If they say "our default is to send the check to you": Please note on the file that I decline that option. Which box on the distribution form is the direct rollover?

You: May I have your name, employee ID, a confirmation number, and the date the check will be cut? Please send me written confirmation of these instructions.

If they resist: I'd like to speak with a supervisor or the plan administrator, and I'd like a copy of the plan's written distribution procedures.

CHECKLIST **Checklist: Rollover Do/Don't**

- ☐ Do get the four options in writing (stay, new plan, IRA, cash out) before choosing.
- ☐ Do ask whether the plan allows partial withdrawals if you may need money before 59½.
- ☐ Do request a direct rollover, check payable to the custodian FBO you.
- ☐ Do open the receiving IRA first and title it "Rollover IRA," separate from contributory IRAs.
- ☐ Do take this year's RMD before rolling, if you are 73 or older.
- ☐ Do ask about company stock (NUA) and after-tax contributions before moving anything.
- ☐ Don't accept a check payable to you; it triggers 20% withholding and the 60-day clock.
- ☐ Don't do a second 60-day IRA rollover within 12 months of the first.
- ☐ Don't roll to an IRA if you left the job in or after the year you turned 55 and want penalty-free access before 59½.
- ☐ Don't sign anything at a seminar.

The plan protects you in ways an IRA may not

An IRA gives you more investment choices and one statement instead of three. It also quietly removes some protections a workplace plan gave you.

The Rule of 55

If you separate from an employer **in or after the calendar year you turn 55**, you can take money from **that employer's plan** without the 10% penalty. Ordinary income tax still applies. Roll the money to an IRA and the exception is gone. It covers only the plan you left at 55 or later, not an older plan from a job you left at 50, and someone who leaves at 54 and waits until 55 does not qualify. Qualified public safety employees (police, fire, EMS, corrections, and since the 2022 law certain private-sector firefighters) get age 50, or 25 years of service if earlier. Check that the plan allows partial withdrawals; some pay only a lump sum. The plan should code the Form 1099-R with distribution code 2; if it uses code 1, claim the exception on Form 5329.

Net unrealized appreciation

If your plan holds **employer stock**, the shares can move in kind to a taxable brokerage account instead of an IRA. You pay ordinary income tax now on the plan's cost basis; the growth (the "net unrealized appreciation") is taxed as long-term capital gain whenever you sell, however briefly you held it. The rules are strict: the entire balance in all the employer's like plans must leave within one tax year after a triggering event (separation, reaching 59½, disability, or death), and any partial withdrawal in an earlier year after the trigger spoils it. The NUA portion gets no step-up at death (Chapter 7). Ask the plan for the stock's cost basis in writing before you check any box.

72(t) payments

Under 55 and need income from an IRA? Substantially equal periodic payments under section 72(t) avoid the penalty if you take a fixed schedule for the longer of five years or until 59½. Any change (an extra withdrawal, a missed payment, adding money) imposes the penalty retroactively on every prior payment, with interest. Three calculation methods are allowed, with an interest rate up to the greater of 5% or 120% of the federal mid-term rate. Set it up with a professional and do not touch the account.

Creditor protection

Money in a 401(k), 403(b) with employer contributions, or pension is protected from creditors without limit under federal law. An IRA is protected in **bankruptcy** up to $1,711,975 (cases filed April 1, 2025 through March 31, 2028), except that money rolled over from an employer plan, and its earnings, is protected without limit. Outside bankruptcy, IRA protection from an ordinary judgment depends on state law and varies widely; some states protect IRAs broadly, others only what is "reasonably necessary for support." Two habits preserve the most: leave money in the plan if you can, and keep rolled-over money in a separate account titled "Rollover IRA" so its unlimited protection stays traceable.

Who is advising you, and under what duty

The Department of Labor's 2024 rule that would have made a one-time rollover recommendation fiduciary advice was vacated by the courts, and the department published the vacatur on March 20, 2026. A broker or insurance agent recommending that you roll your plan into their product is not necessarily a fiduciary. Other rules still apply (the SEC's Regulation Best Interest for brokers, the fiduciary duty of registered investment advisers), but the question below is the fastest way to learn which you are dealing with.

PHONE SCRIPT **Phone Script: Asking an Advisor the Fiduciary Question**

You: Before we go further, I have a few questions I ask everyone, and I'd like the answers in writing. First: for this rollover recommendation, are you acting as a fiduciary, legally required to put my interest ahead of your own?

Them: I always act in my clients' best interest.

You: I appreciate that. My question is whether you are a fiduciary for this recommendation, yes or no, and under which law: the Investment Advisers Act, ERISA, or state law. Could you put that in an email today?

Them: I'm a fiduciary on the advisory side.

You: Is this recommendation on the advisory side or the brokerage or insurance side? If any part is a commission product, what is the commission, and is there a surrender charge?

You: Second: what will I pay, in dollars, in year one, including fund expenses? Third: what does my current plan charge? Fourth: have you compared all four options, staying, a new plan, an IRA, and cashing out, and may I see that comparison?

If they say "the paperwork covers that": Please point me to the page and paragraph. I'll read it before I sign anything.

If they will not answer in writing: Thank you for your time. I'll take that as my answer.

You: May I have your full name, firm, CRD or license number, and your supervisor's name?

Fill the last working years

If you are still earning, the years right before retirement carry the highest contribution limits you will ever see.

Account	2026 base limit	Catch-up
401(k), 403(b), 457(b), TSP	$24,500	$8,000 at 50+; $11,250 at ages 60–63
Traditional or Roth IRA	$7,500	$1,100 at 50+
HSA, self-only / family	$4,400 / $8,750	$1,000 at 55+
SIMPLE IRA	$17,000	$4,000 at 50+; $5,250 at 60–63

The "super catch-up" applies to people who turn 60, 61, 62, or 63 during the year; at 64 you drop back to $8,000, and the plan must offer it. IRA contributions for 2026 are due April 15, 2027, no extensions, and a non-working spouse can contribute the full amount on a joint return.

New for 2026: if your Social Security wages from your employer in 2025 were over $150,000, your 401(k) catch-up contributions must go into the Roth side of the plan. If the plan has no Roth feature, you cannot make catch-ups there at all. Ask HR now.

HSAs have a deadline of their own. You cannot contribute for any month you are enrolled in any part of Medicare, and Part A enrollment after 65 is retroactive up to six months. So stop HSA contributions at least six months before you apply for Medicare or Social Security after 65. The money already inside stays yours for medical costs, including Medicare premiums.

Social Security: the review questions

Chapter 3 covers the claiming deadlines, but the review has to include the basics, because the claiming date sets the length of your conversion window.

Birth year	Full retirement age
1943–1954	66
1955–1959	66 and 2 to 10 months
1960 and later	67

- Claiming at 62 cuts a worker's own benefit 25% (FRA 66) or 30% (FRA 67), permanently.

- Waiting past FRA earns delayed retirement credits until 70. After 70 there is nothing to gain, and filing late gets you at most six months of back pay, never before FRA.
- If you claim before FRA and keep working, the earnings test withholds $1 for every $2 you earn over $24,480 in 2026 ($1 per $3 over $65,160 in the year you reach FRA). Withheld months are credited back at FRA.
- If you were born on or after January 2, 1954, filing for your own benefit or a spousal benefit is deemed to be filing for both; you get the higher. Survivors are exempt: a widow or widower can take one benefit and switch to the other later.
- Tax is not withheld from Social Security unless you ask. File Form W-4V (Voluntary Withholding Request) with Social Security.

Account hygiene

Retirement accounts multiply: two old 401(k)s, a 403(b) from the hospital years, a SEP, three IRAs. Each has its own beneficiary form, its own login, and its own way of being forgotten. Part of the review is tidying.

- **Consolidate, with two exceptions.** Fewer accounts means fewer beneficiary forms to get wrong. Keep a plan where you want the Rule of 55 or the strongest creditor protection, and keep rollover money separate from contributory IRA money.
- **Read every beneficiary form.** They override your will (Chapter 4). Name a contingent. In a workplace plan your spouse is the automatic beneficiary unless he or she signs a notarized waiver.
- **Name a trusted contact** at every brokerage and IRA custodian (Chapter 1). It costs nothing and gives the firm someone to call instead of freezing the account.
- **Check the insurance.** FDIC and NCUA insure $250,000 per depositor, per institution, per ownership category. A joint account with two owners is covered to $500,000. A POD or trust account is covered at $250,000 per beneficiary, up to five, for a maximum of $1,250,000 per owner per bank; credit unions adopt that same trust rule on December 1, 2026. Cash inside an IRA at a

bank is its own category. The FDIC's EDIE calculator will run your exact accounts.

- **Title accounts correctly.** "Rollover IRA" for rolled money. An inherited IRA keeps the deceased owner's name in the title (Chapter 7). Never retitle an IRA into a trust.

WORKSHEET **Worksheet: Retirement Account Inventory**

List every retirement account you and your spouse own, one block per account. Use extra sheets as needed. Update every January.

Account 1 nickname: ____________________

Type (401k / 403b / IRA / Roth / Rollover IRA / HSA / pension): ____________________

Custodian and phone: ____________________ Owner: ____________________

Balance at Dec 31: $____________________ Form 8606 basis: $____________________

Primary beneficiary: ____________________ Contingent: ____________________

Beneficiary confirmed in writing (date): ____________________

Trusted contact named? [ ] Yes [ ] No Employer stock inside? [ ] Yes [ ] No

Rule of 55 plan? [ ] Yes [ ] No RMD due this year? [ ] Yes [ ] No $____________________

Login stored where: ____________________

Account 2 nickname: ____________________

Type: ____________________ Custodian and phone: ____________________

Balance: $____________________ Basis: $____________________

Beneficiaries (primary / contingent): ____________________

Confirmed (date): ____________________ Trusted contact? [ ] Yes [ ] No

Account 3 nickname: ____________________

Type: ____________________ Custodian and phone: ____________________

Balance: $____________________ Basis: $____________________

Beneficiaries (primary / contingent): ____________________

Confirmed (date): ____________________ Trusted contact? [ ] Yes [ ] No

Totals: Pre-tax $______________ Roth $______________ Accounts I could consolidate: ______

The annual review agenda

Once a year, in October or November, sit down with this page, your inventory, and your year-to-date income. If you use an advisor or tax preparer, send it ahead of the meeting; a good one will be pleased.

CHECKLIST **Checklist: Pre-Retirement Review Agenda**

- ☐ Update the Retirement Account Inventory; confirm every beneficiary in writing.
- ☐ Estimate this year's MAGI against $109,000 / $218,000 (IRMAA) and $75,000 / $150,000 (senior deduction).
- ☐ Complete the Bracket-Filling Worksheet; send the conversion instruction letter by mid-November.
- ☐ Arrange the conversion tax from outside money: December RMD withholding or Form 1040-ES.
- ☐ Confirm Form 8606 is on file for every non-deductible contribution.
- ☐ If retiring within two years, plan to file Form SSA-44 when the IRMAA notice arrives.
- ☐ Review the Social Security claiming date and its effect on the conversion window.
- ☐ Confirm contributions are maxed ($24,500 + catch-up; $7,500 + $1,100; HSA) and check the Roth catch-up rule.
- ☐ Stop HSA contributions six months before any Medicare application.
- ☐ If leaving a job: get the four options, plan fees, stock basis, and Rule of 55 terms in writing first.
- ☐ Ask any advisor the fiduciary question; file the written answer.
- ☐ Check FDIC/NCUA coverage; name a trusted contact everywhere.

KEY NUMBERS 2026 Numbers to Know

- Part B standard premium $202.90 a month; first IRMAA line $109,000 single / $218,000 joint, from the 2024 return
- Top of the 12% bracket: $50,400 single / $100,800 joint taxable income
- Deductions at 65+: $16,100 + $2,050 + $6,000 single; $32,200 + $1,650 per spouse + $6,000 per spouse joint
- Roth conversion deadline December 31; five-year clocks start January 1
- Indirect rollover: 20% withholding, 60 days, once per 12 months across all IRAs
- Contributions: $24,500 + $8,000 (or $11,250 at 60–63); IRA $7,500 + $1,100; HSA $4,400 / $8,750 + $1,000
- Mandatory Roth catch-up above $150,000 of prior-year wages
- IRA bankruptcy protection $1,711,975 through March 31, 2028; rollover money unlimited
- Ages: 55 (Rule of 55), 59½, 65 (stop HSA six months before), 70 (credits end), 73 or 75 (RMDs)
- Deposit insurance $250,000 per depositor per bank per category; trust accounts to $1,250,000

A STORY What Diane Did

Diane used the folder. She called the plan and requested a direct rollover of half her 401(k), check payable to the custodian FBO her, and left the other half in the plan; she liked its low-cost index fund and its unlimited creditor protection. She asked, in writing, whether the plan held company stock. It did not.

She emailed the seminar host the fiduciary question. He replied with a brochure. She filed the brochure.

She converted nothing in 2026. Her worksheet showed the year already at $232,000 of joint income, $14,000 into the first IRMAA tier for 2028 and squarely in the 22% bracket. Instead she penciled in 2027: Ray's $30,000 pension, no salary, Social Security not until 67. Her conversion room to the top of the 12% bracket came to about $110,000.

When the 2028 Medicare notice arrives with a surcharge, Form SSA-44 will already be filled in, "work stoppage" checked, her December 18, 2026 retirement letter attached. Total cost of the review: two phone calls, one email, and a legal pad.

Your Next Steps

CHECKLIST Your Next Steps

- ☐ Complete the Retirement Account Inventory this week; ask each custodian for written confirmation of your beneficiaries.
- ☐ Pull your 2024 and 2025 returns, circle the MAGI line, and compare it with the $109,000 / $218,000 IRMAA table.
- ☐ Download Form SSA-44 if you retire, lose a pension, or lose a spouse within two years; call 1-800-772-1213 for an appointment when the IRMAA notice comes.
- ☐ Run the Bracket-Filling Worksheet in November; send the zero-withholding instruction letter by mid-November.
- ☐ Locate every Form 8606 you have filed; file any missing ones before converting.
- ☐ Calendar December 31 (conversion), April 15, 2027 (IRA and HSA contributions), and your custodian's mid-December cut-off.
- ☐ Before any rollover, use the direct-rollover script; open and title the "Rollover IRA" first.
- ☐ Ask HR whether your 2025 wages exceeded $150,000 and whether the plan offers a Roth catch-up.
- ☐ Stop HSA contributions six months before applying for Medicare; file Form W-4V if you want tax withheld from Social Security.
- ☐ Run your cash accounts through the FDIC's EDIE calculator and name a trusted contact at every institution.

CHAPTER SEVEN

The Handoff — Transferring Assets Without Losing Them

By the end of this chapter you will know how each asset you own passes to the next person, what the wrong route costs, and the exact words that keep an inherited IRA from becoming a tax bill.

A STORY **Lorraine, 72, Grand Rapids, Michigan**

Lorraine has been a widow for three years. The house is paid off and worth about $310,000. There is a brokerage account holding stock her husband Gene bought in the 1990s, an IRA of roughly $240,000, and a checking account at the credit union. Her daughter Lisa lives forty minutes away in Kalamazoo; her son Daniel is in Denver.

Everyone has advice. Her neighbor put her own son on her deed "to skip probate" and thinks Lorraine should do the same with Lisa. Gene's brother says adding a child to a deed "loses half the step-up," whatever that is. A woman at church says the IRA belongs in Lorraine's trust. Lisa says she doesn't want to talk about any of it.

On a Tuesday night Lorraine sits at the kitchen table with a legal pad and writes three questions. Who gets the house, and how? Who gets the IRA, and what do they have to do? And why does everyone say something different about the same account?

This story is illustrative. Lorraine is not a real person. The legal pad is.

THE QUIET RULES **The Quiet Rules in This Chapter**

- *Assets don't move by wish. They move by title, designation, and form.*
- *The beneficiary form beats the will, every time.*
- *A non-spouse never touches inherited IRA money. It moves custodian to custodian, or it is gone.*
- *Inherit and you get today's value; receive a gift and you get yesterday's.*
- *A name on a deed is a gift, and it lands on four fronts: taxes, creditors, Medicaid, and control.*
- *A deed that is not recorded before death is a wish.*
- *Never gift a loss.*

The principle: three ways an asset moves

Every asset leaves your hands by one of three routes. It passes by **title** (a joint account with survivorship, a home held as tenants by the entirety, property in a trust). It passes by **designation** (the beneficiary form on an IRA or life insurance policy, a payable-on-death label on a bank account, a transfer-on-death registration at a brokerage). Or it passes through **the court**, by your will or the state's default rules, in probate.

Your will controls only the third route. A will that says "my IRA goes to my daughter" is overruled by a twenty-year-old beneficiary form naming someone else, and the custodian will follow the form. That is not a loophole; it is the design.

Each route carries its own tax rule and clock. An inherited IRA comes with a ten-year deadline and, often, annual withdrawals. An inherited brokerage account comes with a gift from the tax code called the step-up in basis. A house handed to a child by deed during your life comes with none of that gift and a list of side effects.

Inherited IRAs: the ten-year rule and its cousins

Since the 2019 SECURE Act, most people who inherit an IRA can no longer "stretch" withdrawals over their own lifetime. Final regulations published July 19, 2024, settled the details beginning with 2025 distributions. Who you are, relative to the person who died, decides your rule.

The beneficiary classes

Class	Who	Payout rule
Surviving spouse	Husband or wife	Special options (below)
Eligible designated beneficiary	Owner's minor child (to age 21); disabled or chronically ill person; anyone not more than 10 years younger than the owner	Life-expectancy stretch
Other designated beneficiary	Adult children, grandchildren, most others	10-year rule
Non-designated beneficiary	Estate, charity, a trust that is not "see-through"	5-year rule or "ghost" rule

A minor child stretches until age 21, then the ten-year rule begins, so the account is empty by December 31 of the year the child turns 31. "Not more than 10 years younger" covers an older sibling, a friend, or a partner near your age. An adult child, however loved, is in the ten-year group.

Which clock you inherit

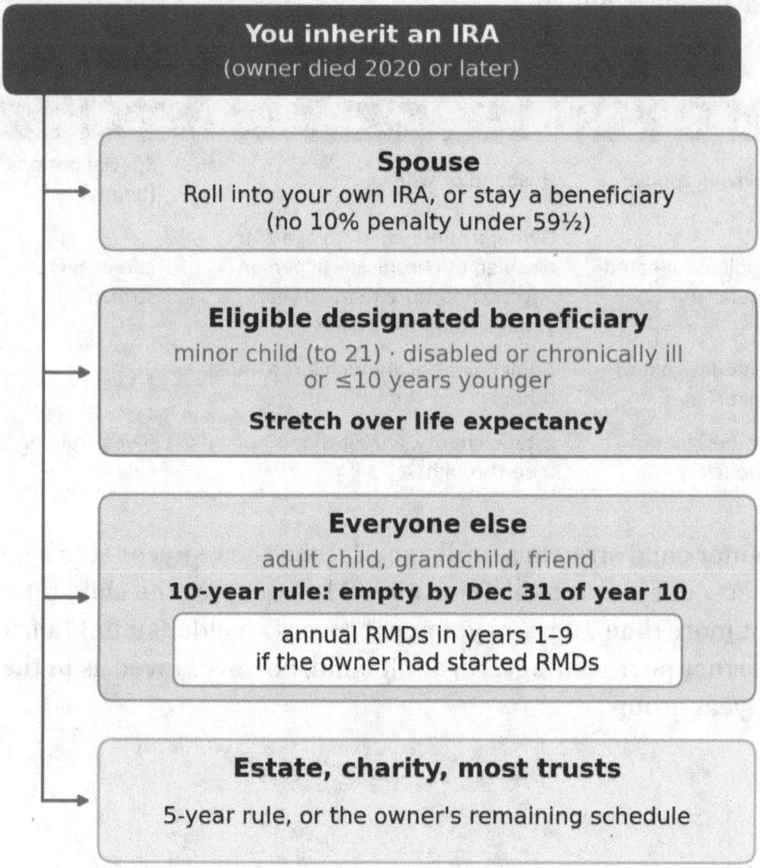

Figure 7.1. *Who inherited the account decides the payout rule that follows*

The ten-year rule, with and without annual withdrawals

Under the ten-year rule the account must be **empty by December 31 of the tenth year after the year of death**. Inherit in 2026, and the deadline is December 31, 2036.

Whether you also owe withdrawals in years one through nine turns on one fact: had the owner reached the **required beginning date** (April 1 of the year after turning 73, or 75 for those born in 1960 or later)?

- **Owner died on or after that date:** you take an annual required minimum distribution in years one through nine, using your Single Life Table factor reduced by one each year, then empty the rest in year ten. The final regulations made this mandatory starting with 2025.
- **Owner died before that date:** no annual withdrawals; only the year-ten deadline. Spreading withdrawals anyway is often the better tax outcome.
- **Inherited Roth IRA:** a Roth owner is always treated as dying before the required beginning date, so no annual withdrawals, but the account must still be emptied by year ten. Since withdrawals are tax-free, waiting is attractive.

If you inherited between 2020 and 2024 and skipped annual withdrawals while the rules were unsettled, the IRS waived the penalty for 2021 through 2024 (Notices 2022-53, 2023-54, and 2024-35), and those amounts need not be made up. The ten-year deadline never moved.

The **5-year rule** applies when a non-designated beneficiary such as the estate inherits from an owner who died before the required beginning date: empty by December 31 of the fifth year after death. If the owner died on or after that date, the estate instead takes payments over the owner's remaining single-life expectancy, the "ghost" rule. Both are usually worse than what a named person gets, which is why an empty beneficiary line is the most expensive blank on the form.

The calendar after a death

- **September 30 of the year after death:** the beneficiary determination date. Anyone paid out in full or who has disclaimed by then is disregarded. This is how a family removes a charity from a shared designation so the individuals get ten years instead of five.
- **October 31 of the year after death:** deadline for a trust beneficiary to deliver the trust document (or a certified list of trust beneficiaries) to the custodian for see-through treatment.

- **December 31 of the year after death:** deadline to split an account with several beneficiaries into separate inherited accounts so each uses their own status; otherwise the oldest beneficiary's status governs everyone. The ten-year count and any annual withdrawals begin this year.
- **Nine months after death:** the qualified disclaimer deadline. The disclaimant must not have accepted any benefit first; taking a withdrawal as beneficiary can spoil it.

One more item, the **year-of-death RMD**. If the owner had reached the required beginning date and died before taking that year's full distribution, the beneficiary takes the rest and reports it on the beneficiary's own return. The deadline is the later of the beneficiary's filing deadline for the year of death (with extensions) or December 31 of the following year, with an automatic penalty waiver if met. Any one of several beneficiaries may take it.

The check that ends everything

This rule matters more than all the others combined. **A non-spouse beneficiary cannot do a 60-day rollover.** If the custodian sends a check payable to you personally, the entire amount is taxable income that year, and it is irrevocable. The IRS has no authority to fix it.

The only safe way to move inherited retirement money is a **trustee-to-trustee transfer** into a properly titled inherited IRA. The title keeps the deceased owner's name on the account, in a form such as "Gene Kowalski (Deceased March 4, 2026), IRA, FBO Lisa Kowalski, Beneficiary." Custodians vary the wording; what matters is that both names and the word "beneficiary" appear.

> WATCH OUT **Watch Out: The Check Made Payable to You**
>
> If a distribution form offers "transfer to inherited IRA" or "pay to beneficiary," the second box is a trap for anyone who is not the spouse. If a check arrives anyway, do not deposit it. Call the custodian the same day, ask them to void it and reissue as a trustee-to-trustee transfer, and get the request in writing. Escalate before the check is cashed, not after.

Three more mechanics. You can never contribute to an inherited IRA or combine it with your own (a spouse electing to treat it as her own is the exception). If the owner had after-tax basis on Form 8606 (Nondeductible IRAs), you inherit a pro-rata share and file your own Form 8606 for the inherited account, so you are not taxed twice. And under *Clark v. Rameker* (June 12, 2014, a unanimous Supreme Court), an inherited IRA is **not** protected in bankruptcy the way your own IRA is; a spouse who rolls the money into her own IRA generally regains that protection. Some states protect inherited IRAs by statute; ask an attorney in your state before assuming.

PHONE SCRIPT **Phone Script: Opening an Inherited IRA by Trustee-to-Trustee Transfer**

You: Hello. I am the named beneficiary on an IRA belonging to [OWNER'S FULL NAME], who died on [DATE]. I want to open an inherited IRA in my name as beneficiary and move the assets by trustee-to-trustee transfer. I do not want a check made payable to me.

Them: We can send you the distribution paperwork.

You: Before you do, please confirm three things. The new account will be titled with the deceased owner's name and my name as beneficiary. The transfer will be custodian to custodian, with no check to me personally. And no tax will be withheld, because nothing is being distributed.

Them: That's correct. / **Them:** Our process is to mail a check.

If they say they mail checks, you say: A check payable to me would be a taxable distribution I cannot reverse. Please make it payable to [RECEIVING CUSTODIAN] for the benefit of my inherited IRA, or transfer electronically. If that is not possible, I need a supervisor or your retirement-transfer department.

You: May I have your name, employee ID, and a case number? Please send written confirmation of the account title and transfer method before anything moves, and confirm whether the owner's required distribution for the year of death was taken.

Trusts and successors, briefly

A trust can be an IRA beneficiary, but only a **see-through trust** (valid under state law, irrevocable at death, identifiable beneficiaries, paperwork delivered by October 31) lets the people behind it count as designated beneficiaries. A **conduit** trust counts only the current income beneficiary; an **accumulation** trust generally counts primary and residual beneficiaries. Never retitle an IRA into a trust during your life; that is a taxable distribution of the whole account (see Chapter 4, The Four Documents).

A **successor beneficiary** gets no fresh start: ten years from the first beneficiary's death if that beneficiary was stretching, or the remainder of the original ten years if not.

If you are the spouse

A surviving spouse has choices no one else gets, and the mistake is making them fast (Chapter 2, The First 90 Days, walks the timeline).

- **Treat as your own or roll it over.** Only a spouse may. RMDs then start at your own RMD age using the Uniform Lifetime Table. Usually best if you are over 59½ or older than your spouse was.
- **Stay a beneficiary.** No 10% early-withdrawal penalty at any age, and required withdrawals wait until the year your spouse would have reached RMD age. You may roll to your own IRA later, once any RMD due that year is taken.
- **The new spousal election.** Since 2024 (SECURE 2.0 §327), a spouse who stays a beneficiary may elect to be treated as the deceased owner, using the Uniform Lifetime Table (smaller required withdrawals) and delaying until the deceased would have reached RMD age. In employer plans this is the default when the owner died before the required beginning date. Roll to your own IRA after your own required beginning date and a "hypothetical RMD" catch-up applies; ask the custodian to compute it first.

Rolling over reflexively is irreversible. A fee-only planner or elder-law attorney can confirm which option fits your age and state.

WORKSHEET **Worksheet: Inherited IRA Date Sheet**

One sheet per inherited account. Keep it with the custodian's written confirmations.

Owner's name: ____________________ Date of death: ____________________

Owner's date of birth: ____________ Reached the required beginning date? [ ] Yes [ ] No [ ] Unsure

Account type: [ ] Traditional IRA [ ] Roth IRA [ ] 401(k)/403(b) [ ] Other: __________

Custodian and phone: ____________________ Account (last 4): _______

My relationship: [ ] Spouse [ ] Minor child [ ] Disabled/chronically ill [ ] Not more than 10 years younger [ ] Adult child/other [ ] Trust/estate

My payout rule: [ ] Stretch [ ] 10-year with annual RMDs [ ] 10-year, no annual RMDs [ ] 5-year [ ] Spousal option: __________

Year-of-death RMD: [ ] Taken on ______ [ ] Not required [ ] Still owed; deadline ______

Inherited account title (exact wording):
____

Trustee-to-trustee transfer confirmed in writing? [ ] Yes, date ______

September 30 of the year after death: ___________ October 31 (trust paperwork): ____________

December 31 of the year after death (split accounts; first RMD if required): ____________

Nine-month disclaimer deadline: ____________ Final depletion deadline (year 10 or 5): ____________

Decedent's Form 8606 basis: $__________ My share: $__________

Contingent beneficiary I have named on this account: ____________________

CHECKLIST **Checklist: When You Inherit an IRA**

- □ Request a copy of the beneficiary form on file and confirm you are named.
- □ Determine whether the owner had reached the required beginning date (April 1 after turning 73, or 75 if born 1960 or later).
- □ Take any remaining year-of-death RMD by the later of your filing deadline (with extensions) or December 31 of the following year.
- □ Open an inherited IRA titled with the owner's name and yours as beneficiary; move assets only by trustee-to-trustee transfer.
- □ Refuse any check payable to you personally, and get the correction in writing.
- □ Split into separate inherited accounts by December 31 of the year after death if there are several beneficiaries.
- □ Deliver trust documents to the custodian by October 31 of the year after death, if a trust is the beneficiary.
- □ Decide about a disclaimer with an attorney before nine months pass and before any withdrawal.
- □ Request the decedent's last Form 8606 and file your own if there was after-tax basis.
- □ Name your own contingent beneficiary, and calendar the annual RMD and the year-ten deadline.

The beneficiary form: the document that beats the will

Every IRA, 401(k), annuity, and life insurance policy has one. Most people signed it the day they opened the account and never saw it again. The custodian will read it carefully on the day you die.

The errors list

- **No beneficiary named.** The estate inherits: probate, creditor exposure, and the five-year or ghost rule instead of ten years.
- **The estate named on purpose.** Same result, chosen.
- **An ex-spouse still named.** Under *Egelhoff v. Egelhoff* (2001) and *Kennedy v. Plan Administrator for DuPont* (2009), an ERISA plan pays the named ex-spouse regardless of state revocation-on-divorce laws or the divorce decree.
- **A minor child named directly.** The custodian will demand a court-appointed guardian. Name a custodian under your state's Uniform Transfers to Minors Act, or a trust, instead.
- **No contingent beneficiary.** If the primary dies first and you never update, you are back to "no beneficiary named."
- **Per stirpes on the IRA and per capita in the will**, or the reverse (example below).
- **An outdated form** after a custodian change, plan merger, or rollover. A new account has a new, blank form.
- **A trust named that has since been revoked.**

One rule applies only to employer plans. Under ERISA your **spouse is automatically the beneficiary** of your 401(k) or pension unless the spouse signs a notarized waiver. IRAs have no such rule, except in community-property states.

Per stirpes vs per capita: the Okafor family

Grace has a $300,000 IRA and three adult children, Ada, Ben, and Chidi, named "in equal shares." Ben dies before Grace, leaving two children. What happens to Ben's third depends on two Latin words.

- **Per stirpes** ("by the branch"): Ben's share passes down his branch. Ada receives $100,000, Chidi $100,000, and Ben's two children $50,000 each.

- **Per capita** (often worded "pro rata among survivors"): Ben's share is redistributed among the surviving named beneficiaries. Ada and Chidi receive $150,000 each. Ben's children receive nothing from the IRA.

Neither answer is wrong. What is wrong is not choosing, or choosing one on the IRA and the other in the will, and letting the family discover the difference at the worst moment. If the form has no box for it, most custodians accept a written attachment.

The beneficiary audit

Once a year, and after every marriage, divorce, birth, death, or account move, ask each custodian to tell you in writing who is on file. You are not asking what you wrote; you are asking what they have.

LETTER TEMPLATE **Letter Template: Beneficiary Designation Confirmation Request**

[DATE]

[CUSTODIAN OR PLAN ADMINISTRATOR NAME]

[BENEFICIARY SERVICES DEPARTMENT]

[STREET ADDRESS]

[CITY, STATE ZIP]

RE: Request for written confirmation of beneficiary designations — Account ending [LAST 4 DIGITS], owner [YOUR FULL NAME], [DATE OF BIRTH]

Dear Beneficiary Services:

I am the owner of the account referenced above. Please send me a written statement of the primary and contingent beneficiaries currently on file, including each beneficiary's name, relationship, percentage share, whether the designation is per stirpes or per capita, and the date you received it.

If your records show no beneficiary on file, or a designation dated before [DATE OF MY MOST RECENT FORM], please say so explicitly and enclose your current beneficiary designation form so I can correct it.

Please also confirm whether any spousal consent or waiver is on file and whether this account is governed by ERISA.

Please respond in writing, to the address below, within 30 days of the date of this letter, and enclose a copy of the designation itself if available.

Sincerely,

[YOUR SIGNATURE]

[YOUR PRINTED NAME]

> [MAILING ADDRESS]
> [DAYTIME PHONE]
> Enclosures: Copy of photo identification; first page of most recent account statement

> QUIET TIP **Tip: One Folder, One Page Per Account**
> Keep one page per account: institution, last four digits, how it is titled, the beneficiaries on file, and the date of the custodian's written confirmation. When something changes, replace the page. Your executor will find it in five minutes instead of five months.

The step-up: why inheriting beats receiving

The most valuable rule in this chapter lives in Internal Revenue Code §1014. When you die, assets included in your estate take a new tax basis equal to fair market value on the date of death (or six months later, if the estate elects the alternate valuation date). The gain built up during your lifetime is never taxed. Your heir starts fresh.

What steps up, and what does not

Steps up at death	Does not step up
Stocks, bonds, and funds in a taxable brokerage account	Traditional IRAs and 401(k)s (income to the heir)
Real estate, including your home	Annuities (the gain is income to the heir)
Other capital assets: land, art, a business interest	Net unrealized appreciation on employer stock under the NUA rules
The decedent's half, or all, of a joint account (rules below)	Accrued interest on U.S. savings bonds

The step-up also runs in reverse. An asset worth less than you paid "steps down" at death, and the loss vanishes. Hence a rule below: sell losers while you are alive.

The picture worth $37,500

Suppose Gene bought stock in 1996 for $50,000, and it is worth $300,000 today. Lorraine can hand it to Lisa two ways.

If Lorraine **gifts** the shares during her life, Lisa takes Lorraine's $50,000 basis (IRC §1015, the carryover rule). When Lisa sells, she owes capital-gains tax on $250,000. At the 15% long-term rate, which applies above $49,450 of taxable income for a single filer in 2026 ($98,900 for a couple), that is $37,500 of federal tax, before state tax or the 3.8% net investment income tax that begins at $200,000 of modified adjusted gross income for singles ($250,000 for couples).

If Lisa **inherits** the same shares, her basis becomes $300,000. She can sell the next morning and owe nothing on the $250,000 of lifetime gain.

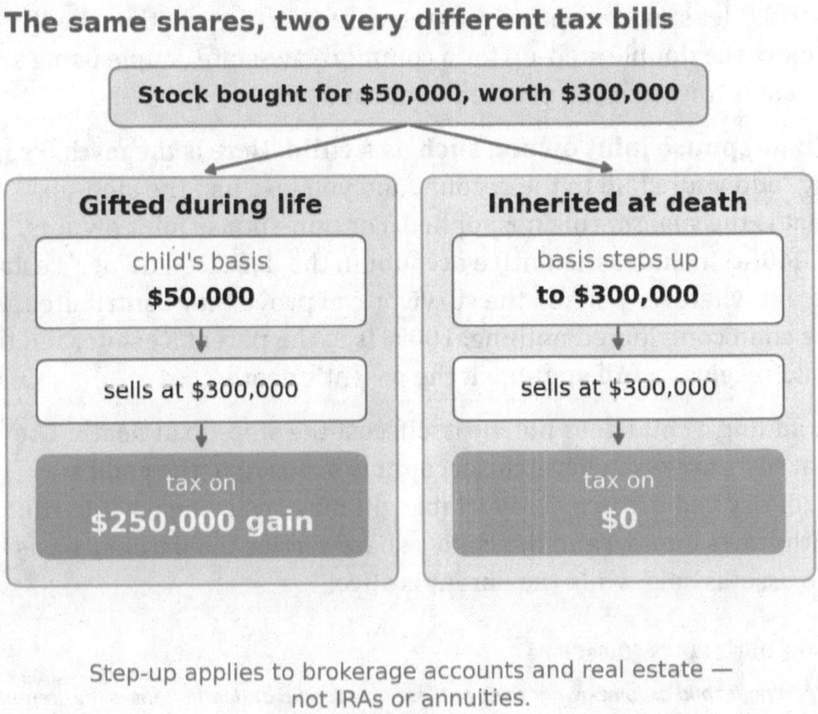

Figure 7.2. *The same $300,000 of stock, gifted during life or inherited at death, produces a $250,000 taxable gain or no gain at all*

The lesson is not "never give." It is: give cash, give assets with little built-in gain, and let the appreciated ones pass at death.

Joint accounts: who gets the step-up, and how much

Here the family rumor mill does its worst work, so here are the three cases precisely.

Spouses in a common-law state. Under §2040(b), exactly one-half of a joint spousal account is included in the first spouse's estate, so **half** the account steps up. The survivor's half keeps its old basis.

Spouses in a community-property state. Under §1014(b)(6), **both halves** step up at the first death, including the survivor's half. This "double step-up" applies in Arizona, California, Idaho, Louisiana, Nevada, New Mexico, Texas, Washington, and Wisconsin. A few other states (among them Alaska, Tennessee, South Dakota, Kentucky, and Florida) let spouses opt in by agreement or trust; whether the IRS honors the double step-up for a common-law-state couple using such a trust is unsettled, so proceed with counsel.

A non-spouse joint owner, such as a child. Here is the myth. People say "add your child to the account and you lose half the step-up." That is the *spousal* rule misapplied. For non-spouse joint owners, §2040(a) includes the **entire** account in the deceased owner's estate, except whatever portion the survivor can prove they contributed. If the child contributed nothing, 100% is in the parent's estate, and the child receives a **full** step-up at the parent's death.

So adding a child does not, by itself, cost the step-up at death. The real costs are elsewhere: the account is exposed to the child's creditors and divorce; a reportable gift may occur the day the child withdraws money; and the child's share carries the parent's basis if the asset is sold while the parent is alive.

> **THE QUIET RULES Quiet Rule**
>
> *Adding a child as joint owner does not lose the step-up at death. It loses the step-up on any sale during your life, and it hands a stranger's creditors a key.*

Gifts: carryover basis, and the one-year rule

Because a gift carries your basis with it, the rule for losing positions is absolute. Gift shares worth less than you paid and the recipient faces a "dual basis": your cost for computing a gain, the lower gift-date value for computing a loss. The loss in between is lost to everyone. **Sell the loser yourself, take the loss on your return (up to $3,000 a year against ordinary income, the rest carried forward), and gift the cash.**

One wrinkle: give appreciated property to someone who dies within one year and leaves it back to you, and §1014(e) denies the step-up. The tax code anticipated the deathbed shuffle.

> WATCH OUT **Watch Out: Never Gift a Loss**
>
> A gift of a losing stock wastes the loss for both of you; a gift of a winning stock hands your heir your old tax bill. Losses: sell first, gift the cash. Big gains: keep them for the step-up. Modest gains to someone in the 0% capital-gains bracket (taxable income up to $49,450 single or $98,900 joint in 2026) can make sense, but a gift to an individual is still a transfer for Medicaid's 60-month look-back.

TOD registration and the basis records your heirs need

Every state and the District of Columbia except **Louisiana** has adopted the Uniform TOD Security Registration Act, so a brokerage account can pass to a named beneficiary outside probate with the step-up intact. Ask your brokerage for its transfer-on-death form; it is free. Name contingents, because a TOD registration does nothing if the beneficiary dies first or becomes incapacitated, and check that the shares match your will's intentions.

Then do your heirs one favor. Brokers report cost basis to the IRS only for "covered" securities: stocks bought in 2011 or later, mutual fund and reinvested-dividend shares from 2012. For anything earlier, the taxpayer must prove the basis. Heirs get a step-up and will not need the old numbers, but if you sell first, you will. Find the confirmations for every pre-2011 lot and put them in the folder.

Deeds: the house is the hard one

The house is usually the largest asset, the one with the most sentiment, and the one people move most carelessly. A deed is easy to sign and expensive to unsign.

Adding a child to the deed

Adding a child as joint owner is a **completed gift** of half the property. On a $400,000 house, that is a $200,000 gift. Anything over $19,000 to one person in 2026 requires **Form 709 (United States Gift and Generation-Skipping Transfer Tax Return)** by April 15 of the following year. No tax is owed until lifetime gifts exceed $15,000,000 under the 2025 law, but the return is mandatory.

Then count the side effects.

- **Basis.** The child's half carries your basis. Sell while you are alive and the child owes gain on that half, without your §121 home-sale exclusion unless the child also lives there. At your death a non-contributing child generally receives a full step-up, though the family should expect to document who paid for what.
- **Creditors, lawsuits, divorce, bankruptcy.** The child's half is the child's asset, reachable by a judgment creditor, a divorcing spouse, or a bankruptcy trustee. You could find yourself negotiating with your son-in-law's lawyer over your own kitchen.
- **Medicaid.** A gift is a transfer inside the 60-month look-back for nursing-home Medicaid. The penalty is the value transferred divided by your state's monthly divisor. Using 2026 divisors of roughly $10,645 in Florida, $11,500 in Pennsylvania, and $7,900 in Texas, a $200,000 gift produces roughly 19, 17, or 25 months of ineligibility. The $19,000 gift-tax figure is irrelevant here (see Chapter 5, The Calendar).
- **Property taxes.** In California, parent-child transfers on or after February 16, 2021, keep the low assessment only for a family home the child makes a principal residence (filing the homeowners' exemption within one year), and only up to the assessed value plus $1,044,586 for transfers between February 16, 2025, and February 15, 2027; rentals and second homes are fully reassessed. File Form BOE-19-P within three years. In Florida, a poorly worded transfer can forfeit the homestead exemption and the 3% Save Our Homes cap. Your county assessor can tell you your state's trigger.
- **Control.** Once your child is on the deed, you cannot sell, refinance, or borrow without your child's signature.

One reassurance: adding a child does not let the lender call your mortgage. The Garn-St Germain Act generally bars a lender from enforcing a due-on-sale clause when a spouse or child becomes an owner, when property passes at death to a relative or joint tenant, or when you move the home into a revocable trust you remain the beneficiary of and keep living in.

CHECKLIST **Checklist: Before You Add Anyone to a Deed**

- ☐ Write down why (probate, convenience, caregiving) and check whether a TOD deed, Lady Bird deed, POA, or trust solves it without a gift.
- ☐ Estimate the gift (half the value for one added owner); Form 709 is due April 15 of the next year if it exceeds $19,000.
- ☐ Ask an elder-law attorney how the transfer is treated under your state's 60-month Medicaid look-back and estate-recovery rules.
- ☐ Ask the county assessor whether the transfer triggers reassessment or loss of a homestead exemption or cap.
- ☐ Ask the person you are adding, plainly, about their debts, pending lawsuits, and marriage.
- ☐ Ask your title insurer whether the new owner is covered and whether a quitclaim affects the policy.
- ☐ Copy the full legal description from the current recorded deed, not the mailing address.
- ☐ Record the deed with the county recorder and keep the stamped copy.

The traditional life estate deed

A life estate deed keeps you in the home for life and gives the "remainder" to your children now. The remainder is a completed gift (Form 709 if over $19,000). You cannot sell or mortgage without every remainderman's consent, their creditors and divorces can attach their interests, and a transfer within the five-year look-back triggers a partial Medicaid penalty valued by actuarial tables. Sell during your life and the state may claim your share of the proceeds. The one real advantage: the home is included in your estate under §2036, so your heirs receive a full step-up.

The Lady Bird deed

An "enhanced life estate," or Lady Bird deed, keeps what the traditional version gives away. You retain the right to sell, mortgage, or change your mind without anyone's signature, and because there is no completed gift, there is generally no Medicaid look-back penalty. At death the home passes outside probate. It is recognized in practice in **Florida, Texas, Michigan, Vermont, and West Virginia** only.

The transfer-on-death deed

A TOD (or "beneficiary") deed names who receives the house at your death, changes nothing during your life, and can be revoked. As of September 1, 2026, it is available in **35 jurisdictions**, counting the District of Columbia. Everywhere, it must be **recorded before death** and notarized (some states add witnesses); the beneficiary does not sign. An unrecorded TOD deed in a drawer transfers nothing.

State	TOD deed status in 2026
Arizona, California, Colorado, Illinois, Minnesota, Missouri, Ohio, Texas, Virginia, Washington, Wisconsin, D.C., and 18 others	Available
Georgia, New Hampshire	Available since July 1, 2024
New York	Since July 19, 2024; 2 witnesses plus a notary; equal shares only
Delaware	Since December 5, 2025
Maryland	From October 1, 2026 (an earlier-recorded deed works only if the owner dies on or after that date)
Florida, Pennsylvania, New Jersey, Michigan, Massachusetts, North Carolina, Tennessee, and others	Not available; Pennsylvania's bill still pending at this writing

PHONE SCRIPT **Phone Script: Asking the County Recorder or a Title Company About a TOD Deed**

You: Good morning. I own a home at [ADDRESS] in [COUNTY]. I am considering a transfer-on-death deed. Does this state recognize them, and does your office record them?

Them: Yes. / **Them:** No, not in this state.

If no, you say: Thank you. Does this state recognize an enhanced life estate, sometimes called a Lady Bird deed? If not, I will speak with an attorney about a trust.

If yes, you say: What are the execution requirements here: notary only, or notary plus witnesses? Is there a required statutory form? What is the recording fee? If I name two beneficiaries, may I set unequal shares? And must the deed be recorded before my death to be effective?

You: May I have your name and a reference number for this inquiry, and is there a written guide or form you can mail me?

If you are calling a title company: If I record a TOD deed, will my owner's title policy still cover me, and can my beneficiary get title insurance at my death without probate? I would like that answer in writing.

Closing line: Thank you. I will see an attorney before I sign anything, but this tells me which door to walk through.

The revocable trust, tenancy by the entirety, and the paperwork itself

A revocable living trust avoids probate for whatever is titled in it, and the home is usually the first thing retitled. Two chores follow the deed: tell your homeowner's insurer to add the trust as an insured, and notify your lender (Garn-St Germain protects the transfer). The step-up is unaffected. The trust's great failure is the unfunded one, where nothing was retitled and the pour-over will sends everything through the probate the trust was meant to avoid (Chapter 4 covers funding).

If you are married and live in one of the **25 states plus D.C.** that recognize tenancy by the entirety, holding the home that way passes it automatically to your spouse and shields it from the creditors of one spouse alone.

A **quitclaim** deed conveys whatever interest the signer has, with no warranties, and is the form most often used to add a family member.

Practitioners commonly warn that a quitclaim may not extend your title insurance to the new owner; ask the title company before signing. The classic clouds on title are an **unrecorded deed** and a **wrong legal description**. Copy the description word for word from the last recorded deed, and record the new one.

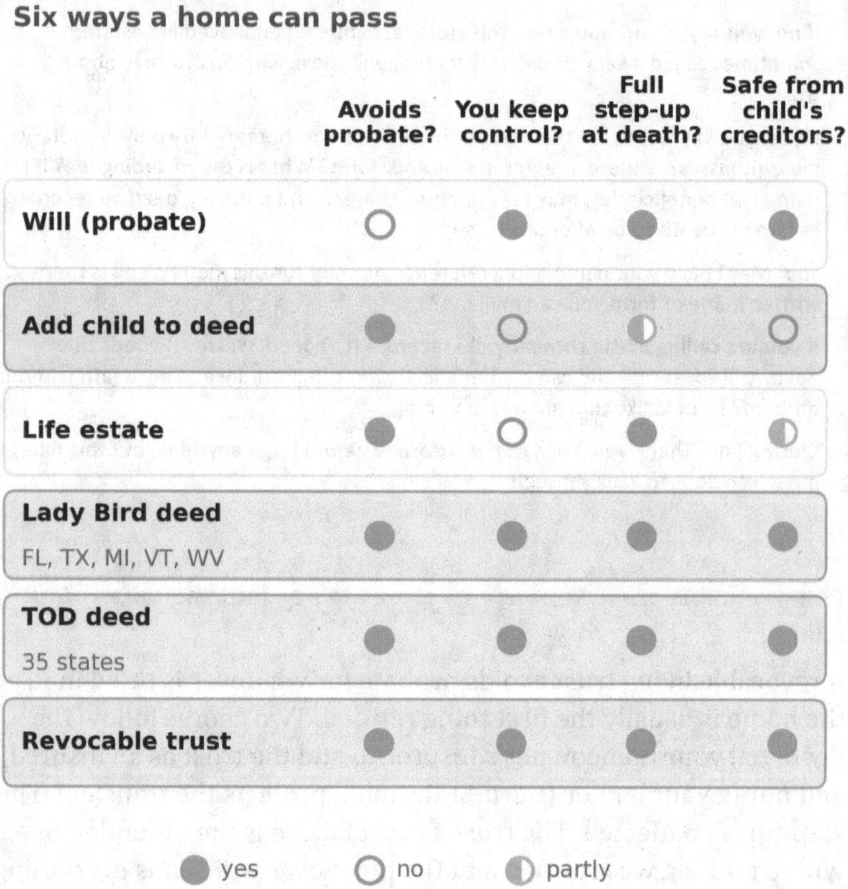

Figure 7.3. *Six ways a house can pass, compared on control, probate, step-up, Medicaid, and creditor exposure*

Option	Probate avoided?	Step-up at death?	Main catch
Will only	No	Yes	6–18 months of probate

Option	Probate avoided?	Step-up at death?	Main catch
Joint tenancy with a child	Yes	Generally yes (non-contributing child)	Gift now; child's creditors; Medicaid penalty; lost control
Traditional life estate	Yes	Yes	Can't sell without remaindermen; partial Medicaid penalty
Lady Bird deed	Yes	Yes	Only FL, TX, MI, VT, WV
TOD deed	Yes	Yes	35 jurisdictions; must be recorded before death
Revocable trust	Yes	Yes	Must retitle; notify insurer and lender

If there is a reverse mortgage

A home with a Home Equity Conversion Mortgage runs on its own clock at death. The servicer sends a "Due and Payable" letter within 30 days of learning of the death; respond within 30 days. Heirs then have **6 months** to sell, refinance, or pay off the loan, and HUD may approve **two 90-day extensions** (12 months total) with proof of active marketing or financing. Heirs who keep the home pay the lesser of the loan balance or **95% of appraised value**; otherwise they may sign a deed in lieu. An eligible non-borrowing spouse may remain under a deferral as long as taxes, insurance, and upkeep continue.

> QUIET TIP **Tip: The Deed Is Not the Only Paper**
>
> File the recorded deed, the homeowner's policy, the latest property-tax bill, and any mortgage or reverse-mortgage statement with your beneficiary confirmations. If there is a reverse mortgage, add the servicer's number and the 30-day, 6-month, and 95% figures. Your family will read that folder on a bad day.

State taxes and portability, briefly

Federal estate tax touches almost no one: the exemption is $15,000,000 per person in 2026, indexed after this year, with no sunset. Twelve states and the District of Columbia have their own estate tax, with exemptions as low as $1,000,000 in Oregon, and five states (Kentucky, Maryland, Nebraska, New Jersey, and Pennsylvania) tax inheritances; Pennsylvania taxes children at 4.5% and siblings at 12% while exempting spouses. Chapter 5 carries the full tables.

For a married couple, the one federal filing worth remembering is **portability**: the deceased spouse's unused exemption passes to the survivor only if Form 706 (United States Estate Tax Return) is filed within **9 months** of death, extendable **6 months** on Form 4768. Estates below the filing threshold that missed it may use the simplified late election under Rev. Proc. 2022-32 up to the fifth anniversary of death. Filing freezes values and preserves the survivor's combined $30,000,000 shelter, and some families are worth more than they think.

WORKSHEET **Worksheet: Asset Handoff Map**

One block per asset. "Passes by" is title, designation, or will. Update yearly and after every life event.

Asset 1: ____________________ Institution: ____________________

How titled (sole / joint with spouse / joint with other / trust / TBE): ____________________

Beneficiary or TOD/POD on file: ____________________ Confirmed in writing on: ________

Passes by: [ ] Title [ ] Designation [ ] Will/probate

Steps up at death? [ ] Yes [ ] No (IRA, annuity, NUA, savings-bond interest) [ ] Half (spousal joint, common-law state)

Value: $__________ Basis (taxable accounts): $__________ Action needed: ____________________

Asset 2: ____________________ Institution: ____________________

How titled: ____________________ Beneficiary or TOD/POD on file: ____________________

Passes by: [ ] Title [ ] Designation [ ] Will/probate Steps up? [ ] Yes [ ] No [ ] Half

Value: $__________ Basis: $__________ Action needed: ____________________

Home: ____________________ Deed type on record: ____________________ Recorded: ________

Mortgage? [ ] None [ ] Mortgage [ ] Reverse mortgage; servicer: ____________________

Deed plan: [ ] Will [ ] Joint with child [ ] Life estate [ ] Lady Bird [ ] TOD deed [ ] Trust

Pre-2011 basis records located: [ ] Yes [ ] Still looking

Per stirpes or per capita, consistent across all forms? [ ] Per stirpes [ ] Per capita [ ] Not yet decided

KEY NUMBERS **2026 Numbers to Know**

- **10 years:** a non-eligible beneficiary empties an inherited IRA by December 31 of the tenth year after death; annual withdrawals in years 1–9 if the owner had reached the required beginning date.
- **5 years:** the deadline when the estate or a non-see-through trust inherits from an owner who died before the required beginning date.
- **9 months:** the disclaimer deadline, and the Form 706 portability deadline, extendable 6 months.
- **September 30, October 31, December 31** of the year after death: beneficiary determination, trust paperwork, split-accounts deadline.
- **$15,000,000:** federal estate and lifetime gift exemption per person; $30,000,000 per couple with portability.
- **$19,000:** annual gift exclusion per recipient; more requires Form 709 by April 15 of the next year.
- **60 months:** the Medicaid look-back, which ignores the $19,000 figure entirely.
- **35 jurisdictions** offer a TOD deed, counting D.C. and Maryland from October 1, 2026.
- **95%** of appraised value (or the loan balance if lower) keeps a home with a reverse mortgage.
- **6 months** to resolve a reverse mortgage after death, plus up to two 90-day extensions.

A STORY What Lorraine Did

Lorraine took the legal pad to an elder-law attorney she found through her Area Agency on Aging (see Chapter 4). The first thing she learned was that Michigan has no transfer-on-death deed but does recognize the Lady Bird deed. She signed one naming Lisa and Daniel. She keeps the house, can sell it or change her mind, has made no gift, has started no Medicaid clock, and the house will pass outside probate with a full step-up.

The brokerage account got a free TOD registration naming both children equally, per stirpes, with contingents. She found Gene's 1996 confirmations in a shoebox and put them in the folder. The IRA stayed out of the trust; its beneficiary form now names Lisa and Daniel, per stirpes, matching her will, and the custodian's written confirmation is filed behind it.

Then she did the thing she had been putting off. She got both children on a video call and said one sentence: "If you ever inherit the IRA, the words are trustee-to-trustee transfer, and you never accept a check." Daniel wrote it on a sticky note. Lisa said she still didn't want to talk about it, and then asked three questions.

Your Next Steps

CHECKLIST Your Next Steps

- ☐ Mail the Beneficiary Designation Confirmation Request letter to every IRA, 401(k), annuity, and life insurance custodian, and file the replies.
- ☐ Choose per stirpes or per capita, and make every beneficiary form and your will say the same thing.
- ☐ Name contingent beneficiaries everywhere, and replace any minor child with a UTMA custodian or trust.
- ☐ Register your taxable brokerage account transfer-on-death (every state except Louisiana), with contingents.
- ☐ Locate basis records for every security bought before 2011 (funds before 2012) and put them in the handoff folder.
- ☐ Sell any losing position before gifting; gift the cash, never the loss.
- ☐ Call the county recorder or a title company with the script to learn whether your state offers a TOD deed or Lady Bird deed before adding anyone to a deed.
- ☐ Complete the Before You Add Anyone to a Deed checklist, including the Form 709 and 60-month Medicaid questions, before signing.
- ☐ Tell your beneficiaries, in writing, that an inherited IRA moves only by trustee-to-trustee transfer and that a check payable to them is irreversible.
- ☐ Complete the Asset Handoff Map worksheet and review it every January and after any marriage, divorce, birth, death, or account move.

CHAPTER EIGHT

The Fine Print — Seven Bank Legal Traps

By the end of this chapter you will know the seven clauses and clocks buried in your deposit agreement that can quietly cost you money, the deadline attached to each, and what to say and file to stay on the right side of every one.

A STORY **Charlotte, 68, Traverse City, Michigan**

Charlotte keeps a tidy house and a tidy checkbook, but she reads bank statements the way most of us do: when the envelope gets thick. On a snowbound afternoon in late March, she opened three months of paper at once.

Two things were waiting. On the January statement was a $612 debit-card charge to a home-goods store in Nevada. Charlotte has never been to Nevada. On the February statement, a line she almost skipped: her three-year certificate of deposit had matured February 9 and "renewed for a like term." The new rate was nearly a full point below what a one-year CD paid at the same bank that week.

She had planned to use that CD money for a new furnace this summer.

Charlotte did what careful people do. She set the statements aside to deal with properly on Monday. Monday became Thursday. By the time she picked up the phone, it was April 2. For the debit charge, the date mattered a great deal. For the CD, it was too late for the easy fix, though not for a good one.

Charlotte is a composite, and her story is illustrative. The rules she ran into are real.

> **THE QUIET RULES The Quiet Rules in This Chapter**
>
> - *Your bank may pay itself from your deposits, but not for its own credit card.*
> - *A CD that matures while you are not looking renews itself, at whatever the rate is that day.*
> - *The error clock starts when the statement is sent, not when you read it.*
> - *A joint owner owns the money, and so do that owner's creditors.*
> - *An account you never touch becomes the state's to hold.*
> - *Deposit insurance follows the ownership category, not the number of accounts.*
> - *The bank may close the door without saying why; keep a second door.*

The Document You Signed Without Reading

When you opened your checking account, someone slid a booklet across the desk, or a link appeared on a screen, and you agreed to it. That booklet is the deposit agreement. It is a contract, and it is the source of most of what follows.

Federal rules set floors: how long a bank can hold a deposit (Chapter 1, The Freeze), how long you have to dispute a debit-card charge, what a bank must tell you before a CD renews. State law adds the rules on checks, setoff, and unclaimed property. Everything in between is the agreement, and the bank wrote it.

You do not need to read all of it. You need to find five clauses.

1. **Setoff.** "Right of setoff" or "we may apply funds": whether the bank can pay itself from your account for a debt you owe the same bank.
2. **Statement review.** "Reasonable promptness" or "you must notify us within": many agreements shorten your window for reporting a forged check.
3. **Inactivity.** "Dormant" or "inactive," and the months before a fee starts.
4. **CD maturity.** "Automatically renew," "grace period," "early withdrawal penalty," each with its days.
5. **Arbitration.** Many agreements send disputes to a private arbitrator rather than a court. Some let you opt out by writing to

the bank within a short window after opening. Your state attorney general's consumer office can explain what the clause means where you live.

One more habit: under the Truth in Savings rules, a bank generally must give **30 days' notice** before a change in terms that lowers a rate or raises a fee. Those notices arrive as thin envelopes. Open them.

WORKSHEET **Worksheet: Deposit Agreement Audit**

Ask the branch for the current deposit agreement, or find it under "disclosures" online. One worksheet per bank.

Bank or credit union: ____________________

Account type(s): ____________________

Clause 1 — Setoff

[ ] Agreement allows setoff for debts to this bank

Do I also have a loan, credit line, or credit card here? [ ] Yes [ ] No

Clause 2 — Statement review

Days I have to report a forged or altered check: ______

Clause 3 — Inactivity

Months of no activity before "inactive" status: ______

Inactive-account fee: $______ per ______

Clause 4 — CDs

Grace period after maturity: ______ calendar days

Early-withdrawal penalty (by term): ____________________

Clause 5 — Arbitration

Arbitration clause present? [ ] Yes [ ] No

Opt-out window (if any): ______ days from opening

Other

Stop-payment fee: $______

Date completed: ____________________

With the agreement in hand, the seven traps come into focus. Each has a rule behind it, a number attached, and a fix that takes an afternoon or less.

Figure 8.1. *The seven bank legal traps at a glance, with the clock attached to each*

KEY NUMBERS 2026 Numbers to Know

- **$50 / $500 / unlimited** — your maximum loss on an unauthorized electronic transfer, reported within 2 business days, later, or after 60 days from the statement (Reg E)
- **60 days** — from the statement date, to dispute an electronic error (Reg E) or a credit-card billing error (Reg Z)
- **10 business days** — for the bank to decide a Reg E claim or give provisional credit
- **30 days / 1 year** — UCC 4-406 windows for forged checks
- **6 months** — a check goes stale (UCC 4-404); **10 days** — after a death, checks may still be paid (UCC 4-405)
- **30 calendar days** — notice before a CD over one year renews; **7–10 calendar days** — typical grace period
- **3–5 years** — dormancy before an account goes to the state
- **$250,000** — insurance per depositor, per bank, per ownership category; **$1,250,000** for a POD or trust account with 5 beneficiaries
- **15% or the amount over $750** — the most Treasury can offset from Social Security for a federal non-tax debt
- **$10,000** — cash above which a Currency Transaction Report is filed; splitting a withdrawal to avoid it is a crime

Trap 1: The Right of Setoff

The rule

If you owe money to a bank and keep money at the same bank, the bank can, in most states and under most account agreements, reach into your deposit account and pay itself. This is the right of setoff. It is old, it is legal, and you agreed to it. It generally requires a **matured** debt (a payment is actually late) and **mutuality** (the same person owes the debt and owns the deposit). A bank cannot take your money for your daughter's car loan. It can take your money for your own.

The numbers

Federal law draws one bright line. Under Regulation Z, section 1026.12(d), a card issuer **may not** offset a credit-card balance against your deposits at the same institution, unless you signed up in writing for an **automatic periodic payment plan** (revocable), gave a consensual security interest, or the bank won a court judgment the ordinary way. A missed credit-card payment does not empty your checking account. A missed payment on a personal loan, an overdraft, or a home-equity line at the same bank might.

What about Social Security? Federal law, 42 USC 407, says benefits "shall not be subject to execution, levy, attachment, garnishment, or other legal process." Whether a bank's *own* setoff is "legal process" is contested. Several federal appeals courts have said it is not, at least when the bank is recovering the customer's own overdrafts and fees; some states, California among them, restrict it by statute. Do not assume your Social Security deposits are safe from setoff at a bank that also holds your loan. An elder-law attorney can tell you where your state stands.

The better-known protection, 31 CFR Part 212, covers something different: a **third-party garnishment**. When a bank receives a garnishment order, it must within **2 business days** look back **two months** for direct-deposited Social Security, SSI, VA, Railroad Retirement, or federal civil-service benefits. The protected amount, the lesser of those deposits or the balance that day, cannot be frozen. If anything is frozen, you get notice within **3 business days**. The rule does not protect benefits you moved to another account or received by paper check, and it yields to an IRS levy or a state child-support order.

The federal government can also take a slice. Under the Treasury Offset Program, a delinquent **federal non-tax debt** (a defaulted federal student loan, most often) can be collected from Social Security retirement benefits: the lesser of the debt, **15%** of the monthly benefit, or the amount by which the check exceeds **$750**. SSI is exempt, and written notice comes first. An IRS levy runs through a separate program at 15% with no $750 floor.

An illustration

Earl, 71, in Chattanooga, Tennessee, had his Social Security deposited to the credit union that also held his truck loan. When he fell two payments behind after a hospital stay, the credit union set off $840 from his account. His daughter, sure the money was "untouchable," got a polite reading of the account agreement. Earl's fix was not a lawsuit; it was moving his direct deposit.

The fix

Quiet Rule: If you owe a bank money and might fall behind, do not keep your deposits there.

- Keep everyday checking at an institution where you have no loan, credit line, or overdraft plan.
- Check your card settings for an automatic-payment authorization you have forgotten.
- If a garnishment order arrives, ask the bank in writing to confirm it applied the 31 CFR 212 lookback and to state the protected amount.
- If Treasury offsets a federal debt, call the number on the notice before the first offset; Chapter 3, The Silent Deadlines, covers the timing.

Trap 2: CD Auto-Renewal

The rule

Most certificates of deposit renew themselves. When the term ends, the bank gives you a short grace period; if you do nothing, the money rolls into a new CD of the **same term** at **whatever the bank is paying that day**. Your five-year CD from a high-rate year becomes a five-year CD from a low-rate one, and getting out costs money.

The numbers

Under Truth in Savings, 12 CFR 1030.5(b), a renewing CD **longer than one year** requires full disclosures for the new term at least **30 calendar days before maturity**, or **20 calendar days before the end of the grace period** if the grace period is at least 5 calendar days. A CD of **one year or less but more than one month** gets a shorter notice on the same timing. A CD of one month or less gets none. A non-renewing CD longer than a year gets a maturity notice at least **10 calendar days** before.

The grace period is not set by federal law. Typically it runs **7 to 10 calendar days** after maturity, during which you can withdraw or change the term without penalty. Miss it, and you are inside a new CD with a penalty. Penalties are bank policy, usually expressed as days of interest.

CD term	Common early-withdrawal penalty	Can it touch principal?
1 year	60–180 days' interest	Yes, if little interest has accrued
3 years	90–180 days' interest	Yes
5 years	150–365 days' interest	Yes

That last column deserves a pause. Break a five-year CD three months after it renewed with a 365-day penalty, and the bank takes the three months of interest you earned and the rest **from your principal**.

An illustration

Charlotte's $40,000 three-year CD matured February 9. The required notice had gone out in early January; it was in the thick envelope. The grace period ended February 19. By April 2 the CD had been a new three-year certificate for six weeks at a lower rate. The penalty was 180 days' interest, about $700 at the new rate; she had earned about $180. Breaking it would have cost roughly $520 of principal.

The fix

Quiet Rule: Every CD goes on the calendar twice: the maturity date, and the last day of the grace period.

Two habits end this trap. Put every CD on a written calendar with both dates. And consider a **ladder**: several smaller CDs maturing in different years, so no single rollover carries all your money.

PHONE SCRIPT **Phone Script: Calling About a CD Maturity or Grace Period**

Have the CD number and maturity date in front of you.

You: I'm calling about certificate of deposit number [NUMBER]. I want to confirm the maturity date and grace period, and give instructions for what happens at maturity.

Them: The maturity date is [DATE] and the grace period is [X] days.

You: Calendar days or business days? And on what exact date does the grace period end?

You: Please note on the account that at maturity I want the funds [transferred to my checking ending in NUMBER / renewed for a one-year term]. Can you confirm you've recorded that?

If they say instructions can only be given during the grace period:

You: Understood. Please tell me the first and last calendar day of the grace period. I'll call again on [FIRST DAY].

If the CD has already renewed:

You: What is the early-withdrawal penalty today, in dollars, and how much interest has accrued since renewal? Would any of the penalty come out of principal?

You: Please give me your name, an employee ID or extension, and a reference number for this call, and send written confirmation to the address on file.

Polite escalation:

You: I'd like a supervisor or deposit operations, because I need this instruction on the record before the maturity date.

CHECKLIST **Checklist: CD Maturity Calendar**

- ☐ List every CD by bank, amount, rate, and maturity date on one sheet
- ☐ Call each bank and confirm the grace period in calendar days and its exact last day
- ☐ Set two reminders per CD: 14 days before maturity, and the first day of the grace period
- ☐ Decide now, in writing, what you want at maturity: cash out, one-year term, or ladder rung
- ☐ Ask whether the bank will honor a standing maturity instruction automatically
- ☐ Watch for the Truth in Savings notice 30 calendar days before maturity; if it does not arrive, call
- ☐ Note each CD's penalty in days of interest and whether it can invade principal
- ☐ Review the sheet every January and July

Trap 3: The Error Windows

The rule

Every kind of bank error has a clock, and the clock starts when the bank **sends** your statement, not when you open it. Report inside the window and the law is on your side; report outside it and the loss is often yours, no matter how obvious the fraud. There are three rulebooks.

Electronic transactions: Regulation E

Regulation E covers debit-card purchases, ATM withdrawals, ACH transfers, and app-based transfers from your bank account. Your maximum liability for an **unauthorized** transfer depends entirely on speed.

When you report	Your maximum loss
Within 2 business days of learning your card or code was lost or stolen	$50
After 2 business days, within 60 days of the statement	$500
More than 60 days after the statement was sent	Unlimited, for transfers after day 60 and before you give notice

Under section 1005.11, you must notify the bank within **60 days after it sends the statement** showing the error. The bank then has **10 business days** to investigate and decide (20 for accounts open less than 30 days). If it needs longer, it must give **provisional credit within 10 business days** and may take up to **45 days** total, or **90 days** for new accounts, point-of-sale debit transactions, and foreign-initiated transfers. It reports results within **3 business days** and corrects a confirmed error within **1 business day**.

A phone call starts the clock. The bank may ask for written confirmation within 10 business days; send it. Deadlines must be extended for "extenuating circumstances" such as hospitalization or long travel, so say so if it applies.

> WATCH OUT **Watch Out: Being Tricked Is Not "Unauthorized"**
>
> Reg E protects you when someone else moved your money without permission. It does not, in general, protect you when you were talked into sending it yourself. A Zelle-type transfer to a "grandson in jail" or a "bank fraud investigator" is treated as authorized, because you pressed the button. Some banks reimburse such losses voluntarily, and the CFPB has pushed them to, but there is no right to it. Report it anyway, quickly, to the bank, to the FTC at ReportFraud.ftc.gov, and to the FBI's IC3. The real protection is the pause: no legitimate bank, agency, or relative needs money by app in the next twenty minutes.

Credit cards: Regulation Z

A credit-card billing error is disputed **in writing within 60 days** after the first statement showing it. The issuer must acknowledge within **30 days** and resolve within **two complete billing cycles, not more than 90 days**. Liability for unauthorized use of the card is capped at **$50**. Use the "billing inquiries" address on the statement, not the payment address.

Paper checks: UCC Article 4

Checks are governed by state law, the Uniform Commercial Code, adopted everywhere with minor variations. Section 4-406 asks you to examine statements "with reasonable promptness" and report forged or altered checks. Two numbers matter:

- **30 days.** If the same wrongdoer forges more than one check, you lose your claim on later ones paid after a reasonable period, "not exceeding 30 days," from the first statement showing a forgery. Comparative negligence applies if the bank also lacked ordinary care.
- **1 year.** After one year from the statement being made available, the claim is gone regardless of anyone's care.

Here the deposit agreement bites: many agreements shorten the 30 days, sometimes to 14. That is Clause 2 on your audit. A related rule, section 4-404, says a bank has no obligation to pay a check presented more than **six months** after its date, but it *may* pay one in good faith and charge your account. A check you wrote that never cleared has not died quietly; put a stop payment on it.

Altered checks, where a thief changes the payee or amount, are common enough to have a nickname, "check washing." Businesses can buy a matching service called positive pay; few banks offer it to consumers. Your positive pay is the monthly statement, read the week it arrives. The windows line up like rungs on a ruler.

Figure 8.2. *The reporting-window ruler: 2 business days and 60 days under Reg E, 60 days under Reg Z, 30 days and 1 year under UCC 4-406, 6 months for a stale check, 10 days after death, and 3–5 years to dormancy*

Rulebook	What it covers	Your deadline
Reg E (federal)	Debit card, ATM, ACH, app transfers	2 business days for the $50 cap; 60 days from statement
Reg Z (federal)	Credit-card billing errors	60 days from statement, in writing
UCC 4-406 (state)	Forged or altered checks	30 days (or less by agreement); 1 year absolute
UCC 4-404 (state)	Stale checks	6 months from the check's date

An illustration

Charlotte's January statement was sent about February 3. The Nevada charge was an unauthorized debit-card transaction, so Reg E applied and her 60 days ran to about April 4. She called April 2. Two days to spare. One more week and the bank could have refused the claim, and any further charges on that card after day 60 would have been hers until she called.

The fix

Quiet Rule: Read every statement the week it arrives; dispute by phone the same day, then in writing.

PHONE SCRIPT **Phone Script: Disputing an Unauthorized Electronic Transaction (Reg E)**

Call the number on the back of your debit card. Have the statement date, transaction date, and amount ready.

You: I'm reporting an unauthorized electronic transaction under Regulation E. On [TRANSACTION DATE] there is a debit of $[AMOUNT] to [MERCHANT] that I did not make or authorize. The statement showing it was sent on [STATEMENT DATE], so I am within the 60-day window.

Them: We'll open a dispute.

You: Thank you. Please give me the case number, your name, your employee ID or extension, and the date you are recording as my notice date.

You: If you cannot resolve this within 10 business days, I understand I'm entitled to provisional credit within 10 business days while you investigate.

If they say provisional credit is not available:

You: Under section 1005.11 of Regulation E, if the investigation runs past 10 business days the bank must provisionally credit my account. Please note my request on the case and tell me who I can speak with about it.

If they ask for written confirmation:

You: I'll send it within 10 business days. What address or secure-message channel should I use?

You: Please cancel this card and issue a new one, and tell me in writing when the investigation is complete and what you found.

Polite escalation:

You: Please escalate this to your fraud department today and give me a supervisor's name. If I have no resolution or provisional credit within 10 business days, I'll file with the Consumer Financial Protection Bureau at 1-855-411-2372.

LETTER TEMPLATE **Letter Template: Written Notice of Error Under Regulation E**

[DATE]

[BANK NAME]

Attn: Disputes / Error Resolution

[ADDRESS ON STATEMENT]

RE: Notice of error under Regulation E, 12 CFR 1005.11 — Account ending [LAST 4], Dispute No. [CASE NUMBER]

Dear Sir or Madam:

This letter confirms my telephone notice of [DATE OF CALL] and serves as written notice of an error on my account. My statement dated [STATEMENT DATE] shows an electronic transaction on [TRANSACTION DATE] for $[AMOUNT] to [MERCHANT]. I did not make or authorize this transaction. This notice is given within 60 days after the statement was sent.

Under 12 CFR 1005.11, please investigate and report your determination within 10 business days of my notice. If you require more time, please provisionally credit my account for $[AMOUNT], plus related fees and interest, within 10 business days, and complete the investigation within 45 days.

Please confirm that the debit card ending [LAST 4] has been canceled and a replacement issued.

Please respond in writing to the address below with the name and contact information of the person handling this matter. If you determine no error occurred, please provide a written explanation and copies of the documents you relied on.

Sincerely,

[YOUR NAME]

[ADDRESS]

[PHONE]

Enclosures: statement page with the transaction marked; police report (if any); notes of the telephone call with case number and employee name

LETTER TEMPLATE **Letter Template: Notice of Forged or Altered Check Under UCC 4-406**

[DATE]

[BANK NAME]

Attn: Check Fraud / Deposit Operations

[ADDRESS ON STATEMENT]

RE: Notice of unauthorized signature or alteration — Account ending [LAST 4], Check No. [NUMBER], paid [DATE], $[AMOUNT]

Dear Sir or Madam:

I am giving notice under Section 4-406 of the Uniform Commercial Code, as adopted in [STATE], that the check described above was [not signed by me / altered after I signed it]. The check appears on my statement dated [STATEMENT DATE], and I am reporting it with reasonable promptness upon discovering it.

The check was [forged / altered as follows: ORIGINAL PAYEE AND AMOUNT versus PAID PAYEE AND AMOUNT]. I have not authorized anyone else to sign checks on this account.

Please recredit my account for $[AMOUNT] and related fees, refuse any further items bearing a signature that does not match the signature card, and close this account and open a replacement with a new number.

Please provide, in writing within 10 business days, a copy of the front and back of the paid item, your determination on recredit, and the name of the person handling this claim. I have filed a report with [POLICE DEPARTMENT], report number [NUMBER].

Please respond in writing to the address below.

Sincerely,

[YOUR NAME]

[ADDRESS]

[PHONE]

Enclosures: statement page; check image (if available); police report; affidavit of forgery (if the bank provided a form)

CHECKLIST **Checklist: Monthly Statement Review**

- ☐ Open every statement within 7 days of arrival and note the statement date
- ☐ Check each debit-card and ATM line against your own record; circle anything unfamiliar
- ☐ Check every paid check image for your signature, the payee, and the amount
- ☐ Look for new recurring charges you did not set up
- ☐ Call the same day about any unfamiliar electronic transaction (Reg E script) and get a case number
- ☐ Send the written Reg E notice within 10 business days of the call
- ☐ Report any forged or altered check the same day by phone and letter (UCC 4-406 template)
- ☐ Stop payment on any check you wrote more than 5 months ago that has not cleared

Trap 4: Joint Account Exposure

The rule

When bills get hard to manage, the most common move is to add an adult child or a friend to the checking account "so they can help." At most banks that means a new signature card reading **joint with right of survivorship**. From that moment the helper is not a helper. The helper is an owner.

The numbers

An owner can withdraw all of it, legally. An owner's creditors can reach it. An owner's divorce can put it on the table. And when you die, a survivorship account passes to the surviving owner by contract, outside your will, even if the will says "equally to my three children."

The theft risk is not hypothetical. In its 2024 analysis of a year of elder-exploitation reports, FinCEN found adult children were the perpetrators in about **40%** of elder-theft reports. Most adult children are wonderful. The account structure should not depend on it.

Some states recognize a **convenience account**, where a second signer can write checks but has no ownership and no survivorship right; Florida, Illinois, New York, and Texas have statutes, and the Uniform Probate Code has a similar provision. But if the card you signed says "joint with survivorship," courts often honor the card over what you meant. Ask the bank which card you signed.

An illustration

Bettina, 79, in Albuquerque, New Mexico, added her son Paul to her checking account in 2023 so he could pay her bills from out of state. Paul is honest. Paul also co-signed his daughter's business lease, and when the business failed in 2026 the landlord's judgment creditor served Bettina's bank. The account was joint. Bettina's money was tied up for four months while lawyers sorted out whose it was.

The fix

Quiet Rule: A helper needs a power of attorney, not a share of the account.

The safe structure has three free parts: a **durable financial power of attorney**, filed with the bank on its own form if it has one (Chapter 4, The Four Documents); a **payable-on-death (POD)** designation, whose beneficiary has no rights while you live and collects with a death certificate afterward; and a **trusted contact** the bank can call if something looks wrong (Chapter 1).

If a helper is already a joint owner, ask whether the bank can convert the account. More often the answer is to open a new sole-name account with a POD, move the money, and close the old one. Do it while you are well; a bank cannot remove a joint owner on one owner's say-so.

Trap 5: Dormancy and Escheat

The rule

Unclaimed-property law is state law, and its logic is simple: an account with no owner contact for long enough is presumed abandoned, and the bank must hand it to the state. The state holds it, in most states indefinitely, until you or your heirs claim it. The money is not stolen. It is parked, without interest, in a place you have to know to look.

The numbers

The dormancy period for bank deposits is **3 years** in most states and **5 years** in a substantial minority. California, Texas, New York, Pennsylvania, and Illinois are 3-year states; Florida is 5. Ohio's statute sets 5 years for bank deposits even though general tables often list 3, so confirm the deposit-specific period with your state's unclaimed-property office. Before reporting, the bank must attempt to reach you, typically **60 to 120 days** before it remits.

Two details surprise people. **Interest posting never counts** as activity, and in many states **automatic renewal of a CD does not count either**. A five-year CD that quietly renews can look, to the state, like five years of silence. And the bank's own "inactive account" fee is a separate creature, set by the agreement (Clause 3); the CFPB notes dormancy is a common reason banks close accounts.

An illustration

Vernon, 76, in Sioux Falls, South Dakota, opened a $25,000 five-year CD in 2019 as "money I'll never touch." He never touched it. It renewed in 2024. In 2026 he went to cash it and learned it had been reported to the state as unclaimed the year before. He got it back, with a claim form and about eight weeks of waiting, but not the interest it would have earned meanwhile.

The fix

Quiet Rule: Touch every account once a year, in a way the bank records.

> QUIET TIP **Tip: One Contact a Year**
>
> Once a year, on a date you will remember, do something at each bank that counts as owner-initiated activity: log in to online banking, make a small deposit or withdrawal, or send a signed letter confirming your address. Write the date on your account inventory (Chapter 6, The Review). For a CD, call and confirm your address the same week you check the maturity date. And search MissingMoney.com, the free multistate database, every couple of years for yourself, your spouse, and your parents. There is never a fee, and anyone offering to "find your money" for a cut is selling a search you can do at the kitchen table.

Trap 6: The Insurance Limit

The rule

Deposit insurance is generous, but it is counted by **ownership category**, not by account. Two checking accounts in your sole name at the same bank are one category, insured to one limit. The same money at two different banks is insured twice.

The numbers

The FDIC standard is **$250,000 per depositor, per insured bank, per ownership category**. Credit unions have the same figure under the NCUA.

Ownership category	Coverage at one bank	Example
Single (your name alone)	$250,000	All sole-name checking, savings, CDs combined
Joint (two owners)	$500,000	$250,000 per co-owner
Certain retirement accounts	$250,000	IRAs held as bank deposits
Trust (POD, ITF, living trust)	$250,000 per beneficiary, up to 5	$1,250,000 maximum with 5 beneficiaries

Two recent changes matter. Since **April 1, 2024**, the FDIC combines revocable and irrevocable trust accounts, including simple POD accounts, into one category insured at **$250,000 per eligible beneficiary up to five**, a ceiling of **$1,250,000** per owner per bank. Beneficiaries beyond five add nothing. Credit unions adopted the same rule effective **December 1, 2026**; until then, credit-union trust coverage follows the older rules, so ask which apply on the day you ask.

When a joint owner or POD beneficiary dies, the FDIC keeps insuring the account as if that person were alive for a **6-month grace period**. After that, a $500,000 joint account with one surviving owner is a $250,000 single account with $250,000 uninsured. Chapter 2, The First 90 Days, puts this on the timeline.

A caution on brokerage cash: if your brokerage sweeps cash into partner banks, coverage depends on how that program is built. Ask for the brokerage's written explanation rather than assuming.

An illustration

June and Wendell, both 74, in Bethlehem, Pennsylvania, sold a rental property and parked $700,000 in a joint savings account "until we decide." Insured: $500,000. Exposed: $200,000. When Wendell died in March, the 6-month clock started; by September, June's account was insured to $250,000 with $450,000 uninsured, at a bank she had chosen for its parking lot.

The fix

Quiet Rule: Count by category and by bank, not by account.

> QUIET TIP **Tip: The Calculator That Does the Math**
>
> The FDIC's Electronic Deposit Insurance Estimator, EDIE, is free and takes ten minutes. Enter each account at a bank, its type, its owners, and any POD beneficiaries, and it tells you exactly what is and is not insured. Run it once a year and after any death, sale, or large deposit. If you are over the line, the fixes are ordinary: name up to five POD beneficiaries, move part of the balance to a second bank, or put a spouse's share in that spouse's own name. A fee-only planner can confirm the titling for your state.

Trap 7: The Closure and the Silence

The rule

A bank or credit union can close your account without your permission and, under federal law, without advance notice and without a reason. The CFPB says so in plain words. Some states may require notice; no specific state statute could be confirmed for this book, so ask your state banking regulator rather than count on one.

The silence has a cause. If the closure is connected to a Suspicious Activity Report, the bank is **legally barred** from telling you a report was filed. The employee on the phone is not being evasive; the law forbids the answer. Federal regulators warned in 2024 against unfair "debanking" without process, but no rule yet requires notice or reasons.

The numbers

What the bank must do is return your money, usually by check mailed to the address on file. There is no federal deadline for that check. The trap is worst for the person with one bank: direct deposits bounce, autopays fail, and the Medicare premium, the insurance, and the utility all go unpaid while a check for the balance wanders through the mail.

> WATCH OUT **Watch Out: Never Split a Withdrawal**
>
> Some closures trace back to a customer trying to be helpful. Withdrawing or depositing more than $10,000 in cash triggers a routine Currency Transaction Report. It is not a problem and you cannot opt out. But breaking a $14,000 withdrawal into two trips of $7,000 to "stay under the limit" is **structuring**, a federal crime under 31 USC 5324 punishable by up to 5 years, even when the money is entirely legitimate. Banks must report suspected structuring, and a pattern of it is a classic reason an account quietly closes. Cash purchases of cashier's checks and money orders between $3,000 and $10,000 are logged too. Withdraw what you need, in one transaction, and tell the branch a day ahead if it is large.

An illustration

Ellen, 70, in Eugene, Oregon, got a letter in July: her account of 31 years would close in 10 days. No reason. Her Social Security, her pension, and eleven automatic payments ran through it. She spent three weeks opening a new account, giving the new routing number to Social Security and the pension, and calling each biller, while the closing bank's check for $9,300 took twelve days to arrive. Nothing was lost but sleep and a late fee. Ellen now keeps two accounts, at two institutions.

The fix

Quiet Rule: Keep a lifeboat: a second account at a different institution, with two months of bills in it.

If a closure notice arrives:

1. Ask, in writing, for the reason and the exact closing date. You may get neither, but the request is on record.
2. Ask for the balance by cashier's check or transfer to your other account, not by mailed check.
3. Redirect direct deposits the same day: Social Security at 1-800-772-1213 or through your my Social Security account; pensions by their own forms.
4. File a complaint with the Consumer Financial Protection Bureau at 1-855-411-2372 and with your state banking regulator. Neither can force the bank to keep you, but complaints are how patterns get noticed.
5. Do not argue about a SAR. No one can lawfully discuss it.

WORKSHEET **Worksheet: Lifeboat Account Plan**

A lifeboat is a second checking account at a different institution, kept funded, with your direct-deposit and autopay details on file so a closure or freeze costs you a phone call, not a month.

Main bank: ____________________

Lifeboat bank (different institution): ____________________

Opened on: ____________________

Routing number: ____________________

Account number (last 4): ____________________

Target balance (two months of essentials): $______

Current balance: $______

Direct deposits to redirect

Social Security (1-800-772-1213): [ ] Info saved

Pension / annuity: ____________________ Phone: ____________________

Automatic payments that would fail

1. ____________________ Phone: ____________________
1. ____________________ Phone: ____________________
1. ____________________ Phone: ____________________
1. ____________________ Phone: ____________________

Annual maintenance

[ ] One owner-initiated transaction this year, on: ____________________

[ ] Confirmed no loan or credit card of mine at the lifeboat bank (setoff)

[ ] POD beneficiary named: ____________________

[ ] Trusted contact named: ____________________

Date reviewed: ____________________

What Charlotte Did

A STORY **Charlotte, 68, Traverse City, Michigan**

Charlotte called the bank on April 2 about the $612 Nevada charge and said the words "unauthorized transaction under Regulation E." The representative opened a case. Charlotte asked for the case number, the employee's name, and the date recorded as her notice. She mailed the written notice the next morning and kept a copy. On the tenth business day a provisional credit appeared; three weeks later it became permanent, and a new card arrived.

The CD was harder. She was past the grace period, and breaking the new certificate would have cost about $520 of principal. She left it alone, paid for the furnace from savings and a short 0% plan from the contractor, and split the rest of her CD money, which had sat in one large certificate, into four smaller ones maturing in different years. Each pair of dates went on the kitchen calendar.

She also opened a second checking account at a credit union across town, with $3,000 in it and her Social Security details on file. She calls it the lifeboat. She has never needed it, which is the point.

Your Next Steps

CHECKLIST **Your Next Steps**

- ☐ Request the current deposit agreement from each bank and complete the Deposit Agreement Audit for the five clauses
- ☐ Move everyday checking to an institution where you have no loan, credit line, or overdraft plan if you have any doubt about staying current
- ☐ List every CD with its maturity date and grace period and put both dates on the calendar (CD Maturity Calendar)
- ☐ Set a weekly time to review statements, and report any unfamiliar electronic charge by phone the same day (Reg E script) and in writing within 10 business days
- ☐ Stop payment on any check you wrote more than five months ago that has not cleared
- ☐ Replace any "helper" joint owner with a durable power of attorney filed at the bank, a POD beneficiary, and a trusted contact (Chapters 1 and 4)
- ☐ Make one owner-initiated contact at every account this year and note the date
- ☐ Search MissingMoney.com for yourself, your spouse, and your parents, and pay no one to do it
- ☐ Run the FDIC's EDIE calculator for each bank, and ask your credit union which trust-coverage rules apply before and after December 1, 2026
- ☐ Open a lifeboat account at a different institution and complete the Lifeboat Account Plan, including Social Security's number, 1-800-772-1213
- ☐ Save the CFPB complaint line, 1-855-411-2372, and your state banking regulator's number where you can find them

APPENDIX A

The Master Calendar

Two kinds of deadline run through this book. The first kind repeats every year on the same date, and those are laid out below month by month. The second kind starts only when something happens to you: a deposit, a death, a statement, a birthday. Those clocks follow in the second half of this appendix.

Two reminders before you use either table. "Business days" exclude weekends and federal holidays; "days" without a qualifier are calendar days. And every figure here is a 2026 figure; the agencies that own them are listed in Appendix B, so you can check next year's in a few minutes.

The recurring year

January through March

Month	Date	What is due or open	Chapter
January	Jan 1	New Roth five-year clocks start; payments at the new cost-of-living adjustment (2.8% for 2026) begin arriving	5, 3
January	Jan 1–Mar 31	Medicare General Enrollment Period (coverage starts the month after you enroll); Medicare Advantage Open Enrollment	3
January	Jan 15	Fourth-quarter estimated tax for the prior year (Jan 15, 2027 for 2026); new Identity Protection PIN issued	3, 5
January	Mid-Jan	IRS IP PIN online tool reopens; free tax-help sites (AARP Tax-Aide, VITA/TCE) open through April	3
February	Feb 1	File and pay in full by this date to skip the January 15 estimate	3

Month	Date	What is due or open	Chapter
March	Mar 31	General Enrollment Period and Medicare Advantage Open Enrollment close	3

April through June

Month	Date	What is due or open	Chapter
April	Apr 1	First required minimum distribution for anyone who turned 73 (born 1951–1959) the prior year; the two-in-one-year trap	5
April	Apr 15	Form 1040; prior-year IRA and HSA contributions; Form 709 for any gift over $19,000 to one person; first-quarter estimated tax	3, 5
April	Apr 15	Three-year refund window closes (2023 refunds expire April 15, 2027; 2024 refunds April 15, 2028); Form 4868 extension request	3
May	None	No federal deadline; a good month for the Beneficiary Audit Grid and the Deposit Agreement Audit	4, 8
June	Jun 15	Second-quarter estimated tax	3, 5
June	Jun 30	End of the Medicaid minimum spousal allowance year (new figures each July 1)	3

July through September

Month	Date	What is due or open	Chapter
July	Jul 1	Common state effective date (in 2026: Georgia's bank-hold law; Washington's estate-tax change). Reg CC dollar thresholds next adjust July 1, 2030	1, 5
August	None	No federal deadline; run the unclaimed-money search (Appendix B) and confirm one owner-initiated contact on each dormant-prone account	3, 8
September	Sep 15	Third-quarter estimated tax	3, 5
September	Sep 30	Beneficiary determination date for retirement accounts inherited in the prior year	7

October through December

Month	Date	What is due or open	Chapter
October	Oct 1	Common state effective date (in 2026: Maryland's transfer-on-death deed law)	7
October	Oct 15	Extended Form 1040 and Form 709; last day to recharacterize a prior-year IRA contribution or remove an excess contribution with earnings	5
October	Oct 15–Dec 7	Medicare Open Enrollment; changes take effect January 1	3
October	Oct 31	Trust documentation to the custodian for accounts inherited in the prior year	7
November	Nov 1	State effective date (in 2026: Oklahoma's bank-hold law); IRS IP PIN online tool closes mid-November until mid-January	1, 3
December	Dec 1	VA pension rates update; NCUA's $1.25 million trust-account rule takes effect December 1, 2026	3, 8
December	Dec 7	Medicare Open Enrollment closes	3
December	Early Dec	Wire annual-exclusion gifts and start Roth conversions and QCDs now; custodians set internal cut-offs and a gift check must be deposited by year-end	5
December	Dec 31	RMDs (every year after the first); Roth conversions; QCDs; tax-loss and gain harvesting; inherited-IRA year-10 depletion; separate-account split and year-of-death RMD for accounts inherited the prior year	5, 7

Clocks that start when something happens

From a death

Clock	Starts	What must happen	Chapter
Month of death	Date of death	The Social Security payment for the month of death (it arrives the next month) must go back	2
10 days	Date of death	Bank may keep paying checks written before death unless someone with an interest orders a stop (UCC 4-405)	2, 8

Clock	Starts	What must happen	Chapter
30 days	Reverse-mortgage due-and-payable letter	Respond; then 6 months to sell, refinance, or pay, with two possible 90-day extensions	7
60 days	Loss of coverage	Elect COBRA (up to 36 months after a death); ACA marketplace special enrollment	2
6 months	Co-owner's death	FDIC and NCUA keep insuring the account as if the co-owner were alive	2, 8
9 months	Date of death	Qualified disclaimer; Form 706 for estate tax and portability (6-month extension on Form 4768)	2, 7
Sep 30, year after	Year of death	Beneficiary determination date for inherited retirement accounts	7
Oct 31, year after	Year of death	Trust documentation to the custodian for see-through treatment	7
Dec 31, year after	Year of death	Split inherited IRAs into separate accounts; year-of-death RMD (or the beneficiary's filing deadline, if later); first annual beneficiary RMD	7
2 years	Date of death	Apply for the $255 lump-sum death payment; surviving spouse may still use the $500,000 home-sale exclusion	2, 5
5 years	Date of death	Late portability election under Rev. Proc. 2022-32; five-year rule for non-designated beneficiaries when death was before the required beginning date	2, 7
10 years	Year of death	Ten-year rule: inherited account empty by December 31 of the tenth year after death	7

From a bank or brokerage event

Clock	Starts	What must happen	Chapter
2, 7, or 9 business days	Deposit	Reg CC availability: second business day standard; seventh for exception holds; ninth for the excess over $6,725 in a new account	1
15 + 10 + 30 business days	Hold placed	FINRA Rule 2165 brokerage hold, extendable in stages to 55 business days	1
5–30 business days	Hold placed	State bank-hold laws where they exist (Florida 15 + 30; Texas 10 + 30; Georgia 15 + 15 from July 1, 2026)	1
7 + 5 business days	POA presented	Bank must accept or ask for an agent certification, then accept, in UPOAA states (New York and Texas: 10 + 7)	4
2 business days	Learning a card or code is lost	Report to cap Reg E liability at $50 (then $500; unlimited after 60 days)	8
60 days	Statement sent	Reg E dispute of an unauthorized electronic transfer; Reg Z written notice of a credit-card billing error	8
30 days / 1 year	Statement available	Forged-check reporting under UCC 4-406: repeat forgeries after 30 days fall on you; absolute bar at one year	8
6 months	Date on a check	Bank need not pay a stale check (UCC 4-404)	8
7–10 calendar days	CD maturity	Typical grace period; notice is due at least 30 days before maturity on CDs longer than one year	8
2 business days	Garnishment order received	Bank reviews a two-month lookback and protects direct-deposited federal benefits	8
12 months	Treasury check issued	Check becomes void; ask the issuing agency to reissue (IRS: Form 3911)	3

Clock	Starts	What must happen	Chapter
3–5 years	Last owner-initiated contact	Dormancy; funds go to the state as unclaimed property	8

From a birthday, a job, or a return

Clock	Starts	What must happen	Chapter
7 months	65th birthday	Medicare Initial Enrollment Period: 3 months before the birthday month, the month itself, and 3 months after	3
8 months	Month after employment or coverage ends	Part B Special Enrollment Period; COBRA and retiree coverage do not count	3
6 months	First month 65 or older and enrolled in Part B	Medigap open enrollment, once, with no medical underwriting	3
6 months before	Applying for Medicare or Social Security after 65	Stop HSA contributions; Part A enrollment is retroactive up to 6 months	6
70½	Date of the distribution	Qualified charitable distributions allowed, up to $111,000 in 2026	5
73 or 75	Born 1951–1959, or 1960 and later	RMDs begin; the first may wait until April 1 of the following year	5
60 days	Receipt of a retirement distribution	Indirect rollover window; one IRA-to-IRA rollover per 12 months; 20% withholding on plan checks payable to you	6
2 years back	Tax return	IRMAA look-back: 2026 premiums come from the 2024 return; a 2026 conversion hits 2028	6
60 + 5 mailing days	SSA overpayment notice	Form SSA-561 reconsideration deadline; the waiver on Form SSA-632-BK has no deadline	3
60 months	Medicaid application	Look-back on transfers for less than fair value	5

Clock	Starts	What must happen	Chapter
5 years	January 1 of the conversion year	Roth conversion clock for penalty-free access to converted money before 59½	6

APPENDIX B

The Directory

Every phone number and form in this appendix appears in the body of the book and was checked against the agency that publishes it as of September 2026. Websites are given as bare names; type them into your browser directly rather than following a link from an email or text, which is how most impostor scams begin. Where a number is not listed here, it is because we could not verify it, not because it does not exist.

Social Security Administration

Contact	Number or address	Use it for
Main line	1-800-772-1213 (Mon–Fri, 8 a.m.–7 p.m.)	Reporting a death, survivor benefits, overpayments, direct deposit, advance designation
TTY	1-800-325-0778	Same services for callers who are deaf or hard of hearing
Overseas callers	1-855-522-6936	Beneficiaries living abroad
Direct Express card	1-800-967-6857	Prepaid debit card for benefits without a bank account (GoDirect.gov)
my Social Security	ssa.gov	Statements, advance designation, form uploads, one-time security code at ssa.gov/PIN
Extra Help	ssa.gov (Part D Extra Help page)	Apply online, by phone, or on Form SSA-1020
Repayments	pay.gov	Repay an overpayment by card or bank account

Form	Full name	When you need it
SSA-11	Request to Be Selected as Payee	Becoming a representative payee (SSA does not accept a POA)

Form	Full name	When you need it
SSA-44	Medicare Income-Related Monthly Adjustment Amount – Life-Changing Event	Lowering IRMAA after retirement, a spouse's death, divorce, or the other five listed events
SSA-561	Request for Reconsideration	Appealing an overpayment notice within 60 days plus 5 mailing days
SSA-632-BK	Request for Waiver of Overpayment Recovery	Asking SSA to forgive an overpayment; no deadline
SSA-634	Request for Change in Overpayment Recovery Rate	Lowering the 50% default withholding
SSA-1020	Application for Extra Help with Medicare Prescription Drug Plan Costs	Part D low-income subsidy
W-4V (IRS)	Voluntary Withholding Request	Having federal tax withheld from Social Security

Medicare and health coverage

Contact	Number or address	Use it for
1-800-MEDICARE	1-800-633-4227	Enrollment questions, penalties, plan changes, written authorizations
Written Authorization Dept.	1-800-MEDICARE Written Authorization Dept., PO Box 1270, Lawrence, KS 66044	Mailing Form CMS-10106
SHIP	1-877-839-2675 (shiphelp.org)	Free, unbiased Medicare counseling in every state
HealthCare.gov	1-800-318-2596	ACA marketplace special enrollment (60 days after loss of coverage)
Medicare online	medicare.gov	Plan finder, enrollment periods, Medigap timing

Form	Full name	When you need it
CMS-40B	Application for Enrollment in Medicare Part B	Enrolling in Part B during a Special Enrollment Period

Form	Full name	When you need it
CMS-L564	Request for Employment Information	Employer's proof of coverage, filed with CMS-40B
CMS-10106	1-800-MEDICARE Authorization to Disclose Personal Health Information	Letting a family member speak to Medicare for you
SSA-44	(see Social Security table)	IRMAA appeal after a life-changing event

Internal Revenue Service

Contact	Number or site	Use it for
AARP Foundation Tax-Aide	1-888-227-7669 (aarp.org/taxaide)	Free tax preparation, sites open roughly January–April
VITA / TCE locator	1-800-906-9887	Free preparation; TCE prioritizes taxpayers 60 and older
IRS Free File	irs.gov	Free guided software for AGI of $89,000 or less (2026 season)
IRS Direct Pay	irs.gov/payments	Paying balances, estimates, and extensions from a bank account
Estate EIN	IRS.gov/EIN	Getting an employer identification number for an estate online
Identity Protection PIN	irs.gov (IRS Online Account)	Opting in; new six-digit PIN each January

Form	Full name	When you need it
1040-SR	U.S. Tax Return for Seniors	Large-print return for taxpayers 65 and older
Schedule 1-A	Additional Deductions	Claiming the $6,000 senior deduction (2025–2028)
1040-ES	Estimated Tax for Individuals	Quarterly payments: April 15, June 15, September 15, January 15
4868	Application for Automatic Extension of Time to File	Six-month filing extension to October 15 (also extends Form 709)
2210, Schedule AI	Annualized Income Installment Method	Avoiding an underpayment penalty after a late-year conversion

Form	Full name	When you need it
3911	Taxpayer Statement Regarding Refund	Tracing a lost or expired refund check
8822	Change of Address	Moving; 8822-B for estates and businesses
15227	Application for an Identity Protection PIN	Paper route to an IP PIN (AGI under $84,000 single / $168,000 joint)

Form	Full name	When you need it
2848	Power of Attorney and Declaration of Representative	Letting someone act for you before the IRS (a durable POA alone is not enough)
8821	Tax Information Authorization	Letting someone receive your tax information but not act
56	Notice Concerning Fiduciary Relationship	Executor, trustee, or guardian notifying the IRS
1310	Statement of Person Claiming Refund Due a Deceased Taxpayer	Refunds when no surviving spouse files jointly and no court-appointed representative attaches letters
SS-4	Application for Employer Identification Number	Estate or trust EIN (online is fastest)
8855	Election to Treat a Qualified Revocable Trust as Part of an Estate	The §645 election
706	United States Estate (and Generation-Skipping Transfer) Tax Return	Due 9 months after death; required to elect portability
4768	Application for Extension of Time to File a Return and/or Pay U.S. Estate Taxes	Six more months for Form 706

Form	Full name	When you need it
709	United States Gift (and Generation-Skipping Transfer) Tax Return	Any gift over $19,000 to one person; gift-splitting; 529 five-year election
8892	Application for Automatic Extension of Time to File Form 709	Extending the gift-tax return alone
8606	Nondeductible IRAs	After-tax IRA basis, conversions, inherited basis

Form	Full name	When you need it
5329	Additional Taxes on Qualified Plans	Missed-RMD penalty and waiver request; excess contributions; early-distribution exceptions
1099-R	Distributions From Pensions, Annuities, Retirement Plans, IRAs	Reporting a QCD (write "QCD" next to line 4b of Form 1040)
1099-B	Proceeds From Broker and Barter Exchange Transactions	Cost basis on covered securities

Department of Veterans Affairs

Form or site	Full name	When you need it
VA 21-22a	Appointment of Individual as Claimant's Representative	Naming a person to act for a veteran (VA does not accept a durable POA)
VA 21-0845	Authorization to Disclose Personal Information to a Third-Party	Letting VA discuss a claim with a family member
VA 21-0966	Intent to File a Claim	Holding a claim's effective date while you gather records
va.gov	Pension and survivor-pension rate pages	Aid and Attendance rates; the net worth limit ($163,699 through November 30, 2026)

Consumer protection, fraud, and complaints

Agency	Contact	Use it for
Consumer Financial Protection Bureau	consumerfinance.gov	Complaints about banks, credit unions, and debt collectors; the Managing Someone Else's Money guides
Federal Trade Commission	ReportFraud.ftc.gov	Reporting scams and impostor calls
FBI Internet Crime Complaint Center	ic3.gov	Reporting internet-enabled fraud, including crypto-kiosk scams
Adult Protective Services	Through the Eldercare Locator, 1-800-677-1116 (napsa-now.org)	Suspected financial exploitation

Agency	Contact	Use it for
State banking department	Your state's website	Your state's bank-hold law; complaints about state-chartered banks
FTC state hold-law overview	consumer.ftc.gov	The October 2024 table of state transaction-hold statutes
FINRA	finra.org	Rule 2165 (holds) and Rule 4512 (trusted contact) for brokerages

Finding lost money

Tool	Where	What it covers
MissingMoney.com	Free NAUPA multistate search	State unclaimed property; also unclaimed.org for each state's own program
PBGC	1-800-400-7242 (pbgc.gov)	Unclaimed pensions from terminated plans; survivor benefits after a death
Retirement Savings Lost and Found	lostandfound.dol.gov (Login.gov account required)	Private-sector plan benefits you may have left behind; not IRAs
NAIC Life Insurance Policy Locator	naic.org	Lost life insurance policies; allow 90 or more business days
EDIE	EDIE.fdic.gov	Calculating your FDIC coverage across ownership categories
NCUA share insurance	mycreditunion.gov	Credit-union coverage, including the December 1, 2026 trust rule

Legal help and health care documents

Resource	Contact	What it is
Eldercare Locator	1-800-677-1116 (eldercare.acl.gov)	Connects you to your Area Agency on Aging and free legal help for people 60 and older

Resource	Contact	What it is
Legal Services Corporation	lsc.gov	Nonprofit legal aid, generally for income at or below 125% of the poverty guideline
NAELA	naela.org	Directory of elder-law attorneys
Five Wishes	fivewishes.org	Advance directive valid in all 50 states and D.C. (four states add steps)
National POLST	polst.org	Your state's POLST, MOLST, POST, or MOST form
CFPB fiduciary guides	consumerfinance.gov	Managing Someone Else's Money, national and state editions

State forms named in this book

State	Form	What it does
New Jersey	L-8	Self-executing tax waiver for Class A beneficiaries (spouse, children, grandchildren, parents) releasing frozen accounts
New Jersey	L-9	Waiver for real estate
Pennsylvania	REV-1500	Inheritance tax return; delinquent at 9 months, 5% discount if paid within 3 months
Pennsylvania	REV-516	Bank's notice to the Department of Revenue of a decedent's account
California	BOE-19-P	Parent-child reassessment exclusion under Prop 19; file within 3 years

Rules cited by name

Short name	Citation	What it governs
Regulation CC	12 CFR Part 229	Funds availability and deposit holds ($275; $6,725; 2, 7, and 9 business days)
Regulation E	12 CFR Part 1005	Unauthorized electronic transfers; 60-day dispute window; provisional credit
Regulation Z	12 CFR Part 1026	Credit-card billing errors (60 days) and the ban on credit-card setoff
Regulation DD	12 CFR Part 1030	Truth in Savings; CD maturity and change-in-terms notices

Short name	Citation	What it governs
Federal benefit garnishment rule	31 CFR Part 212	Two-month lookback protecting direct-deposited benefits from garnishment
Treasury reclamation	31 CFR Part 210	Return of federal payments deposited after a death
Treasury Offset Program	31 CFR 285.4	Offset of Social Security for federal non-tax debts (15%, $750 floor)
Bank Secrecy Act reporting	31 CFR 1010.311; 31 U.S.C. 5324	Currency transaction reports over $10,000; structuring
Suspicious activity reports	31 CFR 1020.320	SAR filing and the "no tipping off" rule

Short name	Citation	What it governs
UCC 4-404	Uniform Commercial Code	Stale checks (six months)
UCC 4-405	Uniform Commercial Code	Checks paid after a customer's death (10 days)
UCC 4-406	Uniform Commercial Code	Forged or altered checks (30 days; one year)
FINRA Rule 2165	FINRA	Brokerage holds for suspected exploitation (15 + 10 + 30 business days)
FINRA Rule 4512	FINRA	Trusted contact person
Senior Safe Act	Pub. L. 115-174, §303 (2018)	Immunity for trained institutions that report suspected exploitation; no hold authority
Garn-St Germain	12 U.S.C. 1701j-3(d)	Protects transfers to a spouse, children, or a living trust from due-on-sale clauses
RUFADAA	State law (49 states and D.C.)	Fiduciary access to digital accounts
UPOAA	Uniform Power of Attorney Act (2006)	POA acceptance deadlines and hot powers in adopting states

Short name	Citation	What it governs
Section 121	IRC §121	$250,000 / $500,000 home-sale exclusion; two years for a surviving spouse
Section 1014 and 1015	IRC §§1014, 1015	Step-up in basis at death; carryover basis for gifts

Short name	Citation	What it governs
Section 2518	IRC §2518	Qualified disclaimers within 9 months
Section 408(d)(8)	IRC §408(d)(8)	Qualified charitable distributions
T.D. 10001	Treasury Decision, July 19, 2024	Final required-minimum-distribution and inherited-account regulations
Rev. Proc. 2022-32	IRS	Late portability election up to five years after death
Rev. Proc. 2020-46	IRS	Self-certification for late rollovers (12 reasons)
Notice 2025-67	IRS	2026 retirement-plan contribution limits
Rev. Proc. 2025-32	IRS	2026 brackets, standard deduction, and gift and estate figures

APPENDIX C

Glossary

Terms are alphabetical. Where a term has a chapter of its own, the chapter number follows the definition.

Advance designation. A Social Security program that lets a capable adult name up to three people, in order of preference, to serve as representative payee if one is ever needed. Set up through a my Social Security account, by phone, or in person; it is not a power of attorney and does not appoint anyone by itself. Chapter 3.

Agent certification. A signed statement, under penalty of perjury, in which the agent under a power of attorney confirms that the principal is alive, has not revoked the document, and granted the authority claimed. It is the standard cure when a bank calls a POA "stale." Chapter 4.

Annual exclusion. The amount you may give any one person in a year without filing a gift-tax return: $19,000 in 2026. A tax rule only; it has no bearing on Medicaid's look-back. Chapter 5.

Beneficiary designation. The form on file with an IRA, 401(k), insurer, or bank that says who receives the account at death. It overrides the will. Chapters 4 and 7.

Business day. A day that is not a Saturday, Sunday, or federal holiday. Deposit holds, brokerage holds, POA acceptance clocks, and Regulation E liability tiers all count in business days. Chapter 1.

Carryover basis. The rule that a gift keeps the giver's original cost basis in the recipient's hands (IRC §1015), so the recipient pays tax on all the gain when selling. The reason never to gift a loss position. Chapter 7.

Case-by-case hold. A bank's decision to use its full Regulation CC time on a particular deposit, so funds arrive on the second business day instead of sooner under its normal policy. Notice is required. Chapter 1.

Community property. Marital property law in nine states (Arizona, California, Idaho, Louisiana, Nevada, New Mexico, Texas, Washington, Wisconsin) under which both halves of a couple's property receive a step-up in basis at the first death. Chapter 7.

Community Spouse Resource Allowance (CSRA). The assets a spouse may keep when the other spouse qualifies for nursing-home Medicaid: between $32,532 and $162,660 in 2026, depending on the state. Chapter 3.

Convenience account. An account with a second signer added only to help pay bills. The helper has no ownership and no survivorship right, but if the bank's signature card says "joint with survivorship," courts often honor the card. Chapters 4 and 8.

Currency Transaction Report (CTR). The report a bank files with the Treasury for any cash transaction over $10,000 in a business day. Routine, not accusatory, and not something you can opt out of. Chapter 1.

Deemed filing. The Social Security rule that anyone born January 2, 1954 or later who files for a retirement or spousal benefit is treated as filing for both and gets the higher. It does not apply to survivor benefits. Chapters 2 and 6.

Direct rollover. A transfer of retirement money straight from one custodian to another, or by a check payable to the new custodian for your benefit. No withholding, no 60-day clock, no once-a-year limit. Chapter 6.

Disclaimer. A written refusal to accept an inheritance, made within 9 months of death and before taking any benefit, so the asset passes as if you had died first (IRC §2518). Irrevocable. Chapters 2 and 7.

Dormancy. The period of no owner-initiated activity or contact, usually three to five years depending on the state, after which a bank must turn an account over to the state as unclaimed property. Interest posting does not count as activity. Chapter 8.

DSUE. Deceased Spousal Unused Exclusion: the part of a first-to-die spouse's $15,000,000 estate exemption that passes to the survivor, but only if Form 706 is filed. Chapter 2.

Durable power of attorney. A power of attorney that keeps working after the principal loses capacity. In Uniform Act states durability is the default; in California and Texas the document must say so. It always ends at death. Chapter 4.

EDIE. The FDIC's Electronic Deposit Insurance Estimator, a free online calculator that shows how much of your money at one bank is insured across ownership categories. Chapter 8.

Eligible designated beneficiary (EDB). An heir who may still stretch an inherited retirement account over life expectancy: a surviving spouse, a minor child of the owner until 21, a disabled or chronically ill person, or anyone not more than 10 years younger than the owner. Chapter 7.

Escheat. The transfer of dormant property to the state, which holds it indefinitely for the owner or heirs. Chapter 8.

Estate recovery. A state's required claim against the estate of a Medicaid recipient age 55 or older for long-term-care costs, deferred while a spouse or a minor or disabled child survives. Chapter 5.

Exception hold. A Regulation CC hold beyond the second business day, allowed for new accounts, deposits over $6,725, redeposited checks, repeated overdrafts, doubtful collectibility, or emergencies. Funds are normally available by the seventh business day. Chapter 1.

FDIC ownership category. The unit of deposit insurance: $250,000 per depositor, per bank, per category (single, joint, certain retirement, trust). A couple with single and joint accounts at one bank can have more than $250,000 insured there. Chapter 8.

Five-year rule. The requirement that an inherited retirement account with no designated beneficiary (an estate, a charity, a non-qualifying trust) be emptied by December 31 of the fifth year after death, when the owner died before the required beginning date. Chapter 7.

First-dollars-out rule. The first money withdrawn from an IRA in a year is treated as the RMD. Do the qualified charitable distribution before any other withdrawal, or it cannot cover the RMD. Chapter 5.

Full retirement age (FRA). The age at which you receive an unreduced Social Security benefit: 66 for those born 1943–1954, rising by two months per birth year to 67 for those born 1960 and later. Chapters 3 and 6.

Garn-St Germain Act. The federal law that bars a mortgage lender from calling a home loan due when the home passes at death, transfers to a spouse or child, or moves into the owner's living trust. Chapter 7.

Ghost rule. For an inherited account with no designated beneficiary where the owner died on or after the required beginning date: payments continue over the deceased owner's remaining life expectancy. Chapter 7.

Grace period (CD). The window after a certificate of deposit matures, typically 7 to 10 calendar days, when you can withdraw or change terms without penalty. Miss it and the CD renews for the same term at the current rate. Chapter 8.

HIPAA release. A stand-alone authorization letting named people receive your medical information while you can still make decisions. A health care proxy usually activates only at incapacity, which is why both are needed. Chapter 4.

Hot powers. Powers an agent under a POA has only if expressly granted: making gifts, changing beneficiaries, creating or changing survivorship rights, creating or amending trusts, disclaiming property, and, in some states, accessing digital assets. Chapter 4.

Indirect rollover. A retirement distribution paid to you that you redeposit within 60 days. Plan checks lose 20% to mandatory withholding; IRA-to-IRA versions are limited to one per 12 months. Chapter 6.

IRMAA. The income-related monthly adjustment amount added to Medicare Part B and Part D premiums when modified adjusted gross income from two years earlier exceeds $109,000 (single) or $218,000 (joint). A cliff, not a slope. Chapters 3 and 6.

Joint tenancy with right of survivorship (JTWROS). Co-ownership in which the survivor takes the whole account or property at the other owner's death, by contract, outside probate. Chapters 2 and 8.

Lady Bird deed. An enhanced life estate deed, used in Florida, Texas, Michigan, Vermont, and West Virginia, that names who gets the home at death while the owner keeps full power to sell or mortgage it. Not a completed gift. Chapter 7.

Letters testamentary. The court document that authorizes an executor to act for an estate; the paper a bank needs before releasing a sole-name account. Chapter 2.

Life estate deed. A deed that gives the home to the remainder holders at death while the owner keeps a lifetime right to live there. A completed gift; the owner cannot sell without the remainder holders' consent. Chapter 7.

Living will and health care proxy. The two halves of an advance directive: the living will states treatment wishes; the proxy names the person who decides when you cannot. Chapter 4.

Look-back period. The 60 months before a Medicaid long-term-care application during which any transfer for less than fair value creates a penalty period. Chapter 5.

Modified adjusted gross income (MAGI). Adjusted gross income with certain items added back; the definition differs by program. IRMAA, the senior deduction, and ACA subsidies each use their own version. Chapter 6.

Minimum Monthly Maintenance Needs Allowance (MMMNA). The income a community spouse may keep when the other spouse is on nursing-home Medicaid; the 2026 federal maximum is $4,066.50. Chapter 3.

Month-of-death rule. Social Security pays for a month only if the beneficiary lived the entire month, so the payment that arrives after a death (for the month of death) must be returned. Chapter 2.

Net unrealized appreciation (NUA). The growth in employer stock held inside a company plan. Distributed in kind as part of a lump sum, that growth is taxed as long-term capital gain when sold, but it receives no step-up at death. Chapter 6.

Once-per-12-months rule. You may make only one indirect IRA-to-IRA rollover in any 12-month period, across all your IRAs. Direct transfers and conversions do not count. Chapter 6.

Penalty divisor. The state's figure for the average monthly cost of nursing-home care, used to convert a Medicaid-penalized transfer into months of ineligibility. Chapter 5.

Per stirpes and per capita. Two ways to divide a share when a named heir has died first. Per stirpes passes that heir's share to their children; per capita divides it among the surviving named heirs. Chapter 7.

Payable-on-death (POD) and transfer-on-death (TOD). Designations on a bank account (POD) or brokerage account (TOD) naming who collects at death with a death certificate, outside probate. The beneficiary has no rights while you live. Chapters 2, 4, and 7.

POLST. Physician Orders for Life-Sustaining Treatment (called MOLST, POST, or MOST in some states): a signed medical order for the seriously ill, not a substitute for an advance directive. Chapter 4.

Portability. The election, made on a timely Form 706, that lets a surviving spouse add the deceased spouse's unused estate exemption to their own. Chapters 2 and 5.

Pour-over will. A will that sends anything left outside a living trust into the trust at death. Assets it catches still pass through probate. Chapter 4.

Pro-rata rule. When any traditional IRA holds after-tax basis, every conversion or withdrawal is taxed in proportion to the pre-tax share of all your IRAs combined. Tracked on Form 8606. Chapter 6.

Provisional income. Adjusted gross income plus tax-exempt interest plus half of Social Security benefits; the figure that decides whether up to 50% or 85% of benefits are taxable (thresholds $25,000 / $32,000 and $34,000 / $44,000, not indexed). Chapter 3.

Qualified charitable distribution (QCD). A gift sent directly from an IRA to a public charity by an owner age 70½ or older on the date of the transfer, up to $111,000 in 2026. It counts toward the RMD and never appears in income. Chapter 5.

Regulation CC. The Federal Reserve rule on funds availability: $275 next-day, second business day standard, $6,725 large-deposit threshold, seventh business day for exception holds. Chapter 1.

Regulation DD. The Truth in Savings rule requiring CD maturity notices (30 days before maturity for CDs over one year) and 30-day notice of adverse changes in account terms. Chapter 8.

Regulation E. The rule covering debit cards, ATM, ACH, and app payments: 60 days from the statement to dispute an unauthorized transfer, provisional credit within 10 business days, and liability tiers of $50, $500, and unlimited. Chapter 8.

Regulation Z. The Truth in Lending rule for credit cards: 60 days to dispute a billing error in writing, $50 cap on unauthorized use, and a ban on the issuer taking your deposits to pay your card. Chapter 8.

Representative payee. The person Social Security appoints to receive and manage benefits for someone who cannot. The only arrangement SSA recognizes; a power of attorney does not work. Chapter 3.

Required beginning date (RBD). April 1 of the year after you reach RMD age (73 if born 1951–1959; 75 if born 1960 or later). Whether an owner died before or after this date decides the heirs' payout rules. Chapters 5 and 7.

Required minimum distribution (RMD). The amount you must withdraw from traditional retirement accounts each year from RMD age: prior December 31 balance divided by the Uniform Lifetime Table factor. Missed amounts carry a 25% excise tax, reduced to 10% if corrected promptly. Chapter 5.

Roth five-year rules. Two separate clocks: each conversion has its own five years before the converted amount is penalty-free under 59½, and earnings are tax-free only five years after your first Roth contribution or conversion and after 59½. Chapter 6.

Rule of 55. Penalty-free withdrawals from the plan of the employer you left in or after the year you turned 55 (50 for qualified public-safety employees). Lost if the money is rolled to an IRA. Chapter 6.

Section 72(t) payments. Substantially equal periodic payments that avoid the 10% early-withdrawal penalty if continued for the longer of five years or until 59½. Any change triggers the penalty retroactively, with interest. Chapter 6.

See-through trust. A trust that meets four requirements (valid under state law, irrevocable at death, identifiable beneficiaries, documentation to the custodian by October 31 of the year after death) so its beneficiaries are treated as designated beneficiaries of an inherited account. Chapter 7.

Self-proving affidavit. A notarized statement by the will's signer and witnesses that lets a court admit the will without calling the witnesses. Not available in D.C. or Ohio. Chapter 4.

Setoff. A bank's right to take money from your deposit account to pay a debt you owe the same bank. Federal law bars it for credit-card debt without your written authorization. Chapter 8.

Small-estate affidavit. A sworn statement that lets heirs collect assets without formal probate when the estate is under a state threshold (for example, $208,850 in California, $75,000 in Texas, $50,000 in New York). Chapter 2.

Special Enrollment Period (SEP). The eight months after employment or employer coverage ends (whichever comes first) in which you may enroll in Part B without penalty. COBRA and retiree coverage do not count. Chapter 3.

Springing power of attorney. A POA that takes effect only on a future event, usually a doctor's finding of incapacity. Slower in practice; Florida has barred new ones since October 1, 2011. Chapter 4.

Step-up in basis. At death, capital assets in the estate take a new basis equal to fair market value, erasing the gain (IRC §1014). It does not apply to IRAs, 401(k)s, annuities, or NUA. Chapter 7.

Structuring. Breaking up cash transactions to stay under the $10,000 reporting threshold. A federal crime even when the money is legitimate. Chapter 1.

Suspicious Activity Report (SAR). A confidential report a bank files when it suspects illegal or unusual activity. The bank may not tell you it filed one. Chapter 1.

Tenancy by the entirety. A form of joint ownership for married couples, available in about 25 states and D.C., with survivorship and protection from one spouse's individual creditors. Chapter 7.

Ten-year rule. Most non-spouse heirs must empty an inherited retirement account by December 31 of the tenth year after the owner's death, with annual withdrawals in years one through nine if the owner had reached the required beginning date. Chapter 7.

Transfer-on-death (TOD) deed. A recorded deed naming who receives real estate at death, revocable during life, available in 35 jurisdictions (Maryland from October 1, 2026) and not in Florida, Pennsylvania, or New Jersey. Chapter 7.

Trusted contact. A person, age 18 or older, whom a brokerage (required to ask under FINRA Rule 4512) or bank may call to confirm your wellbeing or whereabouts or to address suspected exploitation. The trusted contact cannot transact or make decisions. Chapter 1.

UCC 4-405. The Uniform Commercial Code section allowing a bank, even after learning of a customer's death, to pay checks written before death for 10 days unless someone with an interest orders a stop. Chapters 2 and 8.

UCC 4-406. The section that puts forged-check losses on the customer for repeat forgeries reported more than 30 days after the first statement, and bars all claims after one year. Chapter 8.

Uniform Lifetime Table. The IRS table of divisors for lifetime RMDs: 26.5 at 73, 24.6 at 75, 20.2 at 80, 16.0 at 85, 12.2 at 90. Chapter 5.

Wash sale. Buying substantially identical securities within 30 days before or after selling at a loss, including inside your IRA, disallows the loss. It never applies to gains. Chapter 5.

Widow's penalty. The jump in tax and Medicare surcharges a survivor faces when the same income moves from joint to single brackets and thresholds. The reason Chapter 2 sends you to Form SSA-44 and Chapter 6 to Roth conversions. Chapters 2 and 6.

Year-of-death RMD. The distribution the owner should have taken in the year of death, which the beneficiary must complete by the later of their own filing deadline or December 31 of the following year. Chapters 2 and 7.

APPENDIX D

The Tool Library

Every script, letter, worksheet, and checklist in the book, by chapter. Scripts are meant to be read aloud on the phone; letters are complete templates with bracketed fields; worksheets and checklists are meant to be photocopied. Each chapter's Your Next Steps checklist is listed for completeness.

Introduction

Tool	Type	Use it when
If You Do Only Ten Things	Checklist	You have two hours and want the highest-value moves first

Chapter 1: The Freeze

Tool	Type	Use it when
Calling About a Hold	Script	A deposit or transaction is paused; asks Reg CC or fraud hold, release date, written notice, case number
Pre-Clearing a Large Withdrawal or Wire	Script	You plan a large cash withdrawal or wire and want it to go through the first time
Request for Written Explanation and Release Date of Hold	Letter	The phone call did not produce a release date in writing
Trusted Contact Designation & Institution Log	Worksheet	Naming a trusted contact at every institution and recording who has it on file
Before Any Large Transaction	Checklist	The week before a closing, a car purchase, or a big transfer
If Your Account Is Frozen Right Now (The 72-Hour Plan)	Checklist	The 72-hour plan: call, notice, trusted contact, APS, CFPB, state regulator
Your Next Steps	Checklist	Closing actions for Chapter 1

Chapter 2: The First 90 Days

Tool	Type	Use it when
Reporting a Death and Applying for Survivor Benefits	Script	Calling Social Security at 1-800-772-1213 in week one
Calling the Bank About a Sole-Name Account	Script	An account in the deceased's name alone has been frozen
Notification of Death to a Financial Institution	Letter	Formal notice with the enclosures each institution needs
Credit Bureau Deceased Notification	Letter	Placing a deceased alert; one bureau notifies the other two
The 90-Day Master Tracker	Worksheet	Accounts, contacts, dates, and reference numbers in one place
First 72 Hours	Checklist	Death certificates, the month-of-death payment, the four documents
First 30 Days	Checklist	Survivor benefits, Medicare, pensions, insurance, taxes
Days 30–90	Checklist	Retitling, beneficiaries, the survivor's own documents
Do Not Rush	Checklist	The irreversible decisions to postpone
Your Next Steps	Checklist	Preparing now so your spouse never faces a freeze

Chapter 3: The Silent Deadlines

Tool	Type	Use it when
Calling SSA About an Overpayment Notice	Script	A notice arrived; choosing SSA-561, SSA-632-BK, or SSA-634 before the deadline
Calling 1-800-MEDICARE or SHIP About a Late-Enrollment Penalty	Script	A penalty letter arrived or you suspect a missed window
IRMAA Life-Changing Event Cover Letter (Form SSA-44)	Letter	Sending either form with the evidence attached
My Deadline Sheet	Worksheet	Your personal dates: enrollment window, FRA, RMD year, Open Enrollment, estimated taxes

Tool	Type	Use it when
Annual Government Money Sweep	Checklist	The once-a-year pass through refunds, benefits, and unclaimed property
Your Next Steps	Checklist	Closing actions for Chapter 3

Chapter 4: The Four Documents

Tool	Type	Use it when
Presenting a Power of Attorney at the Bank	Script	Delivering a power of attorney, with the statutory-deadline line
Asking a Doctor's Office About the HIPAA Release	Script	Making sure the release is in the chart before it is needed
Cover Letter Delivering a Power of Attorney to a Financial Institution	Letter	Requesting written acceptance within the statutory time
Four Documents Inventory	Worksheet	Document, date signed, where the original is, who has copies, agents, last review
Beneficiary Audit Grid	Worksheet	Every account, its primary and contingent, and the date confirmed
Document Execution (by State Formalities)	Checklist	Witnesses, notary, and notices required in your state
Annual Review	Checklist	The once-a-year pass through all four documents
Your Next Steps	Checklist	Closing actions for Chapter 4

Chapter 5: The Calendar

Tool	Type	Use it when
Setting Up a QCD and Confirming Your RMD	Script	Before any other withdrawal in the year
Asking Your CPA for a Year-End Projection	Script	The five questions to ask in October or November
QCD Instruction to IRA Custodian	Letter	Directing a transfer straight to the charity

Tool	Type	Use it when
Year-End Money Moves Planner	Worksheet	RMD, QCDs, conversion room, gifts by recipient, losses and gains, contributions
RMD Calculator	Worksheet	Prior-year balance divided by the Uniform Lifetime Table factor
December Checklist	Checklist	Everything that must finish by December 31
April Checklist	Checklist	April 1 and April 15 items
Your Next Steps	Checklist	Closing actions for Chapter 5

Chapter 6: The Review

Tool	Type	Use it when
Requesting a Direct Rollover From a 401(k) Plan	Script	Getting the check made payable to the new custodian, FBO you
Asking an Advisor the Fiduciary Question	Script	Before accepting any rollover or product recommendation
Instruction Letter for a Partial Roth Conversion With Zero Withholding	Letter	Converting a set amount by December 31 and paying tax from outside money
Bracket-Filling Worksheet (2026)	Worksheet	How much room is left in the 12%, 22%, and 24% brackets for 2026
Retirement Account Inventory	Worksheet	Every account, custodian, type, beneficiary, and trusted contact
Rollover Do/Don't	Checklist	Direct vs. indirect, 20% withholding, 60 days, once per 12 months, RMD first
Pre-Retirement Review Agenda	Checklist	The one-page annual meeting agenda for you or your advisor
Your Next Steps	Checklist	Closing actions for Chapter 6

Chapter 7: The Handoff

Tool	Type	Use it when
Opening an Inherited IRA by Trustee-to-Trustee Transfer	Script	The exact words that prevent a check made payable to you

Tool	Type	Use it when
Asking the County Recorder or a Title Company About a TOD Deed	Script	Confirming your state allows it and what it must contain
Beneficiary Designation Confirmation Request	Letter	Asking a custodian for written confirmation of the beneficiaries on file
Asset Handoff Map	Worksheet	Asset, how titled, beneficiary, how it passes, step-up, action needed
Inherited IRA Date Sheet	Worksheet	September 30, October 31, December 31, 9 months, year 10
Before You Add Anyone to a Deed	Checklist	Gift, basis, creditors, Medicaid, reassessment, due-on-sale
When You Inherit an IRA	Checklist	The first calls and the deadlines that follow
Your Next Steps	Checklist	Closing actions for Chapter 7

Chapter 8: The Fine Print

Tool	Type	Use it when
Disputing an Unauthorized Electronic Transaction (Reg E)	Script	Within 60 days of the statement; asks for provisional credit within 10 business days
Calling About a CD Maturity or Grace Period	Script	Before the grace period closes
Written Notice of Error Under Regulation E	Letter	Confirming a dispute in writing with the 60-day and provisional-credit references
Notice of Forged or Altered Check Under UCC 4-406	Letter	Reporting a forgery as soon as it is found
Deposit Agreement Audit	Worksheet	The five clauses: grace period, inactivity, fees, setoff, arbitration
Lifeboat Account Plan	Worksheet	A second account and a direct-deposit redirection plan
Monthly Statement Review	Checklist	The 30-day habit that keeps every error window open
CD Maturity Calendar	Checklist	Every CD, its maturity date, and its grace period
Your Next Steps	Checklist	Closing actions for Chapter 8

www.ingramcontent.com/pod-product-compliance
Lightning Source LLC
LaVergne TN
LVHW030725061126
851857LV00019B/1999
9780557896578